Victorian Ladies at Work

WE'LL SERVE THE SHOP.

VICTORIAN LADIES AT WORK

Middle-Class Working Women
in England and Wales
1850-1914

by

LEE HOLCOMBE

ARCHON BOOKS

1973

Library of Congress Cataloging in Publication Data

Holcombe, Lee.
   Victorian ladies at work.

   Includes bibliographical references.
   1. Women—Employment—Great Britain—History. I. Title.
HD6137.H64   331.4'0942   73-3357
ISBN 0-208-01340-7

©1973 by Lee Holcombe
First published 1973 as an Archon Book
by The Shoe String Press, Inc.,
Hamden, Connecticut 06514

Printed in the United States of America

FOR MY MOTHER
AND FOR TIMOTHY

CONTENTS

ILLUSTRATIONS

ACKNOWLEDGEMENTS

Among many friends and colleagues who have contributed in one way or another to this work, I should like to mention specially the following: Professor Norma Adams of Mount Holyoke College, for her inspiring teaching of history and her sympathetic interest in and concern for her students; the late Professor J. Bartlett Brebner, for wise and kindly guidance in his doctoral seminar at Columbia University, where the studies which led to the writing of this book were begun; Professor R. K. Webb of Columbia University and the *American Historical Review,* for his unfailing courtesy and helpful advice, which greatly encouraged me during my student days and after; Edward Breen, for reasons which he will understand; Professor Virginia Ogden Birdsall of the University of Connecticut, for her sympathetic interest in my project; and Mrs. Helen Lathrop Petty, Librarian of the University of Connecticut, Groton, for her efficient help and continued cheerfulness in the face of my many demands upon her time and energies. I should also like to express my gratitude to Mount Holyoke College and to Columbia University for scholarship aid granted me in the course of my studies, and to the University of Connecticut for financial assistance in the preparation of the final manuscript. I am grateful, too, for facilities afforded me by the library and staff of Connecticut College. Finally, my thanks go to the editors of *Punch* and *The Illustrated London News* for kind permission to reproduce the illustrations.

Victorian Ladies at Work

I
THE WOMEN'S MOVEMENT
AND WORKING LADIES

Of the women's movement in Victorian England, Millicent Garrett Fawcett, later Dame Millicent, an outstanding leader of the women's suffrage cause, had this to say:

> The movement must be regarded as one of the results of the up-heaval of the human mind of which the French Revolution was the most portentous manifestation. The awakening of the democratic spirit, the rebellion against authority, the proclamation of the rights of man, were almost necessarily accompanied by the growth of a new ideal concerning the position of women, by the recognition, more or less defined and conscious, of the rights of women.[1]

And again:

> The idea of the subjection of women . . . has to give way to a new ideal, in which women, adorned with the grace of strength and free-dom, shall regulate and control their own life and conduct. . . . the central point of the new ideal is freedom. . . .[2]

"The subjection of women"—this was the title of John Stuart Mill's classic statement of the women's cause in the nineteenth century, a feminist manifesto which has not been equalled for clarity and force by any other similar work in the century since its first publication in 1869.[3] Significantly, it was Mill's least popular and most criticized work.

"Freedom" was the cry of Mill and of the women for whom he spoke, but what, specifically, did they mean? In its essence, the women's movement was an attack upon the "patriarchal ideal" of Victorian society and the special role of domesticity and dependence, of subjection, which it assigned to the perfect woman.[4] According to generally accepted middle-class views, or rather, views generally accepted in the middle classes, marriage and motherhood were the careers marked out for women by nature, and their own homes furnished the fullest scope for women's abilities. Not for them the workaday world outside. They must be sheltered and supported throughout life by the "stronger sex," fathers and brothers, husbands and sons. In practical terms this meant, for example, that married women could not legally hold property or control their own earnings, since these belonged not to them but to their husbands; the children of a marriage were legally the property and under the control of the father, not of the mother; a wife was subject to her husband's command and discipline (a popular gloss on this common-law doctrine held that a man could beat his wife, so long as the stick he used was no thicker than his thumb).

But far from being wholly occupied with household concerns, middle-class women now found that much of their customary work was slipping from their hands. The rise of factory industry was removing from the home such occupations as the spinning of thread and weaving of cloth, the making of clothes, and the preparation of foods which in earlier times had largely claimed their time and energies. Also, the increasing wealth of the middle classes enabled them to turn over the remaining domestic chores to servants and the care of children to nurses, governesses and tutors. Before the onslaught of the Industrial Revolution, the family had been an economic unit and "marriage was an industrial partnership as well as a relation of affection. . . . But [now] parasitism became the fate of the middle-class women."[5]

In short, the homely middle-class housewife of the past was giving way before the middle-class lady of leisure. Indeed, leisured, or idle, wives and daughters had become expensive status symbols for successful middle-class men. For middle-class women to work seemed "to imply that you had not money enough to pay others to work for you." Now, one woman observed: "A lady, to be sure, must be a mere lady and nothing else. She must not work for profit or engage in any occupation that money can command, lest she invade the rights of the working classes, who live by their labour." The idea gained currency that work for ladies was actually degrading, as another woman forcefully declared: "Now allow me . . . to pass by without notice all *democratic* and *low* arguments about *ladies* working. My opinion is . . . that if a woman is obliged to work, at once she (although she may be Christian and well bred) loses that peculiar position to which the word *lady* conventionally designates."[6] The phrase "working ladies" was, in fact, a contradiction in terms.

In these circumstances, the chief aim of middle-class women was to make a good match, since marriage was the only respectable career open to them. To snare husbands and to be graceful ornaments in the homes over which they would preside they must learn the arts of playing the piano, singing, dancing and the like. They needed no very solid education since they were not to work for a living, and since blue-stockings notoriously frightened away matrimonial prospects. "Strong-minded" was one of the most abusive terms that could be applied to a woman, and even the most dedicated feminists strove to avoid being so labelled, although men never actually claimed that they preferred their women feeble-minded. (For example, a lady wrote to John Stuart Mill declaring that she too favoured women's suffrage but that she was "not a strong-minded female, and should never dream of going to the hustings." Mill replied: "I am sorry to find that you disclaim being strong-minded, because I believe strength of mind to be one of the noblest gifts that any rational creature, male or female, can possess, and the best measure of our degree of efficiency for working in the cause of truth.")[7] Indifferently or frivolously educated, often empty-headed and limited in outlook, idle and dependent upon men for their livelihood and their status in society, middle-class women not unnaturally were considered a subordinate species altogether, while women of intelligence and ability were frustrated by the narrow, stultifying lives which were their lot.

It was against all this that feminists inveighed, led in the early days of the women's movement by a remarkable group of talented, active and attractive young women, now all but forgotten yet deserving of at least a passing mention in any account of Victorian feminism. The "ladies of Langham Place," they have been called, from the site of their London headquarters, the offices of the *English Woman's Journal,* which began publication early in 1858. It would be hard to exaggerate the *Journal's* importance in these early days of the women's movement. It quickly became the major organ of publicity and propaganda for the cause, the first real forum for the discussion of women's problems. Also, by gaining the attention and support of women throughout the country, it served as the nucleus of the practical side of the movement, around which and from which sprang up societies and programs designed to benefit women. Among these was the Society for Promoting the Employment of Women, founded in 1859 with offices in the same building as the *Journal.*[8]

The leader of the Langham Place group was Barbara Leigh Smith (1827-1891), whose grandfather and father alike were noted Radical M.P.'s of Unitarian persuasion. Granted a handsome independent income by her father when she attained the age of twenty-one, she was able both to cultivate her considerable talent as a painter and to engage in a variety of projects for the advancement of women, the cause always dearest to her generous, freedom-loving nature. After her marriage in 1857 to a Frenchman, Dr. Eugène Bodichon, she divided her time between her new home in Algeria and her old home and companions in England. Madame Bodichon was instrumental in bringing before Parliament in 1857 the question of reform of the married women's property law; later she helped to organize the women's suffrage petition which Mill presented in Parliament early in 1866; and later still she was the untiring supporter and chief benefactress of Girton College.[9]

A close personal friend and helper of Madame Bodichon was Bessie Rayner Parkes (1829-1925), a descendant of the Unitarian philosopher and scientist Joseph Priestley, and daughter of the Radical lawyer Joseph Parkes, who had played an important behind-the-scenes part in winning. passage of the Reform Bill of 1832. A great lover of literature, especially poetry, Miss Parkes aspired to a literary career and published several volumes of poems of considerable merit. But her passionate altruism led her to devote much of her time and energy to work in the women's cause, including the founding and editing of the *English Woman's Journal,* until her marriage in 1867 to a Frenchman, Louis Belloc. She was soon left a widow with two small children, a daughter Marie, later Mrs. Belloc Lowndes, a talented novelist and critic, and a son, Hilaire Belloc, later the distinguished man of letters, political thinker and sometime M.P., and champion of the Catholic Church.[10]

Among the supporters of Madame Bodichon and Miss Parkes was Adelaide Procter (1825-1864), daughter of the poet "Barry Cornwall" (Bryan Waller Procter). Before her early death from tuberculosis, Miss Procter had established herself as a poet whose works rivalled in popularity those of Tennyson and were the favourite poetry of Queen Victoria. "A Lost Chord," perhaps her most famous poem, appeared first in the *English Woman's Journal,* which she helped to found and to which she contributed other poetry and articles, and she also helped to organize the Society for Promoting the Employment of Women. This Society, which boasted Lord Shaftesbury as its president, was the brain-child of Jessie Boucherett (1825-1905), the practical-minded and energetic daughter of a Lincolnshire squire, whose chance encounter with copies of the *Journal* brought her up to London to offer her services to the ladies of Langham Place. Later she edited the *Englishwoman's Review,* successor to the *Journal* as spokesman of the women's movement. Yet another recruit to the cause was Maria Susan Rye (1829-1903), who was active in the work of the S.P.E.W. and whose interest in the emigration to the colonies of women and of pauper children later led her literally to the ends of the earth. A sort of elder stateswoman of the Langham Place group was Mrs. Anna Jameson (1794-1860). Deserted in effect by her decidedly peculiar husband, Mrs. Jameson had been forced to support herself, and her parents and four younger sisters as well, by her literary labours, and had won a well-merited reputation as art critic and art historian.[11]

The philosophy of feminism as enunciated by Mill and the ladies of Langham Place was, as Mrs. Fawcett pointed out, a natural development and a logical corollary of the claim for the rights of man. As such it echoed the rallying cry of the eighteenth-century philosophers and of Mary Wollstonecraft's *Vindication of the Rights of Woman* (1792), and as such it reflected the rise of liberalism in the nineteenth century. The feminist philosophy also drew inspiration and strength from Evangelicalism and its outgrowth, the "Victorian conscience." Women, like men, possessed certain inalienable, God-given rights, and they also owed a debt to God and man and other women. However revolutionary their statements and demands might seem to many, the mid-nineteenth-century feminists were identifying themselves with the dominant philosophical trends of their time.

Denouncing the patriarchal ideal of society, Barbara Bodichon declared that the "beautiful dependence of woman upon man, upon which novelists and sentimentalists love to dwell *ad nauseam* . . . is in reality a condition of servitude," while Mrs. Fawcett pointed out that the "qualities of docility, obedience, and dependence" magnified by the patriarchal ideal were "apt to degenerate into feebleness," and that the new feminist ideal was of women endowed with "endurance, foresight, strength and skill." Again and again the general feminist claim was heard: "We must acknowledge an independent self-nature in woman as in man, and a common responsibility, because a common dignity, in both." More specifically, women claimed the right to receive an education as good as men's in order to develop their abilities to the fullest extent, and the right to work in whatever career they chose and for which they were fitted, free from a degrading and debilitating dependence upon men. "Let a woman be permitted . . . to enter into any calling the duties of which she can adequately discharge. Without scorn, or jeer, or libel, let her fairly do that which God has given her power to accomplish."[12]

In voicing these claims, women were well aware of the strength of conventional opposition to them. Bessie Parkes clearly saw that when men dismissed the feminist claims by saying that "the vast majority of women are destined to marry, what they mean—the idea which really lies at the bottom of their minds is, that were it otherwise the whole constitution of modern society would literally go to pieces."[13] The patriarchal ideal of society was inextricably bound up with the ideal of the home, which to the Victorians was not just another social institution but the very heart and soul of society. "It was a place apart, a walled garden . . . a shelter *from* the anxieties of modern life, a place of peace where the longings of the soul might be realized . . . and a shelter *for* those moral and spiritual virtues which the commercial spirit and the critical spirit [in religion and morality] were threatening to destroy, and therefore also a sacred place, a temple." And over this walled garden, this sheltering temple, presided the wife and mother, "the angel in the house."[14]

"Of Queens' Gardens"—this was the apt symbolic title of a lecture delivered by John Ruskin to an audience of ladies and published in 1865 in his *Sesame and Lilies*. This, Ruskin's most popular work, stands at the opposite pole from Mill's *Subjection of Women* as the classic Victorian exposition of the anti-feminist case.[15] The sentiments to which Ruskin appealed were deeply felt, and underlay many another anguished masculine outcry against the women's movement, such as the following:

She must no longer stand in the shade apart, shedding the blessing of peace and calmness on the combatants, when they return home, heated and weary, but she must be out in the blazing sun, toiling and fighting too, and marking every victory by the grave-stone of some dear virtue, canonised since the world began. Homes deserted, children—the most solemn responsibility of all—given to a stranger's hand, modesty, unselfishness, patience, obedience, endurance, all that has made angels of humanity must be trampled under foot, while the Emancipated Woman walks proudly forward to the goal of the glittering honours of public life, her true honours lying crushed beneath her, unnoticed.[16]

The more radical of the women's spokesmen, such as Karl Marx's daughter Eleanor, declared that women were "the creatures of an organised tyranny of men," who wanted to "dominate the revolted slave." Others, more reasonably, held that men opposed the feminist claims simply because they wanted what was best for women themselves and for society generally. The question was whether that which conventional-minded men wanted really was the best, and whether they had the right to decide for women what was best for them. As one woman put it: "What is really good for women must be in the end, really good for men, though it may not be precisely that sort of good that they have wished and prayed for."[17]

In any case, the feminists were willing to meet upholders of the patriarchal ideal on their own ground, and argued that the granting of women's claims, far from subverting homes and family life, would actually improve them. They pointed out that the ideal of the leisured lady took little account of the actual facts of married life. The management of large households, including the supervision of many servants and the care, education and guidance of numerous children, required knowledge and labour and skill, but women were not being trained for this. The frivolous education bestowed upon girls merely prepared them "to *get* married, not to *be* married." And how degrading it was for girls to have to marry in order to gain a respectable livelihood and a recognized status in society, and degrading for men as well, when it was "not easy . . . to distinguish a genuine preference in a woman amidst the general scramble for husbands." Idleness was "not ladylike but unwomanly," "an evil and a snare." Work was a positive good, necessary for women as for men to maintain them in both physical and mental health, for nothing was "so depressing and so painful as to feel that one is in the world of no use." Work outside the home was also an excellent preparation for marriage, a means of education, promoting "increased stability, independence, self-reliance," and "any sort of steady womanly work would be a better preparation for married life than mere dull vacancy." Some supporters of the patriarchal ideal were so foolish as to argue that if given a choice, women would prefer work and shun marriage, and the feminists dismissed these with the contemptuous observation that they must consider matrimony "a most unhappy state— a refuge of the destitute!" In the new conditions which they desired for women, the feminists maintained, marriages would probably increase, for work would "bring persons of congenial tastes into mutual intercourse," and marriages which otherwise would be "flagrantly imprudent" because of financial considerations would be possible, with women now economic assets rather than liabilities. In short, to quote Mrs. Fawcett once more, the feminists' new-model women would "become, in a better sense than they have ever been before, companions and helpmeets to men . . .".[18]

Besides producing better daughters, wives and mothers, the feminists argued that improved education and opportunities for women to work outside the home would benefit society at large. Already, and conservatives never objected to their work, many women of the lower classes were employed as domestic servants and factory hands, and many women of the better classes as governesses, while at the top of the social scale the Queen herself furnished a shining example of a woman combining public work of supreme importance with the traditional roles of devoted wife and mother. (But where the feminists were concerned, Her Majesty was definitely not amused, writing on one occasion: "The Queen is most anxious to enlist everyone who can speak or write to join in checking this mad, wicked folly of 'Women's Rights' . . . *with all its attendant horrors,* on which her poor feeble sex is bent, forgetting every sense of womanly feeling and propriety . . . It is a subject which makes the Queen so *furious* that she cannot contain herself.")[19] Far from being unwomanly and unseemly, the feminists declared, the work of ladies outside their homes was desperately needed to help solve the crying social problems of the time. The scope of private charity at that time was enormous, and ladies were expected to spend considerable time and effort in "visiting the poor." But the feminists wanted to see such amateur ladies bountiful replaced by well-educated, competent women with a sound knowledge of social problems and with the ability to take a meaningful and constructive part in such concerns as the administration of workhouses, of schools and of hospitals. The exercise of such eminently desirable and traditionally feminine qualities as tenderness and nurturing care of the young, the sick and the unfortunate must be raised to a higher plane and expanded far beyond individual circles of family, dependents and friends. This, one of the most telling of the feminists' arguments, was especially well put by Mrs. Jameson in two lectures which she delivered privately in 1855 and 1856 and which were later published, *Sisters of Charity Catholic and Protestant, Abroad and at Home* and *The Communion of Labour.* To her and others like her, women's right to work entailed their duty to serve and to uplift.

Having invoked liberalism in the broadest sense of the word with their appeals for the rights of women as free individuals, the feminists also invoked liberalism in the narrower, economic sense. They appealed to the theory of laissez-faire, to the doctrine of free competition in the labour market, with occupations going to those workers, men or women, who proved themselves most capable. To conservatives who claimed that ladies were too weak, nervous, excitable and the like to be successful workers, the feminists replied that it was actually lack of work, lack of opportunities to use and improve their faculties, that rendered them weak, nervous and so on, if indeed they were. They also pointed out that the great majority of working women were employed in factories and workshops, in fields and at mines, doing hard and competitive physical labour. To those who argued that women were intellectually inferior to men, lacking accuracy and steadiness for work, the feminists retorted that they were not intellectually inferior by nature but by reason of their inferior education. All that the feminists asked for women was "fair field and no favour," the chance to prove themselves, and one observer remarked caustically: "The possibility that women, if adequately educated, may develop powers adapted to employments monopolized by men, has led to a jealousy for female delicacy and elevation above work which is a little suspicious: men have never made an outcry against women's entering upon any occupation however hard or 'degrading,' unless that occupation were one in which they would compete with men!"[20]

There were, in fact, frequent alarmed masculine cries that if middle-class women entered the labour market, they would drive men out of work, or at least men's pay would be reduced by the competition of lower-paid female labour. If this were true, some feminists replied, at least it would be fairer to share suffering, to have men take their portion of misery rather than to cast all of it upon women. Others remarked that although women's competition might diminish some men's earnings, women's work would also relieve some men of their financial burdens, for fathers and brothers would no longer have to support their daughters and sisters. But on the whole the feminists believed that the entire community, men as well as women, would gain by women's increased employment. Women must be supported and their maintenance cost the same, whether or not they worked; if they worked, the country would benefit by the increase in its productive power. The amount of work to be done was not a fixed quantity, nor was the "wages fund" of the classical economists; fresh occupations were continually being opened up to educated workers, with the prospect of ever increasing pay.[21] In short, women as well as men could contribute to and benefit from an expanding economy.

The feminists argued their case well, yet leaders are nothing without a following, nor is a philosophy valid without some practical application to the problems of everyday life. The supporters of women's rights might be charged with voicing merely sentimental grievances and with demanding equality for women merely to satisfy their theories, but the charge was never justified, for they were actually addressing themselves to pressing practical problems. Bessie Parkes summed it up: "Except for the material need which exerted a constant pressure upon a large and educated class, the 'woman's movement' could never have become in England a subject of popular comment, and to a certain extent of popular sympathy."[22] The foundations of the Victorian patriarchy did not crumble because of the feminists' verbal assaults, but because the patriarchal ideal departed so far from reality.

A widely read and very influential article which appeared in the *Edinburgh Review* in 1859 was frequently credited with having first shocked the public into an awareness of the problem of "redundant women," that is, the unmarried. It was written by that renowned Radical, Harriet Martineau, whose name for some thirty years had been almost a household word for instructor of the nation in economic and social affairs, and whose words now inspired Jessie Boucherett to found the Society for Promoting the Employment of Women. Drawing upon the census statistics for 1851, Miss Martineau pointed out that there were over half a million more women than men in Britain, single women who could not hope to "marry and be taken care of" and widows who might not have been left provided for by their husbands. Already a sizeable proportion in the mid-nineteenth century, the number of unmarried women increased steadily throughout the period before World War I, the census of 1911 showing that there were nearly 1,400,000 more women that men in the country. (By 1970 women outnumbered men by an estimated 1,500,000. However, whereas females formerly outnumbered males in every age group, they now do not begin to outnumber them till the age of forty-five.) Moreover, this disproportion between the sexes in Victorian times was greater among the middle classes than among the working classes. To illustrate this fact, a woman writer used the 1911 census statistics to compare the number of men and women in six different boroughs of London representing the different social classes: in the three wealthier neighbourhoods (Hampstead, Kensington and Chelsea) there were 5,758 men and 19,738 women, while in the three working-class neighbourhoods (Woolwich, Shoreditch and Bethnal Green) there were 5,185 men and 3,850 women. It was no coincidence that "a period of great upheaval in the female mind" came at a time when there was an "abnormally large" number of unmarried women of "the discussing, thinking, agitating classes."[23]

The chief reason given to explain this surplus of middle-class women was the excessive emigration of men of their class, who were responding to the calls of far-flung empire and seeking new lives in new worlds. As a member of the Army or Navy stationed abroad, a civil servant, a trader, a colonist, the middle-class English male was "anywhere, and everywhere, except where he ought to be, making love to the pretty girls in England." Moreover, contemporaries noted with alarm the growing disinclination of middle-class men to marry, and the tendency among the middle classes to postpone marriage till late in life. Since middle-class women were expected not to work before or after marriage, they were expensive luxuries, contributing nothing to family resources in a period of rising expectations and standards of living.[24] (For the changing pattern of marriage in the twentieth century, see Appendix, Table 6g and comment.)

Yet even those middle-class Victorian women who did marry had no certainty of a secure and sheltered existence. Professional men, on whose individual exertions and success their families depended, frequently could not make adequate provision for the event of their death or disability. Manufacturers and merchants might go bankrupt or their businesses be wound up after their death. Also, with the growth of large-scale industrial and commercial enterprises, the tendency was for men to become salaried employees instead of independent proprietors, and while a small-scale business might continue after the principal's death, a man's salary did not.[25]

In these circumstances, many women obviously must work or starve. Miss Martineau pointed out that in 1851, of six million women in Britain over the age of twenty, more than two million were independent and self-supporting like men, and she concluded:

The supposition was . . . false, and ought to be practically admitted
to be false;—that every woman is supported (as the law supposes her
to be represented) by her father, her brother, or her husband. . . A
social organisation framed for a community of which half stayed
home, while the other half went out to work, cannot answer the purposes of a society, of which a quarter remains at home while three-
quarters go out to work.[26]

(For the proportions of unmarried, married and widowed women in the
country's labour force, see Appendix, Table 6g.)

The great majority of working women in Victorian England belonged to
the lower or labouring classes, as opposed to those of the middle classes.
(A satisfactory definition of the "middle classes" is difficult to come by,
but one Victorian described them aptly as "that part of the population
which, on the whole, and mainly, has to earn its own living, and to earn it
by headwork rather than by handwork.") Bessie Parkes estimated that of
thirteen units representing the total population of the country, one unit
would represent the aristocracy, three would represent the "middle
ranks," and nine "the masses." Therefore middle-class women would constitute only about one-half of three-thirteenths, or some 12 per cent, of the
total population, and those middle-class women who had to work would
be only a fraction of this proportion.[27] Still, there was a significant and
always increasing number and proportion of middle-class women in the
country's labour force. (See Appendix, Tables 6e and 6f.)

For the Victorian lady who was forced to work for a living, "governessing," said Bessie Parkes, was "the one means of breadwinning to which
access alone seems open and to which alone untrained capacity is equal, or
pride admits appeal." By devoting herself to the care and education of
children, even for hire, a lady could fill the role for which nature had intended her; and by living at home and going out into other homes as a
daily governess, or by working as a resident governess in a girls' boarding
school or in her employers' household, she would still enjoy that sheltering abode deemed to be her proper sphere. Every woman was by nature a
teacher, and the mere fact of being a lady and in straitened circumstances
especially qualified her somehow for teaching. Advertisements such as
these appeared in the newspapers: "A Young Lady, *recently bereaved,*
requires music pupils." *"Bank Failures—In consequence of the above,*
a Married Lady, highly connected . . ." etc. It was estimated that only 6
or 7 per cent of all middle-class women teachers had consciously chosen
teaching as their career.[28]

But however "respectable" and "natural" her occupation, the governess's lot was not a happy one. For those living at home or in girls'
schools the life was hard and lonely, unprepared as they were for the work
and cut off, by the necessity of working, from their former social circle.
As for governesses living with their charges' families, they were usually
expected to act as nurses and maids as well as teachers for the children,
and to make themselves generally useful wherever needed. They were

NO SINECURE.

Proud Mother (to the new Governess). "And here is a Pencil, Miss Green, and a Note-Book in which I wish you to write down all the clever or remarkable things the dear Children may say during your Walk."

often excluded from the family circle as being little better than servants, and were in turn despised by the servants themselves.

Yet the struggle to obtain positions as governesses became ever keener as more and more middle-class women found it necessary to make their own way in the world. Moreover, they had to face the added competition of women of the lower classes who had had elementary-school teacher training and who were seeking to raise their social position by becoming governesses. One lady reported that she had had over eight hundred applications for a governess's post. Such competition naturally beat down the level of salaries. In London in the 1860's, for example, the highest salary reported was £65 a year, the lowest £10, and the usual pay for governesses was estimated as about £25. With such meager earnings many governesses had to support others besides themselves, fathers and mothers, brothers and sisters, nephews and nieces. They could save little or nothing to provide for times of sickness or of unemployment, often being dismissed simply because they had reached the advanced age of thirty-five or so and being replaced by younger women. In old age they could look forward only to dependence upon the charity of relatives or friends or, as a last resort, the workhouse.[29]

The plight of governesses, "decayed gentlewomen" they were often called, attracted a great deal of sentimental interest and inspired considerable charitable effort. It was not that governesses were the most numerous or the most depressed class of women workers in the country, but unlike women workers in factories and fields, they were highly "visible" to the middle and upper classes, being familiar figures in their homes. Also, as Bessie Parkes remarked: "There is probably no one who has not some relative or cherished friend either actually engaged in teaching, or having formerly been so engaged." The first article in the first issue of the *English Woman's Journal,* written by Miss Parkes, dealt with governesses and drew upon the annual reports of the Governesses' Benevolent Institution, which, she said, had first shocked her and her fellow workers into an awareness of the problems of poor ladies forced to earn their living by teaching: "The frightful record there set forth of the destitution and desolation into which educated women fall was the most heartrending thing she had ever read in her life."[30]

Founded in London in 1841, the Governesses' Institution sought at first merely "to afford relief privately and delicately to ladies in temporary distress" by distributing small sums of money to needy governesses, but its work rapidly expanded. Annuities for the poorest applicants were established, and an asylum for elderly governesses and a home for those temporarily out of work were opened. In 1857, to give but one example, the Institution had 120 applicants for financial aid and admittance to the asylum; of these women, all of them over fifty years old and ninety-nine of them unmarried, thirty-seven had small incomes ranging from £1 to £17 a year, while eighty-three were absolutely destitute.[31] Here was a vicious circle indeed. Middle-class women who were forced to work had open to them only one overcrowded field where conditions were too often deplorable; their generally poor education did not prepare them for any other field of work, nor even for this one; and they were poorly educated because they were not expected to have to work.

All this was bad enough. And yet another damning indictment of patriarchal society was that by denying to middle-class women a sound education and opportunities for work besides governessing, it consigned many of them to "that pestilence 'which walketh in darkness,'" that is, to prostitution.[32]

The solution to these problems was obvious to the feminists. Parents must cease operating on the false assumption that marriage was both the inevitable destiny and the securest haven for their daughters and must prepare them as well as sons, by a sound general education and by further special training if necessary, to make their way in the world. The education of girls must be drastically revised and greatly improved, and the status of their teachers raised from that of the lowly governesses to that of true professionals. Also, all must give up the idea that teaching was the only respectable calling for ladies, must "get rid of all caste feeling, and judge of people by themselves and not by their work." Women should be allowed free entry into all fields of work then closed to them, partly because of convention, partly because of their lack of training. One woman summed up vigourously:

> It is work we ask, room to work, encouragement to work, an open field with a fair day's wages for a fair day's work; it is an injustice, we feel, the injustice of men, who arrogate to themselves all profitable employments . . . and . . . drive women to the lowest depths of penury and suffering. . . . Could Providence have created several thousand superfluous women for the purpose of rendering them burdens on society, as inmates of our prisons, workhouses and charitable institutions? Or is it that there is something wrong in our social arrangements, whereby they are unfairly deprived of occupations . . .?[33]

Clearly a great practical need reinforced the feminists' claims, on theoretical grounds, for better education and more opportunities for work.

To meet this practical need, the ladies of Langham Place set to work with a will. One of the main aims of the Society for Promoting the Employment of Women was to awaken people to the necessity of better education for girls. Articles were published, papers read, even sermons preached on the subject, and within two years of its founding the Society was speaking proudly of the "general moral influence it has brought to bear, upon the press, and upon the opinions of numerous circles in various parts of the kingdom."[34] Fortunately, the climate of the times favoured the demand for improvement in women's education. To the nineteenth century, education generally represented a panacea for many ills. Indeed, the same intellectual trends which flowered in the philosophy of feminism underlay the contemporary desire for education for all. Education would exercise a moral, elevating and liberating influence upon the individual. It would also produce a nation of responsible citizens and intelligent workers. That the century which saw the beginning of the women's movement also saw the coming of universal, compulsory education was more than coincidence, and the "renaissance" of women's education, as it was sometimes called, was but one part of the wider reform of education, extending from the elementary schools to the universities.

Meanwhile, the ladies of Langham Place were nothing if not practical, and in addition to its propaganda work, the Society for Promoting the Employment of Women, both the central office in London and the sprinkling of branches throughout the country, set up a number of pilot projects to train women and employ them, or find employment for them, in fields of work from which they were then excluded. The Victoria Press, a printing business run by women trained by the Society as compositors, was successfully established, and within three years was actually named Printer and Publisher in Ordinary to Her Majesty. Another project was the opening, under the direction of Maria Rye, of a law stationer's office staffed by trained women, which was so successful that two more offices were soon opened. Of much wider scope as possible fields for women's work was employment as shop assistants and as clerks. Jessie Boucherett saw this, but also realized that girls at the time generally were so poorly educated, so ignorant even of simple writing and arithmetic, that they could not function as clerks handling business correspondence and bookkeeping, nor could they even be trusted to make change correctly in waiting on customers in shops. To help remedy this situation she organized classes which provided younger girls with a "solid English education" and older ones with training for clerical work. (These classes continued in existence for nearly forty years, until 1899, when it was decided that they were no longer needed, owing to the general improvement in education which had come about by that time and to the fact that "commercial subjects" were being taught in most schools and in evening classes.) The Society also helped small groups of women to train for and find employment in such fields as hairdressing, engraving, photography, house decoration, proofreading and, an especial favourite, the administration of charitable institutions.[35]

Its work proved what the Society had set out to prove. Speaking of her experience at the law stationer's office, Miss Rye declared: "I am more and more impressed with the conviction that women need only be trained properly to become capable of conducting or working in this or any other business; and that it is only this want of training which keeps so many women poor and in difficulties all their lives." But clearly the Society was much too small an organization to solve by its own efforts the problem of unemployed women. The situation was summed up thus: "It . . . is the public and not the Society that must find employment for women. All that can be done by a Society is to act as pioneer, to make experiments, to inaugurate efforts. The rest remains to be accomplished by the real impetus of the movement: namely, its necessity, its justice, and its expediency . . .".[36]

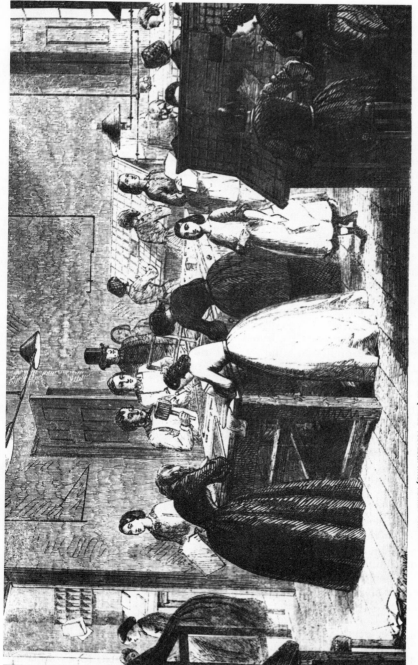

PRINTING-OFFICE (THE VICTORIA PRESS) IN GREAT CORAM-STREET, FOR THE EMPLOYMENT OF WOMEN AS COMPOSITORS.

The wider employment of middle-class women was certainly necessary and even just, but above all it proved to be expedient. England's rapidly expanding economy created a large and increasing demand for labour, a demand which better educated women could supply as well as men—and at a lower cost. (Barbara Bodichon hit upon this last point in an appeal to the self-interest of employers, calling upon them to increase their profits by hiring women workers instead of men, since women expected to receive only about half of men's pay.) The feminists' trust in the country's economic progress and what this would imply for women's opportunities for work was not misplaced, but foreseeing a development is not the same as causing it, and the women's movement cannot be justly credited with bringing about the wider employment of middle-class women. "The great expansion of non-manual [or middle-class] occupations . . . centered on schools, offices, shops and hospitals—an expansion which, deriving from the technological and social diversification of industrialism and satisfying its cheap labour requirements, owed little to pioneering feminists."[37]

Schools, offices, shops and hospitals—these were precisely the places where the early feminists hoped and expected to see an increase in the employment of middle-class women. The growing number of women teachers resulted naturally from the improvements in women's education and, more generally, from the development of a state-supported national system of education. The growth in the ranks of nurses reflected both the progress of medical science and increasing public concern for the health and welfare of the community. The numbers of shop assistants and of clerks swelled to significantly larger proportions of the total working population as a result of the tremendously increased production arising from industrialization and the flourishing state of commerce, nourished by a policy of free trade and the growing wealth and purchasing power of the community. Finally, increasing government activity, itself a response to the growth of an urbanized, industrial society and an awakening social conscience, necessitated the employment of an ever larger army of civil servants. And in three of these fields, shop and clerical work and the civil service, the rate of increase in the number of women employed was substantially above the rate of increase for men, a development which seems best explained, in the final analysis, by the simple fact that women worked more cheaply than men. (Statistics on employment in these five fields are given in the Appendix, Sections 1-5.)

The increasing employment of middle-class women in these fields both contributed to and reflected a major social phenomenon of the later nineteenth and twentieth centuries, the expansion and consolidation of the middle classes of non-manual workers, compared with the manual-labour classes. Between 1861 and 1911 the increase in the total working population of England and Wales was, for men, 77.0 per cent and for women, 44.2 per cent, while the rate of increase for workers in the middle-class occupations of teacher, nurse, shop assistant, clerk and civil servant was 192.3 per cent for men and 307.0 per cent for women. (See Appendix, Section 6.) In turn, the growth of the middle classes was a natural corollary of increasing industrialization. Only an advanced industrial economy can provide employment for large numbers of workers who rank between the masses of manual labourers on the one hand and the aristocracy on the other, and also, as an industrial economy progresses, the number of middle-class or "white-collar" workers increases steadily in proportion to lower-class or "blue-collar" workers.

Clearly the growing numbers of middle-class workers were not recruited, could not be recruited solely from the ranks of the existing middle classes in Victorian England. Although Victorian society was stratified and highly class-conscious, members of the lower classes could always hope to rise in the social scale by entering those occupations traditionally associated with the middle classes, and this became increasingly possible with the advent of popular education. As one Victorian put it: "In these days of diffused education, class runs into class, and it is hard to say where one ends and the other begins, and harder still to define the work which belongs to each."[38] In this connection it should be noted that only a highly developed industrial society has sufficient wealth at its disposal to provide comprehensive schemes of education for the community, education which makes possible the continued growth of the middle classes and which benefits women as well as men. Also, such a society may well be dependent for its continued progress upon large numbers of educated—and, perhaps, lower-paid—women as a necessary source of labour.

Meanwhile, not only were their numbers greatly increasing, but also conditions of work were changing greatly for teachers, nurses, shop assistants, clerks and civil servants. On the one hand, there was a raising of the status of the workers in teaching and nursing, this "professionalization" being a distinctive and widespread phenomenon of the period. The essential feature of a profession has been defined as "special competence, acquired as the result of intellectual training," which "gives rise to certain attitudes and activities." A spirit of solidarity grows naturally among those set apart from the average person by specialized training, and finds formal expression in professional associations. These associations serve as social and educational organizations for their members, and also seek to protect both their members and society at large against untrained practitioners, insisting upon thorough training and recognized tests of proficiency for membership in the profession and enforcing accepted codes of professional ethics. The final step in the evolution or creation of a profession comes with intervention by the government, which sets up a central body, composed of representatives of the profession itself and of the state, to lay down qualifications for admission to the profession and keep a register of those qualified, and to enforce professional discipline by trying those accused of unprofessional conduct and removing from the register the names of those found guilty. Interestingly, it has been suggested that the rise of the professions is one aspect of the democratization or levelling upward of society, a reflection of "the strong desire . . . of the masses . . . to become middle class . . .".[39]

On the other hand, there was a contrary movement, a sort of "de-professionalization," among shop assistants, clerks and civil servants, who in the early part of this period had some of the attributes of professionals and unquestionably enjoyed a status of middle-class respectability. A sound general education and an apprenticeship or a probationary training period were necessary for their work. Many of those in the distributive trades and in clerical work could look forward to going into business on their own and thereby achieving an independent position, which is another distinguishing feature of the professional, while civil servants might rise to the highest government posts. But an expanding economy and universal education changed all this. With the growth of large-scale business enterprises, division of labour swept into shops and offices as it had into factories, and shop assistants and clerks tended to be employed increasingly on work of routine nature for which little special training was necessary, and which offered them little prospect of advancement through promotion and even less prospect of setting up in business for themselves. At the same time, the widening sphere of government activity increased the amount of routine work to be done by civil servants, while regrading of the service tended to confine workers in small compartments with little opportunity of rising to higher posts. Also, with the general improvement in education, men of the middle classes, who had once monopolized these three fields of work, now had to compete for positions both with educated women of their own class and with men and women of the lower classes. In this competitive situation, conditions of work grew worse, and shop assistants, clerks and civil servants tended to sink to the level of a "black-coated proletariat."[40] Their history in the later part of this period is the story of their efforts to improve their lot by means of organization and of government intervention in the form of protective legislation, the two remedies which had done so much to better the position both of the professions and of the manual-labour classes.

Inspired, perhaps, by the claims of the women's movement, often hard pressed by material need, and swept onward if not exactly upward by the swelling tide of industrialization, middle-class working women in the later nineteenth and early twentieth centuries drastically altered both their position and their outlook. In the mid-nineteenth century ladies who had to work for their living were a surplus and depressed minority, who were pitied and who pitied themselves. By 1914 middle-class working women, a respected and self-respecting group, were an essential part of the country's labour force.

II
WOMEN AND EDUCATION

The history of English education in the nineteenth century is the story of the gradual development of state-supported elementary and technical education for the lower classes. It is also the story of the efforts of the middle and upper classes to retain their educational advantages, at first by reforming secondary education themselves and at length by appealing to the state for aid in the struggle. (According to Victorian usage, "elementary education" was synonymous with education for the lower classes, "secondary education" with education for the middle and upper classes, and not with primary and intermediate studies respectively. The lower classes were expected to learn little beyond the three R's, while the classes above them progressed to higher studies.) These developments were of the greatest importance to the women's movement, for the poor education which middle-class women received in the mid-nineteenth century largely explained their sad plight when they were forced to find work, and improvement in their education was the necessary basis of women's progress in all fields.

In 1854 Bessie Rayner Parkes published anonymously a small volume, later reprinted under her name, entitled *Remarks on the Education of Girls*. In it she denounced existing conditions and called for reform in girls' education, but a large section of the press greeted her book derisively as the work of a "strong-minded female." Her criticisms were not officially heeded and substantiated until ten years later, when the Schools Inquiry Commission was appointed under the chairmanship of Lord Taunton to study schools for the middle classes. The Commission's report provided the first comprehensive survey of the sad state of secondary education.[1] Significantly, the Taunton Commission began by ignoring the whole subject of girls' schools. That they were finally included in the inquiry was largely due to the work of a woman who stands second to none in the history of women's education.

Emily Davies (1830-1921), the daughter of a clergyman, was a small, sweet-faced woman of modest manner and unimpeachable respectability, but her background and her personal demeanour belied her iron will and dogged perseverance and her revolutionary convictions.[2] Miss Davies was, in fact, one of the foremost examples of the dedicated feminist who demanded for women the right to be treated as free and equal individuals, and specifically, their right to enjoy the same educational opportunities as men and to enter upon any career of which they proved themselves capable. Apparently Miss Davies's feminist convictions sprang naturally from early resentment of her lot in life. She envied her brothers, who were educated at Cambridge in preparation for professional careers, while she was indifferently taught at home and then was expected merely to amuse herself and be generally useful about the house and in parish work. A chance meeting with Barbara Bodichon's family brought her into contact with the ladies of Langham Place, and during visits to London she took an important part in their activities, serving for a time as acting editor of the *English Woman's Journal* and founding in Gateshead, where her father was rector, a Northumberland and Durham branch of the Society for Promoting the Employment of Women. In 1864, following her father's death, Miss Davies settled permanently in London, ready to devote her life to work in the women's movement and especially to the cause of women's education.

Through a number of influential friends, Miss Davies successfully pressured the Taunton Commission into including girls' schools in their investigations and suggested questions to be asked and possible witnesses to be called, among them John Stuart Mill. At length she was called to give evidence herself, and was followed by eight other women, including two other outstanding feminist pioneers, Frances Buss and Dorothea Beale, the first women ever examined in person as expert witnesses before a royal commission. The Taunton Commission's report, which appeared in 1867, must have satisfied their greatest expectations.

The Commission began by noting the general if usually unavowed belief of parents that girls were "less capable of mental cultivation" than boys. On this vexed question the Commissioners remained non-committal, but they did condemn the prevailing notion of parents that since daughters would marry and be taken care of, they need not be so well educated as sons. They pointed out that in view of the increasing numbers of middle-class women who had to earn their own living, the question of their education was of the utmost importance.[3]

Generally, the Commission found, parents preferred to send their daughters to small schools, usually boarding schools, where supposedly they would enjoy individual attention and a homelike atmosphere. The average number of pupils in girls' schools was estimated to be only twenty-five. Moreover, parents wanted their daughters to associate at school only with the best society, and snobbery was rampant. Schoolmistresses advertised their establishments as "genteel," "exclusive," "limited," and in some cases parents actually dictated to them which girls they must admit and which exclude.[4]

The majority of girls' schools were held in private houses converted for the purpose, where classrooms were frequently overcrowded, poorly ven-

A GENERIC DIFFERENCE.

First Schoolgirl (Sweet Eighteen). "I AM SO TIRED OF WALKING ALONG BY TWOS AND TWOS IN THIS WAY! IT'S AS BAD AS THE ANIMALS GOING INTO THE ARK!"

Second Ditto (ditto ditto). "WORSE! HALF OF THEM WERE MASCULINE!"

tilated, and ill equipped, and the sleeping and washing facilities inadequate. There was usually no provision for play and physical activity. The
girls led sedentary lives indoors, being allowed only a chaperoned daily
walk "in crocodile" as exercise. It is an interesting commentary on the
health of schoolgirls that pallor and crooked spines were supposedly their
distinguishing marks![5]

Owing to the small number of pupils, and the fact that they had to be
accepted at all ages and at all stages of their education, it was difficult to
organize a sensible schedule of properly graded classes in girls' schools.
Some girls went to school for only a few years and then returned home at
an early age. Others were taught at home first, and then attended school
for a year or two to be "finished," many of them when they arrived at
school knowing little more than "how to read and write, and that imper-
fectly."[6] In either case, their schooldays were often interrupted when
parents moved them from one school to another or removed them from
school altogether so that they could pay visits to relatives and friends or
be generally useful at home. Still other girls never attended school at all,
being entirely educated at home by members of their families and occasional masters or mistresses for special lessons, but the Taunton Commission naturally could not investigate this purely domestic education.

As to what the studies of girls should comprise, parents believed, according to the Commission, that "accomplishments, and what is showy
and superficially attractive, are what is really essential for them; and in
particular, that as regards their relations with the other sex and the prob-
abilities of marriage, more solid attainments are actually disadvanta-
geous rather than the reverse." A man-trapping proficiency in music,
drawing, dancing, fancy needlework and the like was important above all.
In more academic studies, for no very clear reason, girls were expected to
excel in such subjects as modern languages, literature, history, astronomy
and botany, while boys concentrated mainly upon the classical languages
and mathematics. One assistant commissioner estimated the amount of
time spent on different subjects in girls' schools as follows: music, 25 per
cent; "miscellaneous information," including mythology, astronomy,
botany, literature and history, 23 per cent; French and German, 16.5 per
cent; and drawing, 6.5 per cent; the remaining 29 per cent was spent on
such subjects of lesser importance as English grammar, writing, arithmetic and geography.[7]

As for the teachers themselves, the Taunton Commission found that the
great majority were totally unqualified for their work, and severely
criticized their "want of thoroughness and foundation; want of system;
slovenliness and showy superficiality; inattention to rudiments." Their
aim seemed to be merely to stuff their pupils' heads with as much information as they could hold. Girls memorized and parroted inferior textbooks,
quoting rules without any understanding of their application and facts
without any knowledge of their logical connection or significance. Moreover, there was little stimulus to study. Girls seldom stood examinations,
for fear that they would become too nervous or develop an "unfeminine

spirit of competition," nor could they, like their brothers, look forward to continuing their education at the universities and to putting their knowledge to practical use in a career.[8]

Paradoxically, parents often paid dearly for this inferior education which their daughters received. Competition among girls' schools did not tend to lower the cost of education, for owing to the small number of their pupils, schoolmistresses had to charge substantial fees in order to meet expenses and make a living.[9]

The Taunton Commissioners found that all the defects characteristic of girls' schools were equally typical of schools for boys, although they believed that the former were worse in every respect. In short, the greater cost of secondary education rather than its superiority distinguished it from the education provided for the lower classes in the elementary schools subsidized by the government.[10]

The increasing provision of elementary schools in the earlier nineteenth century stemmed largely from religious and humanitarian motives, from the desire to provide at least a rudimentary education, and especially to afford moral training, for the children of the lower classes. It was but a matter of time until the state, looking upon this work and finding it good, began to support it. From 1833 Parliament annually voted increasing sums as grants to the Anglican National Society and the Nonconformist British and Foreign Schools Society for the maintenance of elementary schools. In 1839 a committee of the Privy Council took over from the voluntary societies the administration of these grants. Thereafter the committee, reconstituted in 1856 as the Education Department, regulated the course of studies in grant-earning schools by minutes, which after 1860 were embodied in annual codes, and thereby insured a sensible, if limited, curriculum. Significantly, girls received exactly the same education in elementary schools as boys, with the addition of needlework as a compulsory subject, although they were often taught in separate departments and sometimes in separate schools. Government inspectors were appointed to insure that the elementary schools would be maintained in an efficient condition.

In view of the superiority of elementary to middle-class education, the Taunton Commission strongly recommended that the state now take an active part in providing secondary schools. Specifically, the Commission recommended that a strengthened Charity Commission act as a central authority supervising secondary education, analogous to the Education Department supervising elementary education. It also recommended the creation of provincial education boards to deal locally with secondary schools and to levy rates to support them, and the establishment of a central examining council for secondary schools which would do work similar to that of the elementary-school inspectors. But unfortunately, only one of the Commission's specific recommendations bore immediate fruit in legislative action. Created by an act passed in 1869, the Endowed Schools Commission was given powers, which were transferred four years later to the Charity Commission, to use existing endowments to improve secondary education and in particular to provide more endowed schools for girls. In 1869, with endowments for girls' education representing less than 2 per cent of the total, there were but twelve endowed girls' schools, none of outstanding merit, with an average of only fifty pupils each; by 1895, 902 of the total of 1,448 endowments had been reformed, and there were eighty endowed schools for girls.[11]

It was fortunate that voluntary efforts could implement other recommendations of the Taunton Commission, especially their suggestion for the establishment of some external standard to guide middle-class schools, some external examination to determine the curriculum and test the quality of the education offered, as the Education Department laid down the curriculum and its inspectors examined the pupils in elementary schools. The university local examinations had already been established by Oxford in 1857 and by Cambridge in 1858 to test the efficiency of middle-class schools for boys, and these were soon opened to students in girls' schools as well. In 1863 a committee headed by Emily Davies had secured from Cambridge permission for girls to take its local examinations on a trial basis, and shortly afterward prevailed upon the university to open the examinations to girls officially and permanently, an example soon followed by Durham and Oxford. As Miss Davies later declared, the local examinations revolutionized middle-class schools for girls. The high proportion of failures among girls at the earliest examinations forcefully demonstrated the need for radical reform, while the subjects required by the examinations encouraged girls' schools to align their curriculum with that of the best schools for boys and to work out a comprehensive scheme of instruction. In a wider sense, by bringing girls' schools into contact with the universities and with each other, the examinations helped to break down the sense of isolation prevailing among them and their teachers, and fostered a feeling of community and solidarity.[12]

Meanwhile, two institutions dedicated to the higher education of women had developed in London, the prototypes of the new, improved schools for girls of the middle classes.[13] Queen's College, founded in 1848, owed its origin to the scheme for training teachers and granting them certificates of proficiency which the Governesses' Benevolent Institution had begun in connection with the free registry service at its home for unemployed governesses. A Church institution, Queen's always maintained its original close ties with the Anglican King's College, a number of whose professors, notably Frederick Denison Maurice, volunteered to teach and examine women for the Governesses' Institution. In 1849 Bedford College was established, largely through the efforts of Elizabeth Reid, the wealthy widow of a London physician. Mrs. Reid wished to create, in contrast to Queen's, a school without denominational bias in connection with the non-sectarian University College, and to have women associated equally with men in its management, no minor innovation at that time. Incorporated by royal charters and governed by councils, Queen's and Bedford were free from the pressures brought to bear upon the small private-venture girls' schools. Their curriculum included the traditionally masculine studies as well as the usual feminine subjects, and classes were taught originally by King's and University College professors, with older women attending as chaperones in the early days. Students who followed the regular four-year course and passed the required examinations received certificates of general proficiency, while those who entered for individual courses of lectures obtained certificates of proficiency in single subjects. In addition, although its original connection with the Governesses' Benevolent Institution was soon dissolved, Queen's made special provisions for the training of governesses, allowing them reductions in rates, providing evening lectures free of charge, and granting them special teachers' certificates.

Among the teachers trained at Queen's was Frances Mary Buss (1827-1894), one of the great women of English education, who later wrote: "Queen's College began the Women's Education Movement undoubtedly . . . it . . . opened a new life to me and to most of the women who were fortunate enough to become students." The daughter of a London engraver and painter, Miss Buss left school at the age of fourteen to begin her teaching career in the establishment run by her parents, while her brothers continued at school and then went on to the universities. Although sympathizing fully with the views of women like Emily Davies, Miss Buss was more concerned with the practical need for better education for girls than with asserting and proving that girls were the intellectual equals of boys. "As I have grown older," she wrote, "the terrible sufferings of women of my own class, for want of a good elementary training, have more than ever intensified my earnest desire to lighten . . . the misery of women, brought up 'to be married and taken care of,' and left alone in the world destitute."[14]

Miss Buss's two institutions, modelled after Queen's College, furnished the pattern for the reformed girls' schools of the future.[15] The North London Collegiate School, begun by Miss Buss's parents, and the Camden School, which she founded in 1871, represented the antithesis of the girls' schools described as typical by the Taunton Commission. Miss Buss's ideal was a big day school. She disapproved of boarding schools, believing that they "destroyed home feelings," and she preferred operation on a large scale, which would facilitate organization, create a spirit of fellowship and discipline among the students, and not least important, lower the cost of education. The curriculum of her schools, systematically graded for pupils between the ages of six and eighteen, was aligned with that of boys' schools, the "accomplishments" being ruthlessly excluded. Physical training was always a required subject, at first musical drill and later organized games, and when women qualified as medical practitioners, Miss Buss appointed several as consulting physicians to her students. Miss Buss chose her teachers carefully for their sound education and practical ability, and students were tested both by frequent internal examinations and by external examinations, the university locals and later the London matriculation. An elaborate system of marks and prizes further encouraged serious study. The fees charged, about £15 a year, were much lower than those typical of the "best" girls' schools of the day, and ap-

parently anyone able to pay was eligible for admission. One student in the
'80's commented thus on the lack of snobbery: "No one asked where you
lived . . . or what your father was—he might be a bishop or a rat-catcher."[16]
Miss Buss finally realized a cherished ambition when, by investing her
life savings and obtaining further substantial funds from two City Companies for an endowment, and by relinquishing her personal control to a
board of trustees, she transformed her establishments into "public"
schools.

Large public day schools, providing sound intellectual and physical
training, charging reasonable fees, and characterized by a democratic
spirit—such were the girls' high schools which, avowedly emulating Miss
Buss's achievements, now sprang up all over the country. (The name "high
school" apparently originated with the new school for girls at Manchester,
where the first headmistress was a Miss Day and it was felt that confusion
might arise if the earlier name "public day school" was retained.[17]) The
most important organization promoting the establishment of high schools
was the National Union for the Education of Girls of All Classes above
the Elementary, known more simply as the Women's Education Union.
Dedicated to awakening the public to the need for better education for
girls, the Union was founded in London in 1871 through the inspiration of
Maria Shirreff Grey (1816-1906) and her sister, Emily Shirreff (1814-
1897). The daughter of an admiral, Mrs. Grey devoted her life to the
cause of women's education after the death of her husband. She served as
organizing secretary of the Union until the breakdown of her health in
1879, when she became an invalid for the rest of her life. A persuasive
speaker, many of whose speeches were published, she was also the author
of two novels and of two works on education, *Thoughts on Self-Culture
Addressed to Women* (1850) and *The Intellectual Education of Women*
(1858). Miss Shirreff acted as honorary secretary of the Women's Education Union and as joint editor of its *Journal,* and served on the council of
the Union's offspring, the Girls' Public Day School Company. She was
also active in the affairs of Girton College, serving as honorary mistress
of the College in 1870 and as a member of its executive council until her
death.[18]

In 1872 the Girls' Public Day School Company was organized in connection with the Women's Education Union, its aim being to provide for
girls of the middle classes good schools at moderate cost, modelled after
the North London Collegiate School.[19] Voluntary local committees assumed the responsibility of starting schools with capital acquired by the
sale of Company shares, after which the Company's board of directors
appointed the headmistresses and exercised a general supervision over
the schools. Within thirty years the Company boasted thirty-eight schools
with more than seven thousand students. In this case, philanthropy and 5
per cent went exceedingly well together. Similar organizations soon followed the Company's example. On a national scale there was, for instance, the Church Schools Company, founded in 1883, and a number of
local companies also established some excellent schools for girls.[20]

While this outstanding progress was under way in day schools, boarding schools for girls were likewise reformed and given a new lease of life,
largely through the inspiration of another famous pioneer, Dorothea Beale
(1831-1906). The daughter of an affluent London surgeon, Miss Beale
received only a poor and sporadic early education, first from daily governesses at home and then at a school which she left at the age of thirteen
because of ill health. Later she attended the earliest classes at Queen's
College, obtaining a large number of certificates of proficiency in individual subjects, and served as tutor at the College for several years. In 1858
she was appointed principal of the Ladies' College at Cheltenham, a position she was to hold for nearly fifty years. Unlike the dedicated feminist
Emily Davies and the practical-minded Frances Buss, Miss Beale conceived of her mission chiefly in religious terms. To her, the true goal of
education was moral training, and teaching a sacred calling. This was her
creed: "I must behold the Face of the Father, and so become a light to my
children that, seeing the light shine in me, they may glorify the Father."[21]

A small day school which provided the usual ladylike education of the
time and which was, incidentally, the first proprietary school for girls in
England, the Cheltenham Ladies' College seemed on the point of founder-
ing when Miss Beale took charge. Under her competent administration the
College gradually developed into a large residential establishment which
came to approximate the great public schools for boys. Distinctive features of the College were a sound curriculum tested by internal and external examinations and also by inspectors from the universities, emphasis
upon physical training and especially organized games, organization of
students according to the house system, and the prefectorial system of
discipline by the older students, all of which served to foster that *esprit de
corps* and tradition of loyalty which may be called the "public school
spirit."[22]

But despite these outstanding achievements of private enterprise in the
education of girls, the situation remained far from satisfactory, and the
general superiority of elementary to middle-class education, noted by the
Taunton Commission, became increasingly apparent after 1870. Even
heavily subsidized by the government, voluntary efforts of the religious
societies to provide elementary schools had proved inadequate. Also, the
ideal of education for godliness was being transmuted into the ideal of
education for citizenship, an ideal which the state must directly implement. Forster's great Education Act followed hard upon the Reform Bill
of 1867, for, it was said: "We must educate our masters." Under the Act
of 1870, voluntary schools continued to receive government grants as
before. In areas where their facilities proved to be inadequate, school
boards were to be elected, women being eligible both to vote for and to
serve upon these boards, and were empowered to receive grants and levy
rates in order to provide sufficient schools. (Emily Davies was elected to
the London school board in 1870, one of only four women in the whole
country to win election at that time.) Thus the state at last assumed the
responsibility of placing an elementary education within the reach of all

its citizens. An act of 1880 made this education compulsory, and an act of 1891 made it free in both board and voluntary schools.

Meanwhile, there was an increasing concern to provide for the lower classes a more "practical" education than they were receiving. Interest in technical education grew rapidly in the '70's as Britain began to feel the effects of increasing foreign competition. Domestic competition played a part as well, for the middle classes feared that the education of working-class children was too "literary" or "impractical" and consequently tended to draw them away from manual work and into the blackcoated occupations which were traditionally middle-class preserves. As early as 1851 the government had begun to pay to schools grants in aid of technical education which were administered by the Department of Science and Art in South Kensington. Following upon the report of a royal commission on technical education, the Technical Instruction Act of 1889 empowered the newly created county councils and urban authorities to levy a rate to be spent in support of technical education. Another act of 1891 earmarked a portion of the "whisky money," the proceeds from the increased duties on beer and spirits, to be spent on technical education by the county and county borough councils. The Education Department also began to introduce technical subjects into its code for elementary schools. In addition, in 1891 the Department issued a separate code for evening classes, which had been started in connection with and under the same administration as the elementary schools. Originally intended to provide an elementary education for those unable to attend day schools, the evening classes, or evening continuation schools as they came to be called, now ceased to offer elementary subjects and became another avenue of technical education. Technical classes and schools sprang up and flourished all over the country.[23]

From these developments secondary schools benefited directly and indirectly. In the first place, they were eligible to receive both South Kensington grants from the central government and rate aid and whisky-money grants from the local government authorities. Empowered to interpret by minutes the vague statutory definition of "technical education," the Science and Art Department actually sanctioned as "technical" every subject usually offered in secondary schools except classics! Still, the amount of such aid to secondary schools should not be overstated. In 1894, for example, only a little more than £17,000 out of nearly £317,000 spent on technical education by local authorities went to secondary schools.[24] Indirectly, secondary schools benefited as it came to be realized that technical instruction was actually a form of higher education and must be based on a sound secondary education, and as it became increasingly apparent how inadequate was the country's provision of secondary schools.

This inadequacy was pointed out by the royal commission on secondary education under the chairmanship of James Bryce (later Lord Bryce) which was appointed in 1894. The composition and work of the Bryce Commission furnish an excellent illustration of the change in the position of women and the increasing interest in women's questions since the days of the Taunton Commission thirty years before. The Bryce Commission included three women among its seventeen members. Mrs. Sophie Bryant, a teacher at the North London Collegiate School and, after Miss Buss's death, headmistress, was an outstanding scholar who had taken the highest place in the honours division at the first London University examination open to women, and was the first woman to obtain a D. Sc. degree. Mrs. Henry Sidgwick of Cambridge, one of the distinguished Balfour family and sister of the future prime minister, had, together with her husband, taken an active part in the founding and administration of Newnham College.[25] The third woman member of the Commission was Lady Frederick Cavendish. In addition, five of the thirteen assistant commissioners were women, instructed to draw up comprehensive reports on female education to supplement the evidence of the eleven women witnesses heard, among them Dorothea Beale, a representative of the Girls' Public Day School Company, and several of the Company's headmistresses.

The reports of the "lady assistant commissioners," as they were officially dubbed, bore fresh witness to the great improvement in the education of girls during the past three decades—the good effect of the university local examinations on the curriculum of girls' schools generally, and the excellent work of the new high schools, of good private schools organized on the same lines, and of the reformed boarding schools. The lady assistant commissioner reporting on Lancashire, for example, found not one girls' school warranting the general indictment which the Taunton Commission had made of the majority of girls' schools.[26]

But the Bryce Commission discovered that good secondary schools were far too few in number. Moreover, their fees usually placed them beyond the reach of children of the lower middle class, who had to resort to cheap private schools. Such schools for girls exhibited the traditional defects—snobbishness and pseudo-gentility, an outmoded curriculum in which the accomplishments predominated, and incompetent teachers.[27] To supply the need for a good but inexpensive secondary education, school boards in many of the larger towns had developed "higher grade schools" which children of the lower middle class as well as those of the working classes attended in increasing numbers. However, the famous Cockerton judgment of 1900 abruptly cut short the development of these schools, by declaring illegal the school boards' use of rate aid to provide studies beyond the elementary level. This decision lent weight to the recommendation of the Bryce Commission that the state create a national system of public secondary schools.

By the turn of the century it was obvious that the state must take action to bring secondary education within the existing educational structure, and also to resolve the administrative muddle resulting from the piecemeal way in which that structure had been thrown together. To consolidate the central administration of education, an act of 1899 created the Board of Education by amalgamating the Education Department and the Science and Art Department, and transferred to it the educational functions of the Charity Commission. Henceforth the Board controlled all government grants for education and, through the annual codes and regulations which it issued, directed the future development of education throughout the country. The Education Act of 1902 reformed local school administration by sweeping away the school boards and replacing them with education committees of the county and county borough councils and the councils of the more populous boroughs and urban districts. The majority of the committee members were to be members of the councils, but other persons experienced in the field of education could be co-opted, and some of the committee members must be women. In consultation and co-operation with the Board of Education, these new local education authorities were responsible for providing in publicly supported schools education of all levels, elementary, secondary and technical.

To facilitate the organization of public secondary schools, the Board of Education had now to undertake duties long since performed by the state with respect to elementary schools. Until 1911 the Board laid down the curriculum for secondary schools; thereafter, owing to complaints that this curriculum reflected too much the grammar-school ideal of education and was too "impractical" to appeal to working-class children, the local education authorities and the schools themselves took over the drawing up of curricula adapted to their pupils' needs. To insure the efficiency of these schools the Board of Education organized a separate group of secondary-school inspectors, whose work was to be supplemented by that of inspectors appointed by the local authorities. The Board also made government inspection available to private schools, which could apply to be certified as efficient. The county and municipal secondary schools for girls created under the new educational system were modelled after the existing high schools. Indeed, the local authorities took over a considerable number of these schools as publicly supported schools. In 1902 the Board of Education recognized 272 secondary schools with 31,716 students. By 1913 there were 1,027 grant-aided schools with 187,647 students, while 121 schools, with 22,546 students, were not grant-aided but were recognized as efficient.[28]

Perhaps most significant of all, as a reflection of the increasingly democratic temper of the times, the government rejected the connotations of class so long attached to different types of education and sought instead to relate schools to the age of the students and the kind and level of the subjects offered. Secondary schools, once considered the preserve of the middle classes, were defined simply as those offering to students up to and beyond the age of sixteen a general education wider and more advanced than that given in elementary schools. And although secondary education after 1902, unlike elementary education, was neither compulsory nor free, the publicly supported secondary schools apparently were largely filled by children of the lower classes. Of the students in grant-earning secondary schools in 1913, for example, about 64 per cent of the boys and about 60 per cent of the girls had entered from elementary schools.[29]

By 1914 England had created a national system of public education. If she were still far from reaching the goal of a completely democratic or classless system, at least she had taken giant steps in that direction, providing elementary education for all and secondary and technical education for many. And in this progress women, by the educational opportunities afforded them, benefited as much as men.

III
WOMEN IN THE CLASSROOM:
THE TEACHING PROFESSION

The history of teaching in England in the nineteenth and early twentieth centuries is that of the rise of a professional body of elementary-school teachers working in publicly supported schools. It is also the story of efforts by secondary-school teachers working in private schools and by teachers of special subjects in both public and private schools to imitate elementary-school teachers in their professional training and in their effective professional associations. These developments were of special importance to middle-class working women, for in the mid-Victorian era teaching, or "governessing," was considered the only respectable calling for them, and teaching remained throughout this period one of the chief fields of work for middle-class women.

Elementary-School Teachers

In effect, the state created the elementary-school teaching profession in order to supply the large army of efficient teachers needed for the development of a national system of elementary education. In 1875 there were 13,200 elementary schools in the country with 1,873,200 pupils in average attendance, and in 1914, 21,000 schools with 5,392,600 pupils, while the number of elementary-school teachers increased in this period from 23,656 to 165,901. Among these teachers women represented a rapidly growing majority, their numbers increasing by a startling 862.1 per cent, compared with an increase of 291.7 per cent for men, and whereas in 1875 women represented 54.3 per cent of all elementary-school teachers, in 1914 they represented 74.5 per cent.[1] (However, this pattern of employment did not obtain in other branches of the teaching profession, the proportions of men and women employed remaining remarkably stable in the profession as a whole, with women consistently representing about three-fourths of all teachers employed. See Appendix, Section 1.)

The majority of women teachers in elementary schools were probably always recruited from among girls of the working classes. Many of those who previously would have gone into domestic service or factory work now eagerly took advantage of this expanding field of employment to better their economic position and, as they considered it, to rise in the social scale. But as time passed, increasing numbers of women of a higher social class began to take up elementary-school teaching.[2]

Not surprisingly, women of the middle classes generally shrank from the prospect of entering the earliest elementary schools. The mere mention of these called to mind crowded, noisome classrooms where as many as eighty unkempt and unruly lower-class children, often suffering from hunger and disease, had to be subjected to a dull, mechanical round of work and examined periodically by that alarming person, the government inspector. Besides the unattractiveness of the work, middle-class women were also repelled by the prospect of undergoing the training necessary for them to qualify as elementary-school teachers, training which was long and hard and which would involve their mingling with "a class with whom they were not accustomed to associate," a class they considered unintellectual and ignorant, parochial in sympathies, and vulgar in speech and manners.[3]

Under the famous pupil-teacher system instituted by the government in 1846, students completing their elementary education at the age of thirteen were apprenticed for five years in elementary schools recognized by the state for the purpose of their training. They received from the head teachers special instruction, for which the government laid down a syllabus, and helped with the teaching of the younger pupils, receiving small salaries which increased in amount with every year of service. At the age of eighteen pupil teachers could take the Queen's Scholarship examination for admission to the teachers' training colleges established by the voluntary religious societies, which since 1839 had received grants from the government for buildings and maintenance. The government paid most of the Scholarship students' expenses at the training colleges, and effectively dictated the curriculum to be followed by means of its certificate examinations, which students took at the end of their college course in order to obtain teaching certificates.

There were in this period some demands that training colleges be established especially to prepare ladies for elementary-school work, and a few experiments were made in this direction. For example, the Bishop Otter Training College at Chichester for a time made special provision for students who had had a more "ladylike" upbringing than the average pupil teacher, while Dorothea Beale formed a "Government Training Department" at the Cheltenham Ladies' College, but eventually gave it up because of her dislike of official red tape and regulations.[4]

Actually, however, it was not necessary to serve as a pupil teacher, attend a training college and obtain a teaching certificate in order to become an elementary-school teacher. The state had had to open side entrances into the professional edifice which it was busily erecting, and in addition to trained, certificated teachers, there were also employed large numbers of untrained teachers with certificates and of uncertificated teachers. In 1875 trained, certificated teachers represented 70 per cent of the men and 57 per cent of the women, but in 1914 these percentages had fallen to 66 for men and only 32 for women. Untrained teachers with certificates represented in 1875 21 per cent of the men and 30 per cent of the women, and in 1914, 22 per cent and 27 per cent respectively. As for uncertificated teachers, they included in 1875 only 9 per cent of the men and 13 per cent of the women, but in 1914, 12 per cent of the men and no less than 41 per cent of the women.[5]

To obtain certificates without undergoing training, prospective elementary-school teachers took the government's "acting teachers' examinations," instituted as early as 1847. These examinations were open to former pupil teachers who after their apprenticeship had served for three years as assistant teachers, and to others who qualified by passing any of a number of examinations recognized by the government as attesting a sound secondary education, such as the university local examinations. As for uncertificated teachers, the majority were former pupil teachers who had not gone on to a training college or taken the acting teachers' examinations; the rest qualified as uncertificated teachers by passing certain examinations which the government recognized for the purpose. Moreover, there was a large, special class of women among uncertificated teachers. Known variously as supplementary teachers, additional women teachers, or Article 68's (from the code of 1890 sanctioning their employment), their only qualifications were that they were over eighteen, vaccinated, and approved by the school inspector. In the early days of the national system of elementary education, some women of the middle classes attempted the government's acting teachers' examinations for a certificate or the examinations qualifying them to become uncertificated teachers, but many of them failed owing to their poor education.[6]

Calls to social service and responsibility undoubtedly always drew some middle-class women into the elementary schools. Throughout this period they were exhorted to take up the work "in the missionary spirit," to teach the children of the poor throughout the week as many already taught them in Sunday schools. Ladies must not only teach the three R's but also counteract the evil influences of mean homes and streets by instilling in their pupils the virtues of obedience, honesty, truthfulness and thoughtfulness.[7] But of greater importance than such appeals was the gradual but radical transformation of the elementary schools, which made them much more attractive places in which to work and which helped to dispel middle-class prejudice against them. Government building codes increasingly regulated school construction and required the maintenance of healthful conditions. The number of students allowed in each class was reduced, those in need received free food, clothing and medical attention, and handicapped children were provided for in special schools. Gradually a broader curriculum was introduced, and more intelligent teaching methods.

At the same time, great improvements were effected in the professional training of elementary-school teachers. Because of the poor preparation which many pupil teachers received during their apprenticeship in the elementary schools, the government in 1880 sanctioned the creation by school boards of pupil-teacher centers and central classes, staffed by specially selected instructors and catering for students from all the schools of the area. These secondary schools for pupil teachers, for such they were, proved a great success. Moreover, they emphasized the fact that the whole question of teacher training involved the larger question of popular secondary education, the needs of elementary-school teachers thus reinforcing the claim of the middle classes to a place in the national system of education and helping to win the passage of the Education Act of 1902. That Act led to the introduction in 1907 of the so-called bursary system of teacher training, which soon ousted the pupil-teacher system almost completely. Under this new system, prospective elementary-school teachers who had attended a secondary school until the age of sixteen received from the Board of Education bursar grants to enable them to continue their secondary education for another year or two before entering a training college. In addition, most local education authorities provided for pupils under the age of sixteen teaching or probationary scholarships in secondary schools, since many parents could not afford to keep their children at school until they were sixteen.

Another important development in this period was the raising of the professional training of elementary-school teachers to the university level. The training colleges sponsored by the religious societies were never able to provide enough teachers for the country's elementary schools and, being denominational in character, residential in organization, and staffed largely by former elementary-school teachers, they were criticized as producing teachers of generally narrow outlook and of imperfect education and culture. To overcome these difficulties, the Education Department in 1890 began the payment of grants to day training colleges established in connection with the universities and university colleges. Here students continued their general education in the regular university and college classes and received their professional training in special classes. At the end of two years they obtained a university certificate or diploma in education, and the ablest could then remain another year to work for a university degree. In addition, the Board of Education in 1906 began to pay to the new local education authorities established by the Education Act of 1902 grants for the building and maintenance of day training colleges. Many of these affiliated with the universities and university colleges, as did some of the denominational training colleges. In 1890 there were 49 training colleges with accommodations for some 3,700 students; by 1914 there were 89 training colleges—47 voluntary colleges, 20 university day training colleges, and 22 council colleges—with nearly 11,000 students.[8]

As a result of these improvements, elementary-school teachers and professional training rose in the general public estimation. Now identified with a sound secondary education and with a university career, elementary-teacher training became respectable, while the fact that the new training colleges were non-residential helped to remove middle-class qualms about mingling with social inferiors in the denominational residential colleges. At the same time, the general improvement in secondary education for middle-class girls greatly enhanced their chances of passing the acting teachers' examinations and the examinations for uncertificated teachers.

There was also in this period a great improvement in the working conditions of elementary-school teachers. A spirit of solidarity grew naturally among those who underwent training which the government prescribed and heavily subsidized, who were officially recognized as teachers by the government, and who worked together in conditions largely regulated by government codes. This professional feeling led to the formation of associations, and of one in particular, which sought to improve the status of their members and which came to be numbered among the most powerful professional associations in the world.

The National Union of Teachers, the first effective association of elementary-school teachers, was organized in 1870, and from an original membership of only 400 grew to include by 1914 over 80 per cent of the more than 109,000 certificated teachers in the country, certificated teachers only being admitted as members.[9] A number of other national associations developed later, but none approached the great influence of the N.U.T., which today, with some quarter of a million members, is one of the ten largest unions in the country. On the local level similar success was achieved by only one organization, the Metropolitan Board Teachers' Association, founded in London in 1872 to represent teachers in board schools as opposed to those in voluntary schools. In 1903 this organization became the London Teachers' Association, admitting teachers in schools of all grades under the London County Council. Fortunately, the N.U.T. and the L.T.A. worked together harmoniously for the benefit of their members. Their spheres of influence were pretty clearly defined, the former dealing with school boards and school managers and later with the local education authorities outside the metropolitan area, and with the central government, the latter dealing with the London school board and then with its successor, the London County Council. In 1922 the two unions merged, the L.T.A. becoming the London County Branch of the N.U.T.

As in other fields of employment, women were slow to realize and to take advantage of the benefits of professional organization, and they played little part in the early history of the unions. Gradually, however, the tide turned. Realizing the growing importance of women in the profession, the N.U.T. made great efforts to induce them to join its ranks. A Ladies' Committee of the national executive council was set up, and many of the local associations established Ladies' Bureaus, which sponsored social gatherings and speeches to attract women members. By 1914 women constituted 59 per cent of the N.U.T. membership, 52,093 out of a total of 88,404 members, and had won a recognized place in the union's counsels, although their representation in official positions was far from being proportional to their numerical strength in the union. In 1914 seven of the thirty-two members of the national executive council were women. Women were also serving on the executives of twenty-one of the fifty-four county associations of the union, including four women presidents and five vice-presidents, and on the executives of all but about a hundred of the union's 524 local associations, seventy-nine as president and eighty as vice-president. In 1911 the N.U.T. elected its first woman president, Miss Isabel Cleghorn of Sheffield, who in 1914 was appointed one of the union's three trustees.[10]

Both the National Union of Teachers and the London Teachers' Association participated actively and effectively in political affairs. They sent deputations and a constant stream of memorials, documents, petitions and letters to the local school authorities and also to M.P.'s and to the Education Department and its successor, the Board of Education, winning a usually sympathetic hearing for their claims. They campaigned vigourously in Parliamentary and in local elections, and in 1895 the N.U.T succeeded in returning to Parliament as a Liberal its general secretary, and one of its vice-presidents as a Conservative, "a form of political non-partisanship that the Union has preserved to the present day."[11]

A great attraction of the teachers' unions in the early days was their provision of members' benefits. The Teachers' Benevolent and Orphan Fund, established in close connection with the N.U.T. but administered separately and admitting non-union members, provided old-age pensions, widows' annuities, temporary financial aid, and hospital privileges. The Teachers' Provident Society, a friendly society limited to union members, provided sickness and death benefits.

One of the main objects for which the N.U.T. was founded, and one of its greatest triumphs, was the winning of pensions for certificated teachers. As a result of the union's continued agitation, the government in 1875 revived its original teachers' pension scheme, established in 1846 but abolished in 1861. However, this system was far from satisfactory, providing only a limited number of pensions for those teachers retired or disabled after fifteen years' service who applied to receive them and who were specially recommended by the government inspectors and the school authorities. The N.U.T. therefore continued its campaign, and won the recommendation of pensions for elementary-school teachers by a royal commission in 1888, by a select committee in 1892, by a unanimously passed resolution of the House of Commons in 1893, and by a departmental committee in 1894. The Teachers' Superannuation Act was finally passed in 1898, applying to all teachers certificated after its passage and to those already certificated who elected to come under its provisions, the great majority of them so choosing. This Act provided for the payment, from a fund created by contributions both from the state and from teachers, of pensions to teachers beginning at age sixty-five, when their certificates normally expired, and of disability allowances to teachers retired after ten years' service. In 1912 this Act was amended to provide more liberal pension rates. In addition to this national system, several local authorities, notably London, Manchester and Newcastle, had supplementary pension plans or alternative plans providing greater benefits.[12]

The N.U.T. was also successful in its campaign for the abolition of "extraneous duties," that is, duties unconnected with their regular school work which were frequently imposed upon elementary-school teachers. Those employed in voluntary schools, for example, often had to play the church organ, train the choir, teach Sunday school, and take part in other parochial activities. As a result of the union's protests, the education code of 1903 forbade the imposition of extraneous duties as a condition of employment.[13]

The N.U.T. likewise strove to win for teachers greater security of tenure. Although it was customary to give three months' notice of dismissal to head teachers and one month's notice to assistants, teachers in both voluntary and board schools held their positions at the pleasure of the school managers and the school boards and were frequently dismissed for insufficient and capricious reasons. The union failed to obtain remedial legislation in this matter, but it did win from the Education Department an agreement to investigate cases of unjust dismissals of teachers on appeal, and to refuse to recognize for the purpose of grants any teachers whose terms of engagement were not set forth in written contracts. Later, the centralization of local school administration under the county councils by the Education Act of 1902 tended to shield teachers from local prejudices which had led to dismissals in the past. Also, certain councils, notably the London County Council, laid down specific regulations governing the procedure in cases of dismissal, including the right of teachers to be represented by counsel at public investigations. Another grievance of teachers in connection with tenure was the autocratic authority of the government inspectors to suspend or cancel the certificates of allegedly incompetent teachers and to threaten withdrawal of government grants to their schools if they were not dismissed. The N.U.T. also failed to win establishment of a statutory tribunal to which teachers could appeal against decisions of the government inspectors, but did obtain the agreement of the Education Department to inform teachers of the inspectors' charges against them and to give them an opportunity to defend themselves in cases where their certificates were suspended or cancelled. Meanwhile, the N.U.T. had set up funds to cover expenses of legal actions taken and to pay maintenance grants to teachers suffering some injustice. By 1914 it could be said that there were no glaring cases of unjust dismissals.[14]

But women teachers continued to be less secure in their positions than men, for many local education authorities during this period began to impose a marriage bar upon them. Under this restriction no married women were hired as teachers, and marriage, or even the intention of marrying, was automatic cause for prompt dismissal of women teachers.[15]

Elementary-school teachers also complained of limited opportunities of advancement in their profession. Some were able to rise by obtaining teaching positions in secondary schools which were often better paid and

Teacher. "I wonder what your mother would say if she knew how backward you are in geography?"

Girl. "Oh, my mother says she never learnt jogfry and she's married, and Aunt Sally says *she* never learnt jogfry and *she*'s married; and you did and you ain't."

always more prestigious. By 1914 about one-third of the men and one-fifth of the women teachers in grant-earning secondary schools had begun as elementary-school teachers, or at least had had elementary-teacher training. But the chief means of rising was by promotion to the headships of elementary schools and to the headships of departments within elementary schools. In the early days of the national elementary-school system, almost all certificated teachers were head teachers, because their numbers could barely keep up with the number of new schools being built. Moreover, women usually headed both girls' and infants' departments in the elementary schools. However, in the later years of the century the number of certificated teachers increased as the pace of school building slackened, and there was a growing tendency to amalgamate the departments in elementary schools under one head teacher, usually a headmaster. The National Union of Teachers opposed this policy of amalgamation but apparently with little success, and generally a woman had to be much better qualified than a man in order to obtain a headship.[16]

Elementary-school teachers could also rise in the professional scale by obtaining positions in the training colleges, but this also tended to become more difficult as, after 1902, the Board of Education increasingly regulated and raised the standards of the college staffs. Usually the principals had to be university honours graduates, while two-thirds of the teaching staffs had to have approved university qualifications, and these regulations barred the great body of elementary-school teachers from positions in the training colleges. But the Board of Education did give special attention to the claims of women in this field. Previously men had usually headed the women's training colleges, but the Board now provided that in future women only should be appointed as principals in the women's colleges, and that in the coeducational colleges there must be women vice-principals and the staffs must include men and women in reasonable proportions. (Teachers in the training colleges and departments had their own professional associations, the Association of Principals of Training Colleges and the Training College Teacher's Association.)[17]

Another possible avenue of advancement for elementary-school teachers was promotion to the ranks of the schools inspectorate, on both the central and the local government levels. Inspectors appointed by the local authorities apparently were always largely recruited from among elementary-school teachers, but the N.U.T. had to wage a lengthy campaign to gain for its members admission to the central inspectorate, first as sub-inspectors and assistant inspectors, and at last in 1893 as "H.M.I.'s," who had traditionally been drawn solely from among public-school and Oxbridge men. But the Board of Education and the local education authorities alike employed only very small numbers of women as inspectors, and even then organized them separately from the men and used them not in general inspectoral work but on duties deemed especially suitable to women's interests and abilities.[18]

The problem of salaries was one of perennial concern to elementary-school teachers, confronted as they were by financially hard-pressed voluntary school managers and by school boards which were frequently elected, as the saying went, "on a rate-saving principle." The problem was further complicated by the employment of large numbers of uncertificated teachers, who were always paid less than those with certificates, and by the increasing employment of women at salaries substantially below those of men. In 1914 the estimated average salaries of those with certificates were, for head teachers, £176 for men and £122 for women, and for assistant teachers, £127 for men and £92 for women. The salaries of the uncertificated were, for head teachers, £94 for men and £68 for women, and for assistant teachers, £65 for men and £54 for women.[19]

The National Union of Teachers first tackled the salary problem in an indirect manner, seeking to end or at least to limit the employment of uncertificated teachers. Before the Revised Code of 1861, the government had encouraged the employment of certificated teachers by the payment to schools of grants in aid of their salaries, the grants paid for women teachers being two-thirds of the grants paid for men. After 1861 grants to elementary schools were governed by the system of "payment by results," of sinister reputation, that is, grants were paid to schools for each pupil passing a simple examination conducted by the government inspectors. Thus the only stimulus to the employment of certificated teachers was their superior ability in presenting successful candidates for the inspectors' examinations, that is, their ability to earn for their schools a larger grant than uncertificated teachers could. In 1895, after unceasing pressure by the N.U.T., the system of payment by results was abolished and a system instituted of payment of grants for each pupil in average attendance.

Meanwhile, beginning with the code of 1882, the Education Department issued staffing regulations for elementary schools receiving grants under which the staffs were measured by a scale stating the number of pupils which each class of teacher was allowed to teach. That is, the formula for staffing was: total number of teachers times their scale value equals total number of pupils in average attendance. The values initially assigned to teachers were: the certificated, 80 pupils; the uncertificated, 60; and additional women teachers, 40. In 1894 the Education Department introduced the principle of limiting the size of classes, the number of pupils per class being originally restricted to sixty. Failure to comply with these regulations made schools liable to forfeiture of government grants.[20] Although steps in the right direction, these regulations by no means satisfied the demands of the N.U.T., which continued to strive for the elimination from the profession of both uncertificated teachers and untrained certificated teachers.

The N.U.T. had also long campaigned for two other reforms which bore directly upon the question of salaries and which were embodied in the Education Act of 1902. Voluntary schools, with more meager financial resources than the rate-aided schools, had to pay lower salaries,[21] while schools in backward rural areas naturally paid less than those in wealthy urban districts. By making rate aid available to voluntary schools and by using the county as the unit for the local administration of education, the Act of 1902 helped to solve these problems. The new local education authorities, drawing upon the resources of much larger areas than the old school-board districts and being responsible for all publicly supported schools in their areas, were in an excellent position to remove inequities existing between board and voluntary schools and between schools in different types of locality.

After 1902 many of the new local education authorities adopted comprehensive salary scales covering all teachers under their jurisdiction, and the N.U.T. did much work in preparing and circulating information for their guidance, eventually formulating a standard salary scale for certificated elementary-school teachers. More directly, if salaries were not raised in a certain area, the N.U.T. offered to pay the moving expenses of teachers seeking more remunerative positions elsewhere. The union had also, since 1890, maintained a "black list" of undesirable posts, and occasionally published warning notices about such posts.[22]

Still there was growing unrest among elementary-school teachers, as among industrial workers, with the rise in the cost of living in the years immediately preceding the war, and there was a growing spirit of militancy. An initial skirmish took place in 1907, when the West Ham Council decided to reduce its teachers' salaries. The N.U.T. prepared for a strike, but the dispute was soon settled to the teachers' satisfaction. In 1913 the union began a nation-wide campaign to obtain adoption of its salary scale by bringing pressure directly to bear upon the local education authorities. The high point of this campaign was the N.U.T.'s first strike, which was waged in 1914 against the Herefordshire County Council, involved the closing down of sixty schools, and ended with a settlement in the teachers' interests after mediation by the bishop of Hereford. The salary campaign attracted great publicity and enjoyed wide support, and led to improvements in salaries in 149 of the 321 local education areas before the war. Suspended at the outbreak of war, the salary campaign was resumed in 1916 and helped to bring about the creation in 1919 of a joint committee including twenty-two representatives of the local education authorities and an equal number of representatives of the N.U.T., under the chairmanship of Lord Burnham. The Burnham Committee, analogous to the Whitley Council for civil servants, drew up salary scales for elementary-school teachers, which the Board of Education in 1925 required that all local education authorities adopt, unless specifically allowed by the Board to deviate from the scales.[23]

Somewhat surprisingly, the N.U.T. did not during this period adopt a policy of equal pay for women—surprisingly, because it was women's lower pay which seemed to explain both their increasing employment at the expense of men and men's resentment of them. Still, the union's salary scale did represent a considerable improvement in the pay of women relative to that of men. In 1914 the estimated average salary of certificated women assistant teachers was only 72 per cent of men's salary, while under

the union's scale the minimum salary of certificated women assistants
would be about 90 per cent of men's minimum and their maximum salary
about 80 per cent of men's maximum. The union's scale for assistant
teachers was £90-200 for men and £80-160 for women in the provinces,
and £100-250 for men and £90-200 for women in the metropolitan area.
The union had not, by 1914, prepared a salary scale for head teachers,
but the union conference in 1913 had laid down a minimum of £150 for
headmasters and £120 for headmistresses.[24] The reason for setting
women's maximum salary at 20 per cent less than men's, compared with
only a 10 per cent difference in minimum salary, was that far fewer women
than men would attain the maximum, since many women teachers retired
perforce upon marriage, and therefore it was more important that
women's salaries be closer to men's at the bottom of the scale than at the
top. To this extent the N.U.T. moved a long way in the direction of equal
pay for women, a policy which it would soon officially adopt.

While the conditions of elementary-school teachers were generally
being greatly improved, resentment of their special disabilities—lesser
security of tenure, fewer chances of promotion, and lower salaries—led
women teachers to form separate associations to protect their interests.
Apparently the earliest of these grew up in London. A Metropolitan
Board Mistresses' Association was formed in 1882 chiefly to combat a
proposal then before the London school board to exclude married women
from its service. But this Association seems to have become defunct or
moribund, for in 1897 a London Mistresses' Association was "hastily
formed" when the London school board drew up a scheme to raise the
salaries of men teachers but made no mention of rises for women. Representatives of the N.U.T. actually claimed that women did not want
higher salaries! Owing to the organized opposition of women, the school
board retracted the scheme and revised it to include pay increases for
women as well.[25]

About 1903 there was organized the Equal Pay League, which included
men as well as women. The League canvassed candidates for the N.U.T.
executive council and published in *The Schoolmaster,* the union's official
journal, the names of those favouring equal pay for women. The League
also sought to promote the increased representation of women on the
union's executive and at teacher's conferences. The League's work led in
time to the creation of the National Federation of Women Teachers,
representing more than fifty local women's associations which had sprung
up in the country's most populous centers. Most of the Federation's members also belonged to the N.U.T. or the London Teachers' Association,
and the Federation, in conjunction with the London Mistresses' Association, lobbied for equal pay and the increased representation of women
within the two larger organizations.[26]

In 1909 the National Union of Women Teachers was formed when the
London unit of the National Federation of Women Teachers and the
Women Teachers' Franchise Union, a group previously working within

the larger associations for women's suffrage, broke away from the N.U.T. Membership in this new women's union was compatible with membership in the N.U.T., but apparently there was little overlap.[27]

The London women's organizations, especially the Association of London Married Women Teachers, established in 1909, did excellent work, for the London school board and its successor, the London County Council, never refused to employ married women as teachers and made special arrangements for maternity leaves for them.[28] But most other local education authorities continued to impose a marriage bar, which was not made illegal until passage of the Education Act of 1944.

Owing to the work of the women's organizations, both the N.U.T. and the London Teachers' Association in 1919 accepted the principle of equal pay for women. In practice, however, both unions accepted unequal pay for women as embodied in the salary scales drawn up by the Burnham Committee after the war, women's salaries being a little more than four-fifths those of men. It was not until 1955 that the government accepted the principle of equal pay and the Burnham Committee, which had been reconstituted in 1944 to include representatives of secondary-school teachers as well as elementary-school teachers, drew up salary scales providing for extra annual increments to women's salaries, which by 1961 became equal to men's.[29]

Meanwhile, those elementary-school teachers ineligible for membership in the N.U.T. remained unorganized until the formation of the National Union of Uncertificated Teachers in 1913. The fact that nine-tenths of these teachers were women probably explains the late appearance of this union, which was essentially a women's association although not limited to women. Its members objected that the N.U.T. had neglected the interests of uncertificated teachers, especially with regard to salaries and pensions. Uncertificated teachers continued to be relatively poorly paid, and they resented their exclusion from the Superannuation Acts of 1898 and 1912, while they were compelled to come under the provisions of the National Insurance Act of 1911 and "to have a card like a labourer." Many uncertificated teachers enlisted in the special "state section" which was opened by the Teachers' Provident Society of the N.U.T. as an approved society under the Insurance Act and which by 1914 included 4,928 men and 45,226 women. In 1919 the N.U.T. decided to admit uncertificated teachers, and immediately gained some 11,000 new members. The uncertificated teachers' union thus lost its reason for existence, but it lingered on until 1945.[30]

By 1914 certificated elementary-school teachers, women along with men, had definitely achieved the status of professionals, with recognized training and qualifications and with strong associations which had substantially improved their working conditions. And despite the continuing special disabilities of women, which the separate women's associations were seeking to remove, elementary-school teaching was often acclaimed as the field richest in opportunities for them.[31]

Secondary-School Teachers

While elementary-school teaching was being transformed by government policy and action and by the efforts of the teachers' associations, teaching in secondary schools was likewise undergoing a transformation. But here, in the absence of action by the state before 1902, voluntary effort was responsible for the great improvements effected, and women led in the movement to make secondary-school teaching a true profession, pioneering in the provision of professional training and in the formation of professional associations. These associations, speaking effectively if not with one voice for secondary-school teachers, helped both to improve the working conditions of their members and to win a place for secondary schools in the national system of education.

The need to improve the qualifications of secondary-school teachers was of the greatest importance to the whole women's movement, for it led directly to the provision of higher education for women. Queen's and Bedford Colleges had sought to supply women's lack of university degrees, the recognized qualification for teachers in the best schools for boys. But the Taunton Commission found that these colleges still ranked merely as secondary schools, and the governesses to whom they granted certificates of proficiency could not claim an equal standing with university graduates.[32] Now, after the opening of the university local examinations to girls in 1863, the idea gained currency that the universities should open higher examinations to women, particularly those who planned to teach.

Here, however, a rift developed in the feminist ranks. Emily Davies and her supporters held that women should receive the same education as men in the universities, the best education then available, and take the same examinations, just as girls took the same university local examinations as boys. This group was, in fact, less directly concerned with improving the qualifications of women teachers than with proving that women were equally capable with men of profiting by a higher education, and they felt, with reason, that special tests and certificates for women would be, or would be considered, inferior to men's examinations and degrees. The efforts of this group led to the founding in 1869 of Girton College, Cambridge, the first women's college of university stature.[33] In 1881 the university at last formally recognized the little band of women students by officially admitting them to tripos examinations and awarding them certificates.

The other feminist group believed that the existing, severely restricted university curriculum did not represent the best possible education for either men or women, and they were interested mainly in improving the qualifications of women teachers. Consequently, they were more willing to compromise and accept for women special examinations in new subjects and special certificates, which they felt would be better for women themselves and which would also serve eventually to broaden the university curriculum for men.

Among the leaders of this second group was Anne Jemima Clough (1820-1892), daughter of a cotton merchant of Liverpool and sister of the poet, Arthur Hugh Clough.[34] Like Emily Davies, Miss Clough received only a poor education at home and longed for better education for all women. Like Dorothea Beale she was first attracted to teaching by her interest in moral training, and she began her teaching in Sunday schools for the lower classes. And like Frances Buss she experienced the hardships of the middle-class woman forced to earn her own living. To help in the financial difficulties following her father's failure in business and death, she began to take in a few paying pupils and later opened a small middle-class school in Ambleside, the Lake District village to which she had moved with her mother. After her mother's death, Miss Clough gave up her school and resided for a time with her brother's family in London, where she met others interested in the cause of women's education. By 1866 she was again in Liverpool, dedicated to work for that cause, and her efforts helped in the founding of the North of England Council for Promoting the Higher Education of Women, a federated body representing a number of local committees.

In 1869 Cambridge granted the Council's request that the university establish an examination and certificates for women over the age of eighteen (the existing local examinations tested education only up to the age of eighteen), with particular reference to "testing and attesting" the qualifications of teachers. A few years later this "women's local examination" was opened to men and the name was changed to the "higher local examination." Newnham, the country's second university college for women, grew out of the special lectures offered at Cambridge to prepare women for the new examination and the residence hall headed by Miss Clough which accommodated some of the women students.[35]

At Oxford the women's campaign was led by Annie Rogers, daughter of Professor Thorold Rogers, who in 1873, to the dismay of the male candidates, had taken the highest place for classics in the university's local examinations.[36] In 1875 the university established special examinations and teachers' certificates for women. Three years later Miss Rogers helped to organize an association to provide instruction preparing women for these examinations and to serve as a link between the university authorities and the residences which were opened for women students and which gradually developed into regular colleges—Lady Margaret Hall and Somerville (1879), St. Hugh's (1886) and St. Hilda's (1893). Eventually the women gained permission to take the university's regular examinations for the B. A. degree in place of the special women's examinations.

Now London took the lead in the matter of granting degrees to women. In 1878 the university abolished its special examinations and certificates for women, established ten years before, and opened to women on equal terms with men every degree, honour and prize. University College now admitted women to its classes, while King's established a separate women's department. In 1882 Westfield College for women opened, and in

1886 the Royal Holloway College, while Bedford, outstripping its rival Queen's, developed into a full-fledged college of university stature. In 1900 all of these colleges were incorporated as constituent colleges in the reformed University of London. Meanwhile, the Victoria University, chartered in 1880, and Durham University in 1895, admitted women to their classes and degrees. Despite repeated attempts by the feminists, Oxford did not admit women to degrees and full membership of the university until 1919, while Cambridge did so only in 1947.

At the same time, the work of the North of England Council had helped to launch another movement to provide higher education, the university extension program. At the urging of the Council, Cambridge in 1873 assumed official responsibility for extra-mural courses of lectures conducted by university professors. Soon London, Oxford, Durham and Victoria Universities also undertook extension work. So important did the program become that to provide accommodations for the lectures several "university colleges" were established. A number of these eventually received charters of incorporation and took their places as full-fledged universities: the University of Wales, comprising the colleges at Aberystwyth, Bangor and Cardiff (1893); Birmingham (1900); Liverpool and Manchester (1903) and Leeds (1904), these three developing from the university colleges originally comprising the Victoria University, which was dissolved; Sheffield (1905); and Bristol (1909). Like the original extension lectures, the new universities admitted women on equal terms with men.

But the great majority of intending women teachers could not afford a university course, nor could the number of women who did obtain university degrees or certificates supply all the qualified teachers needed for the reformed secondary schools for girls. Moreover, many of the feminist pioneers believed that for good teachers a sound education alone was not enough, that besides a general knowledge of what they would teach they needed special instruction in how to teach. For example, Frances Buss had entered thirteen of her students for the first university local examination to which Cambridge admitted girls as an experiment, and ten of them failed. Shocked at this result, Miss Buss persuaded a mistress at one of the Home and Colonial Society's training colleges for elementary-school teachers to give lessons in teaching methods to the mistresses at her school, and the later success of her students in the local examinations proved the value of such training.[37] There was, then, an obvious need for some professional qualification which would attest both the sound education of women in lieu of a university degree and their ability to teach.

The effective professional training of secondary-school teachers dates from 1876, when the Teachers' Training and Registration Society was organized in connection with the Women's Education Union. In 1878 the Society opened in London the Maria Grey Training College, named in honour of its first organizing secretary. Like the elementary-teacher training colleges after which it was modelled, the new school carried on the general education of its students while providing special instruction in teaching methods and supervised practical experience in teaching. Several other training colleges for women were soon established on the same pattern.

Meanwhile, another method of training was developing, analogous to the pupil-teacher system in the elementary schools. As early as 1871 Maria Grey had suggested that a number of "student teachers" be attached to every large secondary school for girls, where they would continue their general education, receive instruction in teaching methods from the headmistresses, and gain practical experience by taking over classes from time to time. Miss Buss favoured and tried this plan, as did the Girls' Public Day School Company. The student-teacher system achieved its greatest success under Dorothea Beale at the Cheltenham Ladies' College, where by 1885 the teacher-training program had taken concrete form in St. Hilda's College for teachers. By the turn of the century almost all high schools for girls, and many private schools as well, were training student teachers.[38]

Finally, secondary-school teachers sought to connect their professional training directly with the universities, as elementary-school teachers were doing. In 1878 Cambridge established a syndicate to conduct lectures, hold examinations and award certificates in education. The syndicate also inspected institutions training non-elementary-school teachers and awarded certificates to their students, the first school so inspected being the Maria Grey Training College. In connection with the university's lectures on education, the Cambridge Training College for Women was opened in 1885 under the direction of Miss E. P. Hughes, who had just taken a first class in the moral science tripos and who was known as a gifted teacher. The aim of the training college, as envisaged by Miss Buss and Miss Clough, who were largely responsible for its founding, was to give to Girton and Newnham students who were taking the tripos course a year of training before they began to teach, that is, to make professional training a post-graduate course. Following the example of Cambridge, the other universities and university colleges also instituted examinations and certificates or diplomas for secondary-school teachers. The secondary-teacher training colleges now began to prepare their students for these university examinations, and even more important, the university training colleges for elementary-school teachers began to train secondary-school teachers as well, eventually developing into regular university departments of education.[39]

As in the provision of professional training for secondary-school teachers, women likewise led the way in the founding of professional associations for these teachers. The first of these was the London Schoolmistresses' Association, organized in 1866 at a meeting held at the home of Emily Davies, who served as secretary until the Association disbanded in 1888. A second schoolmistresses' association was founded at Liverpool at the suggestion of Anne Clough, and a number of others soon appeared in other cities. These early organizations sought to break down the social isolation of women teachers, many of whom in the early days had scarcely so much as a speaking acquaintance with other members of their profession, and they played an active part in opening the university local examinations to girls. Including head and assistant mistresses in both public and private schools, private governesses, and amateurs interested in women's education, these local schoolmistresses' associations gradually gave way before more strictly professional bodies, organized on a wider basis and representing different classes of teachers.[40]

The earliest of these was the Association of Head Mistresses, founded in 1874 at a meeting of about a dozen teachers called together by Frances Buss, who served as president until her death, when Miss Beale succeeded to the office. By 1914 the Association counted as members 354 headmistresses of public schools for girls, among the most eminent professional women of their day. Always interested in raising the standards of their profession, the members of the Association followed the policy of appointing as assistant mistresses in their schools women with professional training in preference to those not trained, other things being equal. At the same time the Head Mistresses' Association insisted that teacher training should not be a substitute for general education and culture.[41]

The idea of forming a similar organization for assistant mistresses in public schools apparently originated among a group of Newnham students led by Miss E. P. Hughes, later head of the Cambridge Training College for Women. Miss Buss and other educational leaders encouraged the group in their plans, and the Association of Assistant Mistresses was formed in 1884 at a meeting of about 180 teachers held in Cambridge. By 1914 the Association had 1,689 members, representing 379 schools.[42]

The inspiration of women also led to the founding in 1884 of the Teachers' Guild of Great Britain and Ireland, for a time one of the most influential organizations in the field of education. The Guild grew out of plans of the Women's Education Union, the Head Mistresses' Association and the London Schoolmistresses' Association to organize a provident society for teachers. Among its early officials were the omnipresent Miss Buss, Miss Beale, Miss Clough, Mrs. Grey and Miss Shirreff, and about three-fourths of its members were women. Including teachers in both public and private secondary schools, elementary-school teachers, and private teachers, as well as laymen interested in education, the Guild declined in importance as the different classes of teachers turned increasingly to their own separate organizations, and it was dissolved shortly after World War I.[43]

Yet another women's organization was the Association of University Women Teachers, founded in 1883 by Miss Clough, who served as president until her death. By 1914 its membership numbered about 2,700 women who had obtained university qualifications for teaching.[44]

Meanwhile, men teachers in secondary schools long remained indifferent to professional training and slow to organize. Among them the idea persisted that teachers' certificates were the stamp of an inferior grade of teacher, desirable perhaps for elementary-school teachers and for women who could not obtain university degrees, but not for men. The few attempts to provide professional training for men failed miserably, largely because the great majority of headmasters did not support them, evincing no intention of appointing trained assistant masters in preference to those without training.[45]

But gradually the men's attitude changed. As the study of education became a recognized subject of university standard, their prejudice against professional training tended to wane. Even more important, as the century drew to a close it became apparent that the state must soon intervene in the field of secondary education, and that this would probably mean official regulations governing the training and qualifications of secondary-school teachers as of elementary-school teachers. In these circumstances men saw the necessity of evolving a policy with respect to professional training and of forming their own organizations to state their views. The emergence of the men's associations—pre-eminently the Headmasters' Conference, the Association of Head Masters, the Association of Assistant Masters, the Association of Headmasters of Preparatory Schools, and the Private Schools Association—marked the entry of secondary-school teachers into the political arena.[46]

Fortunately, a spirit of friendly co-operation generally prevailed among the various secondary-school teachers' associations. They jointly sponsored conferences to discuss important questions and set up joint committees to decide upon and implement policies of mutual interest. Like the National Union of Teachers, they were in constant communication both with Whitehall and with the local education authorities, and their representations were usually respectfully heeded even if their claims were not always met. Relations among four of the organizations—the Head and Assistant Mistresses' Associations and the Head and Assistant Masters' Associations—were especially close and cordial, and in 1906, together with the Preparatory Schools Association, they resolved to form a Federal Council of Secondary School Associations composed of three representatives from each member organization. The Council was soon joined by the Headmasters' Conference, the Private Schools Association and other professional groups.[47]

The first problem to which the associations turned their attention was that of professional training. Representatives of the associations met in conference at Oxford in 1893 and at Cambridge in 1896 to discuss the question, and a joint committee on teacher training was established in 1897 to elaborate a detailed program. This committee recommended that secondary-school teacher training be a one-year post-graduate course provided by institutions connected with the universities and university colleges, which would be inspected by the central authority for education and would award university diplomas in education. The Bryce Commission on secondary education, said to have been appointed as a result of the Oxford conference of 1893, heard witnesses for the teachers' associations and endorsed their views on professional training.[48]

With the passage of the Education Act of 1902, the state assumed the responsibility of insuring the competence of secondary-school teachers.

Generally, the Board of Education held that for these teachers no standard lower than a university degree should be accepted and, in addition, reserved to itself the right to require that a certain proportion of all new teachers appointed in recognized secondary schools must have had special training in teaching. But the progress of professional training was slow at first. The Board of Education did not define in detail the qualifications for teachers in secondary schools as it did for those in elementary schools, merely stipulating that to be eligible for grants or for recognition as being efficient, secondary schools must have staffs sufficient in number and quality to provide adequate instruction, this to be determined by the government inspectors. Also, government grants for professional training were very limited. In 1908 the Board began the payment of maintenance grants for secondary-school teachers-in-training to university training departments and to training colleges connected with the universities, which after 1911 could admit only students who had already obtained university degrees. In 1913 the Board began to pay grants to recognized secondary schools for the training of student teachers, but the student-teacher training system never developed to any great extent under the Board's regulations. Unlike prospective elementary-school teachers, intending secondary-school teachers did not receive government grants directly, and the cost of their training was high, estimated in 1914 as £52-110 a year in residential colleges and £20-55 non-resident. Consequently the number of students in training remained small, in 1914 only 175 all together, including 167 women. The qualifications of teachers in grant-earning secondary schools in 1914 were as follows: university graduates with training, 27.9 per cent of the men and 29.7 per cent of the women; university graduates, 71.6 per cent of the men and 52.3 per cent of the women; non-graduates with training, 37.5 per cent of the men and 47.4 per cent of the women, of whom only 9 per cent of the men but 47 per cent of the women had had secondary-school training, the remainder having had elementary-school training or, in the case of women, kindergarten training. Only in 1925 did the Board of Education begin the payment of grants directly to intending secondary-school teachers to cover the cost of four years at a university, in order to help achieve the goal of making three years' work for a degree and another year's work for a diploma in education the recognized qualification for the profession.[49]

Meanwhile, there was, of course, no compulsory or officially approved training for teachers in private schools or for private governesses. However, to meet the competition of good public schools, especially after 1902, and particularly if they wished to be recognized as efficient by the Board of Education, private schools had to improve their standards of teaching by employing well-qualified mistresses. Also, the increasing numbers of well-educated women seeking positions not only raised the standard of teaching among private governesses but also improved their employers' estimate of them and the treatment they received.[50]

Although never so "trade-unionist" in practice as the National Union of Teachers and the London Teachers' Association, the secondary-school teachers' associations always concerned themselves with improving working conditions in their profession. One of their chief attractions in the early days was their provision of members' benefits. The Teachers' Guild, originally established to encourage teachers to make provision for sickness and old age, collected information about insurance and investments for its members, and in some cases obtained for them reductions in insurance premiums and in stockbrokers' fees. The Head Mistresses' Association and the Assistant Mistresses' Association engaged in similar activities. The Teachers' Guild also established a Benevolent Fund for the relief of members in distress in temporary and unforeseen circumstances.[51]

In addition to such voluntary efforts, the secondary-school teachers' associations were interested in establishing a compulsory national pension system for their members in place of the existing piecemeal provisions for pensions. By 1912 only 126 grant-earning secondary schools—39 council schools under the larger and wealthier local education authorities, 25 Girls' Public Day School Company schools and 62 foundation and other schools—had pension plans covering some 1,000 teachers out of the 1,813 they employed. In addition, even where no pension system existed, schools often granted pensions to retiring teachers, especially head teachers, as an act of grace. The question of pensions came into prominence with the discussions on the National Insurance Bill of 1911. Secondary-school teachers failed to obtain exemption from the operation of the Act when it passed, but did win the provision that they would be exempted if future legislation created a separate pension system for them. As a result of the Insurance Act, delegates from five teachers' associations—the Teachers' Guild, the Assistant Masters' Association, the Assistant Mistresses' Association, the Association of University Women Teachers, and the Association of Teachers in Technical Institutions—resolved to form the Secondary, Technical and University Teachers' Insurance Society. The "state section" of this Society, an approved society under the Insurance Act, catered for those teachers compulsorily insured under the Act's provisions, and by 1914 had a membership of 10,350, including 1,750 men and 8,600 women. The Society's "dividend section" afforded to those not compulsorily insured an opportunity to obtain voluntary insurance with larger benefits, and had by 1914 between 300 and 400 members.[52]

Meanwhile, to continue the agitation for a separate pension system for secondary- and technical-school teachers, the Federal Council of Secondary School Associations and the Association of Teachers in Technical Institutions set up a joint committee. This committee drew up a pension plan which was recommended to the government both by the Chancellor of the Exchequer and by a departmental committee which reported in 1914.[53] The war intervened before legislation could be passed, but secondary- and technical-school teachers at last achieved their goal of a state-supported pension system with passage of the Teachers' Superannuation Act of 1918.

Secondary-school teachers were also concerned to establish security of tenure. Representatives of the Assistant Masters' Association stated in evidence before the Bryce Commission that their greatest grievance, greater even than that of low salaries, was the excessive power of headmasters in dismissing assistants without interference by the school governors, just as the governors could dismiss headmasters at their discretion. In contrast to this, headmistresses in public secondary schools usually could dismiss assistant teachers only with the approval of the governors, to whom the assistants could appeal their cases if they felt unjustly treated. This policy, approved by both the Head Mistresses' Association and the Assistant Mistresses' Association, apparently was a legacy of the days when women were unaccustomed to positions of public authority and it was deemed wise for men to supervise their exercise of that authority. The Bryce Commission recommended that the system obtaining in public girls' schools be extended to boys' schools as well. The system of appeal against dismissal continued in public girls' schools after the Education Act of 1902, but this advantage was now offset by the fact that women serving in schools under the local education authorities often became subject to the marriage bar, outlawed only in 1944.[54]

The position of private-school teachers and of private governesses with respect to tenure was, of course, quite different from that of public-school teachers. Written agreements setting forth the terms of engagement apparently were rare, and in their absence private teachers could theoretically be dismissed at the pleasure of their employers. In practice, however, the custom of granting notice of one term or of half a term had become widespread, and could be enforced by the courts in suits for damages brought by teachers who felt themselves unjustly dismissed. Even in cases where this customary notice was not recognized, the courts could still require "reasonable notice in all the circumstances."[55] Thus private teachers enjoyed substantial legal protection

Like those in elementary schools, women teachers in secondary schools complained of the limited prospects of advancement in their profession. To become heads of private schools, women always had to be able to purchase existing schools or to establish their own, while the number of public schools for girls before 1902 was infinitesimal compared to the number of women in teaching. Another problem in this connection was that few headmistresses over the age of thirty-five were appointed, this apparently a relic of the bad old days when governesses past the age of thirty-five were dismissed because of their declining faculties. After 1902 the number of girls' schools increased steadily, so that the avenue of promotion to headmistress-ships broadened considerably. But there was a tendency, as in elementary education, to combine schools for boys and girls under headmasters. The Associations of Head Mistresses and Assistant Mistresses sent at least one deputation to the Board of Education to protest this policy, maintaining that mixed schools were undesirable in localities where there were enough pupils for two good schools, and that where a mixed school was necessary there should be a sort of condominium of the headmaster and the senior assistant mistress. Actually, however, the tradition of coeducation and amalgamation of schools under headmasters never obtained to the same extent in secondary as in elementary education, and in this respect women secondary-school teachers enjoyed a decided advantage over women in elementary schools. Women might also rise in their profession by obtaining positions in the secondary-teacher training colleges. (The staffs of these colleges had their own professional association, the Teachers' Training Association, which by 1914 had little more than a hundred members, and they could also join the Training College Teachers' Association, which originally catered primarily for those in elementary-teacher training colleges.) At the same time, women in secondary-school teaching had little chance of becoming government inspectors. The Head Mistresses' Association sent a deputation to the Board of Education to protest the small numbers of women inspectors and their limited sphere of action and inferior status, and to demand that duly qualified women be made eligible for all grades of the inspectorate, but without success.[56]

For women secondary-school teachers, as for all teachers, the subject of salaries was one of perennial interest. In the '70's and early '80's the level of women's pay rose considerably both in the new public schools for girls and in good private schools, which competed to attract teachers with university or other good qualifications. It was said that women with the equivalent of a first or second class at Cambridge could "command their own prices," usually receiving £120 a year to begin and rising after two or three years to £150. From the middle '80's, however, salaries tended to remain stationary and then declined. Few new girls' schools were being opened, vacancies in existing schools were rare, and the number of well-qualified applicants for positions was increasing.[57]

The Bryce Commission heard a considerable amount of evidence on the subject of salaries. A joint committee of the Associations of Head and Assistant Mistresses collected information showing that salaries of assistant mistresses ranged between an average of £84 a year in the lowest paying schools to £147 in the best paying; the estimated average in small schools was £112, in the largest schools £117, and in Girls' Public Day School Company schools £113. The Assistant Masters' Association presented comparable figures on its members' salaries: average in small schools, £150; average in the largest schools, £200; and average in all schools, £135. On the basis of the evidence presented, the Bryce Commission concluded that the level of pay was too low, and noted with concern that women's salaries lagged so far behind men's, stating that although "positive recommendations can hardly be made," they hoped that school authorities would "deal more liberally than has hitherto often been the case with women teachers," that they would have regard to "the desirability of encouraging both by good salaries and by prospects of promotion, the entrance of the most capable women into the work of teaching."[58]

The question of equal pay for women in secondary-school teaching never became a burning issue and a rallying cry as it did among elementary-school teachers. Unlike the elementary schools, where boys and girls were educated together and the number of women teachers increased at the expense of men, coeducational secondary schools remained the exception rather than the rule, so that men and women teachers did not compete with each other, and women did not replace men because of their lower salaries. For example, in 1914 there were in grant-earning secondary schools 6,609 men teachers and 6,321 women.[59] (For the numbers of men and women in the teaching profession as a whole, see Appendix, Section 1.) While never evolving a common policy with respect to salaries, the men's and women's associations of secondary-school teachers loyally supported one another's demands for higher pay. Their harmonious relations were disturbed on only one occasion, early in 1914, when the Head Masters' Association proposed that the payment of government grants to schools be based on the teachers' salaries rather than on the number of pupils attending. The Associations of Head Mistresses and Assistant Mistresses naturally opposed this scheme, under which girls' schools would receive only about 75 per cent of the grants for boys' schools, since the salaries of women teachers were only about three-fourths those of men. The women's organizations favoured simply an extra government grant in aid of salaries.[60]

After 1902 a good number of the new local education authorities adopted salary scales covering their secondary-school teachers as well as their elementary-school teachers. Once fearful of being considered "vulgar" if they raised the question of pay, the Head Mistresses' Association and the Assistant Mistresses' Association now issued frequent statements of their salary claims, sometimes singly and sometimes jointly, and urged them upon the local authorities. Shortly before the war the women's associations were demanding for assistant mistresses salaries of £100-180 for non-graduates with professional training and of £120-220 for graduates with professional training, and for headmistresses salaries of £300-700 depending upon the size of their schools. Unfortunately, only the salaries paid by the London County Council, always the leader of the country in educational affairs, equalled those demanded by the women's associations. The famous White Paper of 1911 on secondary-school teachers' salaries and superannuation showed that the average salaries in grant-earning secondary schools were £438 for headmasters and £332 for headmistresses, and for assistants, £168 for men and £123 for women. That is, women's average salaries were little higher than the minimum salaries demanded by the women's associations, and these salaries were still only about two-thirds to three-fourths the average salaries of men. After the war a joint (Burnham) committee representing the local education authorities and the teachers' associations, like that for elementary-school teachers, was established for secondary-school teachers, and under the salary scales which it established women received roughly four-fifths the salaries of men. Women teachers in secondary schools, like those in elementary schools, had to wait till 1955 for the government to accept and begin to implement a policy of equal pay.[61]

Teachers in public secondary schools represented a large and increasing proportion of those engaged in secondary education, but by 1914 it was estimated that half the secondary-school teachers in the country, numbering perhaps 15,000, were still employed in private schools. For these private-school teachers there was a great range in salaries. Evidence presented to the Bryce Commission showed that high-class private schools offered salaries approximating those in the best public schools, while cheap private schools catering for the lower middle class, "the nadir," often paid salaries below the subsistence level. For example, the lady assistant commissioner reporting on Lancashire found that in one large private day school for girls salaries ranged between £80 and £155, with an average salary of £110, while in expensive boarding schools, where most of the teachers lived in, salaries were in the £50 range, room and board being calculated as equal in value to the amount of salary paid. In cheap private schools a salary of £45 was considered handsome, since many teachers in such schools received only £20-30.[62] For the later years of this period, information on private-school salaries is difficult to obtain. Probably, however, the trend was for private schools to meet the competition of public schools, especially after 1902, by offering equivalent salaries in order to attract competent teachers, or to go under.

Meanwhile, the salaries of private governesses generally lagged behind those of all other teachers. About the time of the Bryce Commission it was estimated that governesses with good qualifications could command salaries equivalent to those offered in the best public and private schools, £50-100 or more as resident governesses and £100 and up as non-residents. However, the majority of governesses probably continued to come from that class of ladies who were equipped for teaching by genteel poverty rather than by academic attainments, and who could not obtain positions in regular schools. Their competition tended to drag down the salary level of well-qualified private teachers, a number of whom met at Queen's College in 1912 to organize a Union of Private Governesses to protect their interests in the face of such competition.[63]

It is interesting that the best women teachers, in pressing for higher pay, based their claims usually on three considerations. Good teachers must receive enough to repay them for their large expenditure of time and money in equipping themselves for their profession—school fees till the age of nineteen and the cost of three years at a university and of one year of professional training. Also, they must receive enough to maintain themselves in their proper station in life, to enable them to buy books, to afford recreation and travel, and to mingle with their social equals—in short, to enjoy a comfortable, cultured life. Finally, their salaries must be high enough to meet the competition from other occupations, the training for which was shorter and less expensive and which offered pay equally or even more enticing than secondary-school teaching (elementary-school teaching and secretarial work were often mentioned in this connection).[64] So far had the pendulum swung since the days when "decayed gentlewomen," ignorant and pitied, turned to teaching as their sole chance of survival, thankful for whatever pittances they could obtain!

Teachers of Special Subjects

Alongside teachers in elementary and secondary schools there had grown up a third group, the teachers of "special subjects." Actually, however, to describe such teachers as a distinct section of the profession is merely a matter of convenience, for they were by no means a homogeneous group. Engaged in eight fields of work, some of which had developed in connection with the elementary and secondary schools' curricula and others in response to demands for technical education, these teachers differed widely among themselves in their qualifications, in the degree of professional organization attained, and in their conditions of work.

One of the first special subjects to develop, and one in which women enjoyed an absolute monopoly, was that of kindergarten or infant-school teaching. Many of the earliest elementary schools made some provision for the teaching of very young children and when, after the Education Act of 1870, school attendance became compulsory at the age of five and permissible at the age of three, it became common to set up separate infant schools or infant departments in elementary schools, headed and staffed by women.

As early as 1854 the Education Department authorized the elementary-teacher training colleges to provide special courses for infant teachers and awarded them special certificates. But the real development of infant-teacher training dates from 1874, when the London Froebel Society was founded, largely through the efforts of Maria Grey and Emily Shirreff. Similar societies soon developed in other localities, and in 1887 they joined to form the National Froebel Union. The Education Department soon officially recognized the Union's examinations for infant-teachers' certificates, and to prepare students for these examinations a number of special kindergarten-training colleges were established, while some of the secondary-teacher training colleges and some secondary schools organized special kindergarten-training departments.[65]

The London Froebel Society and the National Froebel Union were not professional associations in the fullest sense, for they did not concern themselves directly with the working conditions of teachers. But since the great majority of infant teachers were employed in public elementary schools, they did not lack effective spokesmen. Large numbers of them joined the National Union of Teachers or the London Teachers' Association, benefiting from the improvements gained by those vigourous organizations.

Increasing interest in the physical fitness of the community at large and of the school population in particular was an outstanding characteristic of this period, and the elementary schools always provided physical training. In the early days this was usually only a weekly period of Ger-

MORE SWEDISH INSTRUCTION.

Instructress (to exhausted class, who have been hopping round room for some time). "Come! Come! That won't do at all. You *must* look cheerful. Keep smiling all the time!"

man military drill conducted by a retired drill sergeant or one of the regular class teachers, and was considered chiefly a means of inculcating mechanical obedience rather than of developing the physical faculties. Gradually this kind of training was superseded throughout the country by the Swedish gymnastic system of Ling, which had been introduced into its schools by the London school board as early as 1878 and which entailed the employment of specially qualified teachers. From their beginning the reformed secondary schools for girls also provided physical training, at first calisthenics and later organized games, which further increased the demand for trained teachers. Also, there was great scope for such teachers outside the schools, in private-venture gymnasia, girls' clubs, evening classes, and home lessons.[66]

It is interesting that women represented a large majority among physical-training teachers. Probably this was due to the fact that, beginning in 1885, a number of private colleges were established to provide special instruction in physical training for women, for which training the Board of Education began to issue a syllabus in 1902, and to award certificates to trained women, while the first such college for men opened only in 1912. Soon four examining bodies were founded to award certificates to those teachers trained in approved colleges—the British College of Physical Education (1891), the National Society of Physical Education (1897), the Incorporated Gymnastic Teachers' Institute (1897), and the Ling Association (1899).[67]

Besides these four associations, which had relatively small memberships and did not engage in "trade-union" activities, physical-training teachers apparently developed no other professional organizations. Nevertheless, owing to the great demand for trained teachers, they seem to have enjoyed a generally enviable position with good salaries. Theirs was, in fact, acclaimed as one of the best-paid women's occupations.[68]

Concern for the health of schoolchildren also aroused interest in the teaching of the physically and mentally handicapped, and resulted in legislation empowering education authorities to establish special schools for such children, who previously had been taught in the ordinary elementary schools or not at all. The elementary-teacher training colleges were authorized to provide special courses for teachers in these schools, but few did so, and the special schools were staffed at first by those holding ordinary elementary-teaching certificates. Later special colleges officially approved by the Board of Education developed to provide training, such as the college for teachers of the deaf at Ealing and the Royal Normal College at Upper Norwood for teachers of the blind.[69]

Apparently there were only two professional associations, the National Association of Teachers of the Deaf and the Union of Teachers of the Deaf on the Pure Oral System, which catered specially for teachers in this field. However, these special-school teachers could also join the larger teachers' associations, such as the National Union of Teachers, and their position and pay seem to have been good, at least as good as that of regular elementary-school teachers, if not better.[70]

Music was a subject universally taught, in elementary and secondary schools and in the universities, and in private schools and lessons, and music teachers represented all grades and classes. Consequently, it was almost impossible to establish recognized professional qualifications and to form effective professional associations. Bogus examining bodies flourished, while even the *bona fide* schools represented a bewildering number and variety, and the music associations which did develop represented different grades of teachers, or were not confined to teachers and primarily concerned with protecting their interests, so that none could claim to speak for music teaching as a profession.[71]

Like music, "art" was a subject always taught in the elementary and secondary schools, but the great interest in art and in the training of art teachers came with the rage for technical education in the later nineteenth century. Stimulated after 1851 by the Science and Art Department grants which were given to encourage the study of mechanical drawing and of design in its practical applications to industry, a large number of independent schools of art sprang up all over the country. Later the school boards began to establish evening classes in art and to introduce the subject into their higher-grade schools, and later still the county and municipal authorities began to encourage the study of art by whisky-money grants and rate aid.[72]

The earliest recognized qualifications for art teachers were the certificates awarded by the Royal College of Art (originally the School of Design, established in London in 1837) both to its own students and to those trained in local schools of art approved by the College, the examinations for these certificates being open to women equally with men. Later a number of other examining and certificate-awarding bodies developed.[73]

Three professional associations grew up among art teachers. These were the all-male National Society of Art Masters and the small Royal Drawing Society, both founded in 1888 and concerned mainly with examining and granting certificates to teachers, and the Art Teachers' Guild, a largely social organization established in 1900, the great majority of its members being art mistresses in colleges and high schools for girls.[74] None of these associations was actively trade-unionist, and about the conditions of art teachers it is difficult to generalize, since they were employed both in different types of schools and as full-time and part-time instructors.

Interest in the teaching of domestic subjects, another field in which women enjoyed an absolute monopoly, stemmed, like the interest in art, from concern for more practical education for the lower classes. In 1874 the National School of Cookery, the earliest school for training in domestic subjects, was established in South Kensington. Similar schools soon developed in other large cities, and in 1876 they joined to form the Northern Union of Schools of Cookery, later known as the National Union for the Technical Education of Women in the Domestic Sciences, which held examinations and granted diplomas to teachers. At the urging of the Union, the Education Department recognized cookery and later laundry work and "housewifery" as subjects which could be taught in the elementary schools and in evening classes under the school boards, while technical classes supported by the county and municipal authorities also began to offer instruction in these subjects. Only very gradually did the reformed secondary schools for girls follow suit, their curricula representing initially a revolt against the solely domestic interests of old-fashioned women. Reflecting the changing attitude in girls' secondary schools, Oxford began to set papers in domestic science for its local examinations, and King's College for Women of the University of London established a department of "Home Science and Economics." After 1902 the Board of Education required that girls' secondary schools offer domestic subjects or lose the government grant.[75]

To insure the competence of teachers of domestic subjects in the public schools, the Education Department at first required that they must have certificates of training from schools approved by the Department. These schools, which after 1907 became eligible for government grants, usually offered a one-year course for certificated elementary-school teachers who wished to specialize, a two-year course for prospective elementary-school teachers, and a three-year course for secondary- and continuation-school teachers. After 1914 the Board of Education itself took over the examination and certification of domestic-subjects teachers.[76]

These teachers are particularly interesting as being the one group among specialist teachers who organized a single, strong professional association of their own. The Association of Teachers of Domestic Subjects, founded in 1897, admitted women holding diplomas from recognized training schools and other teachers especially approved by its council. By 1914 it had more than 1,300 members, including teachers in elementary and secondary schools, technical institutes and training schools. The Association concerned itself primarily with the techniques of the subjects taught, using its considerable influence to effect improvements in the curriculum sanctioned by the Board of Education, but it also interested itself in the working conditions of its members. The Association made special arrangements with an insurance company whereby its members could insure against sickness and purchase deferred annuities at reduced rates, and took an active part in the temporarily unsuccessful campaign to win a government pension system for secondary-school and specialist teachers. The Association also drew up and urged upon the local education authorities an approved salary scale for its members: in 1914, a scale of £85-150 for those in elementary schools, £110-220 for secondary schools, £120-220 for technical institutes, and £110-250 for training schools.[77]

Like the teaching of domestic subjects, the teaching of manual training first appeared in English schools in response to the enthusiasm for practical education for the lower classes. Gradually, however, the realization grew that manual training could be an educational medium for the mental development of children of all classes. Originally restricted to such studies as woodworking, manual-training programs came to include drawing, metalwork, clay-modelling and basket-weaving, and were offered in elementary and secondary schools as well as in technical institutions and classes. The first manual-training teachers were mostly skilled artisans, but gradually the more progressive local education authorities began to require that their teachers have the usual professional training in addition to special qualifications in manual training. Instruction for these teachers was provided by some of the elementary-teacher training colleges and technical institutes, and by special classes and vacation courses sponsored by the local education authorities and other interested bodies. The Board of Education officially recognized the certificates for manual-training teachers granted by the City and Guilds of London Institute, and by the joint examination board set up by the Sloyd Asociation and the Educational Handwork Union, organizations which had been formed to propagate the study in England of the Swedish woodwork system of Sloyd.[78]

Two professional associations developed among these teachers. The National Association of Manual Training Teachers, organized in 1891, claimed by 1914 nearly 1,000 members out of an estimated 1,500 to 2,000 full-time instructors. Its chief aim was to assert its members' claim to recognition as equal in status to the other teachers in the schools where they were employed, and particularly their right to similar salaries, for their pay lagged far behind that of regular teachers in elementary schools and especially that of teachers in secondary schools. A less distinctly specialist and trade-unionist organization was the Educational Handwork Association, formed in 1904 by the amalgamation of the Sloyd Association and the Educational Handwork Union. By 1914 it claimed nearly 7,000 members, most of them not full-time manual-training teachers but elementary- and secondary-school teachers, the great majority of them women attracted by their amateur interest in handicraft and by the realization that the subject was becoming increasingly important in schools.[79]

Enthusiasm for the teaching of commercial subjects was yet another example of the growing interest in technical education. Commercial classes offered by secondary and technical schools, by evening continuation classes, and by private-venture day and evening schools flourished with the increasing demand for a large army of clerks. Certificates of competence in commercial subjects were granted by various examining bodies, such as the Royal Society of Arts and the London Chamber of Commerce. To supplement these, a number of associations grew up to hold special examinations and award certificates to teachers of commercial subjects, and also to protect the interests of these teachers. Unfortunately, these associations tended to proliferate, disagreeing among themselves as to what the qualifications of teachers should be, largely because of the wide range of commercial subjects taught—commercial English, business practice, arithmetic, shorthand, typing, bookkeeping, accounting, banking, commercial geography, history, commercial law, modern languages, economics, and secretarial work and practice. Women were employed in this field chiefly as teachers of languages and of typing. Moreover, teachers of commercial subjects were employed in many different kinds of schools, and they included many part-time instructors, perhaps as many as one-third being accountants, bookkeepers, clerks, civil servants, and elementary- and secondary-school teachers supplementing their incomes by teaching in evening classes. As a result, the associations catering for them attracted relatively few members and could do very little to improve their working conditions.[80]

In addition to the various specialist organizations catering for them, teachers of special subjects working in elementary and secondary schools could also join the elementary- and secondary-teachers' associations. On the other hand, those employed solely in technical schools remained unorganized as such until the establishment in 1904 of the Association of Teachers in Technical Institutions. By 1914 this Association had grown to include 800 out of an estimated 2,500 teachers, 1,700 men and 800 women, employed in grant-aided technical schools, and engaging actively in politics and having an effective legal department, it had become one of the strongest organizations in the field of education.[81]

The Association's primary goal was to secure control over the curriculum which its members had to teach. This was achieved in 1911, when the Board of Education began to allow technical institutions to draw up their own courses of studies and to issue their own diplomas and certificates in lieu of those awarded by various external examining bodies, such as the Board itself, the Royal Society of Arts, and the City and Guilds of London Institute. The Association also worked hard to improve the conditions of its members. It concentrated especially upon limiting their hours of work and upon drawing up and obtaining the adoption of an approved salary scale. The Association worked closely with other specialist organizations, notably the Association of Teachers of Domestic Subjects, with which it was formally affiliated, and with the secondary-teachers' organizations in the campaign for increased government grants for teachers' salaries and for a state-aided pension scheme.[82] Technical-school teachers, like secondary-school teachers, gained pensions under the Superannuation Act of 1918, and for them also a Burnham Committee was established after the war to draw up salary scales.

Teachers of special subjects constituted, then, a highly diversified professional group, and generalization about them is difficult. However, it is noteworthy that within this group of teachers, women were concentrated mainly in those fields—infant teaching, physical training, and the teaching of domestic subjects—which had attained a high degree of recognized professional training and of professional organization, and in which generally good working conditions prevailed.

University Teachers

About women teachers in the universities little need be said, or indeed can be said, for the simple reason that they were relatively so few in number. The majority of university women teachers were, of course, employed in the women's colleges, which were very small in number compared to the colleges for men, while even in the women's colleges women usually competed with men for positions. Indeed, to uphold the principle for which women always contended, that academic appointments should go to the best qualified persons regardless of sex, one women's college had to adopt officially the rule that all posts were open to men as well as women. In most of the new coeducational universities, teaching positions were nominally open equally to women with men, but in practice a woman had to be exceptionally well qualified and much more distinguished than a man in order to gain an appointment.[83]

The number of women holding professorships could be counted almost on one hand, and they owed their positions to long service in struggling institutions rather than to open competition when these institutions attained university status. There was a somewhat larger sprinkling of women in the junior positions of lecturer, assistant lecturer and demonstrator, a definite inducement to their appointment being that able women were often obtained at the same salaries which inexperienced men would have demanded. For example, by 1914 the staff of Bedford College for Women included twelve men and six women serving as heads of departments, and six men and twenty-nine women serving as assistants.[84]

Professors were appointed by the university councils and enjoyed life tenure, while appointments to junior positions were made by the heads of departments and were either for a three-year period or merely subject to terminal notice. Women professors received salaries estimated in 1914 as ranging between £300 and £700, while women serving as junior staff members received salaries between £150 and £250. Salaries in the women's colleges tended to be lower than those in the coeducational universities.[85] The Federated Superannuation System for the Universities, established shortly before the war, provided pensions at age sixty for faculty members, who could also insure voluntarily with the Secondary, Technical and University Teachers' Insurance Society.

During this period, university teachers as such formed no professional associations of their own, and it is interesting that the only organization catering for but not limited to this group was the Association of University Women Teachers.[86]

The Registration of Teachers

No account of women in the teaching profession would be complete without some mention of the teachers' registration movement.[87] However, this movement was important not for its success, teaching being unique among the professions in that an effective professional register was never created, but because it finally united the different groups of teachers in a great co-operative effort and thereby enabled them to gain their ends by other means.

Originated by and for secondary-school teachers but soon eagerly espoused by elementary-school and specialist teachers as well, the registration movement sought to attain two ends, improvement in the quality of teachers and the creation of a representative body speaking for the profession. The proposed teachers' registration council would lay down the

qualifications required of teachers and keep a register of those duly qualified, and, eventually to be elected by registered teachers, the council
would advise the government on its educational policy. There was, however, no necessary connection between the two goals sought, and perhaps
for this reason the registration movement was doomed to eventual failure.

The Education Department had long laid down the qualifications required of elementary-school teachers and had begun to establish standards
for different groups of specialist teachers as well, and after 1902 the Board
of Education became responsible for insuring the competence of teachers
in all grades of government-supported schools. The government now
would not, could not, delegate to an independent professional body the
duty of determining the qualifications of teachers, for this would mean,
in effect, that employees would be dictating to that greatest of employers,
the state.

At the same time, the course of the registration movement had shown
that no new professional body was, in fact, needed to speak for teachers.
The registration system created in 1902 proved a miserable fiasco because
it formalized the existing divisions between elementary- and secondary-
school teachers and because the former opposed it so bitterly, winning
abolition of the system in 1907. The second teachers' register was created
in 1912 only because elementary- and secondary-school teachers and
specialist teachers had at long last managed to sink their differences and
join together in forcing the government to accede to their demands. (Although this register also was ineffective, it continued in existence until
1949.) Obviously the existing professional associations, if they continued
to co-operate among themselves, were strong enough to protect their
members vis-à-vis the state.

In the years after World War I co-operation among the various teachers' associations continued and grew ever closer, as did the co-operation
between these associations and the government, exemplified by the creation of the Burnham Committees in 1919. Even without an effective registration system, teachers gained a considerable measure of control over
entry into their profession and an increasing voice in winning improved
working conditions.

IV

WOMEN IN WHITE:
THE NURSING PROFESSION

Like teaching, nursing was always considered to be women's work and was, moreover, exclusively a women's occupation, so mid-Victorian feminists did not have to make out a case for the suitability and desirability of women's employment. Rather, nurses, like governesses, had fallen upon evil days, and women reformers faced the same problem that they did in the case of teaching, that of raising a depressed class of women workers to the status of true professionals. This goal was triumphantly achieved, and no aspect of the women's movement is more striking or important than the transformation of nursing from a refuge for the outcast into an honourable and skilled calling, and a very popular one as well.

The Days of Sairey Gamp

In the mid-nineteenth century young ladies of the middle classes were revolted by the idea of becoming nurses, a reaction easily understood in view of the conditions of the time. The nurses of the day lived and worked in appalling surroundings; their work was considered a particularly repugnant form of domestic service for which little or no education and special training were necessary; their living was meager indeed; and not surprisingly, their ranks were recruited from among the very lowest classes of society.

People entering hospitals for the first time were often seized with nausea as a result of the so-called "hospital smell," then considered unavoidable but actually the result of insanitary conditions. The wards were bare and gloomy, poorly heated and ill ventilated, crammed with beds that were sometimes dirty and vermin-infested, peopled by patients of the poorest classes who not infrequently were drunk and disorderly, and periodically swept by epidemics which carried off large numbers of both patients and nurses.[1]

The nominal heads of the nursing staffs in voluntary hospitals were the matrons. Some had been upper servants in the households of persons connected with the hospitals, through whom they obtained their posts, but apparently most were educated women of good position who were forced to find work. They were essentially head housekeepers, who engaged and were supposed to supervise all the hospital servants, including the nurses. Actually, however, few hospital matrons had had experience in nursing, and they visited the wards only occasionally, the supervision of the nurses being left to the medical staffs.[2]

The doctors themselves and the medical students performed most of the skilled nursing work which trained women later undertook, while the nurses did the routine and menial chores. The head nurses, often called "sisters" (a relic, presumably, of the days when members of religious orders performed most nursing work), were each responsible for the management of an entire ward. Many were promoted from the ranks of nurses, sometimes called "assistant nurses," below them, while some had been servants in gentlemen's households and some came from the lower middle class, such as the widows of small tradesmen and clerks. The sisters assumed such domestic duties as caring for the linen and superintending the cooking in their wards, and at the same time were directly responsible for the care of patients to the doctors, whom they accompanied on their daily rounds to receive orders regarding treatment and medicines. Some sisters were, in fact, very capable women, who gained much knowledge and skill from the doctors' instructions and long experience. The assistant nurses combined actual attendance on patients with the work of scrubbing and cleaning the wards and bathrooms, making beds, cleaning the utensils and washing bandages, cooking for the patients and sisters and for themselves, and washing the dishes.[3]

Sisters usually were on call at all times, and slept in rooms adjacent to their wards. Assistant nurses served for fourteen or fifteen hours at a stretch, sleeping in basement rooms or in cupboards on the stairs and sometimes actually in the wards. Sisters received salaries estimated at £20-50 a year, and nurses £14-25 or even as little as £10-12. In addition, nurses usually received an allowance of food, and sometimes an allowance for uniform.[4]

The best hospital matrons tried to select as sisters and nurses women of good character and preferably those with some hospital experience, but the difficulty of attracting applicants was usually so great that women had to be accepted without any testimonials. A famous surgeon recalled of his early experience at St. Bartholomew's Hospital in London that "the ordinary nurses were for the most part rough, dull, unobservant, and untaught women." And one eminent matron later reminisced about her early days in hospital: "The 'nurses' were drawn from the lowest denizens of the surrounding neighbourhood, such as preferred sick-nursing to street-walking, and perhaps they were able to combine the two trades."[5]

By general agreement the besetting sin of nurses was drunkenness. One doctor at a large London hospital stated flatly: "The nurses are all drunkards, sisters and all, and there are but two nurses whom the surgeons can trust to give the patients their medicine." It was not uncommon to see nurses returning late at night from the public houses to the hospitals, drunken and rowdy. Within hospital walls nurses smuggled in supplies of spirits in defiance of the strict rules against the practice, or simply appropriated for themselves the supplies then prescribed in considerable quantities to keep up the strength of patients.[6]

An equally grave and very common charge against nurses was that of sexual promiscuity. They came into daily contact with doctors and medical students and with male patients, who were generally presumed to be a corrupting influence upon them or, alternatively, an easy prey to unprincipled and immoral women. A sister in one London hospital told Florence Nightingale that "there was immoral conduct practiced in the very wards," and gave her "some awful examples."[7]

Such women were hardly noted for their kindly attentiveness to patients. Among the less extreme examples of the nurses' heartlessness were their practices of taking the patients' pillows and blankets for their own use and of pilfering the patients' food. In the circumstances, families and friends of patients and even doctors frequently bribed the nurses with money and drink to insure that their charges received good care.[8]

The best hospitals tried to attract a better class of women as nurses by hiring wardmaids and scrubbers to perform the heavier work, and by improving the nurses' living conditions and raising their salaries. But much more sweeping reforms were necessary to transform hospital nursing into a respectable calling.

The organization of nursing in military and naval hospitals was quite different from that in voluntary hospitals. Most of the nursing was done under the direction of the medical staffs by a few male orderlies, aided by men withdrawn from the ranks for the purpose, by convalescent patients, and sometimes by pensioners living in the neighbourhood of the hospitals. Inefficient as this system was, service hospitals at least enjoyed an advantage over their civilian counterparts in that they were more orderly, the patients and male attendants being under strict military discipline. Relatively few women were employed as nurses, some of them wives and widows of servicemen, some merely camp followers, for so disreputable were most women who applied for positions that the authorities of many service hospitals decided to do without women nurses altogether. When the Crimean War broke out, the government at first decided to employ no women as nurses, claiming that those available would have been even more callous than men in the treatment of the suffering.[9]

The bad conditions prevailing in voluntary and in service hospitals were as nothing compared to those in workhouse infirmaries. These institutions had become in fact great state hospitals, yet they were considered merely as "receptacles for pauperism" rather than places of healing for the poor. They came under workhouse management, which was based on deterrent principles, and under the administration of boards of guardians more concerned with the care of the rates than with the care of pauper patients. Unfortunately the original plan of the new Poor Law of 1834 had not been realized—that workhouse infirmaries should care only for able-bodied paupers lodged in workhouses who fell ill, while serious and chronic cases and mental patients would be cared for in voluntary hospitals and in separate Poor Law infirmaries and asylums. Because of the limited accommodations of the voluntary hospitals and the failure to establish separate Poor Law institutions, workhouse infirmaries had to admit the great majority of those needing Poor Law medical relief. Here the seriously ill and the convalescent, acute and chronic cases, the contagious and the non-contagious, lying-in cases and mental cases were all jumbled together in the same crowded and dirty accommodations and receiving the same rough pauper fare as the healthy.[10]

As for the nursing in workhouse infirmaries, only a few paid women were employed, usually the dregs of the population who could not obtain work even in hospitals, and who "strutted about the wards in dirty finery to show that *they* were not paupers." Most of the nursing was done by inmates of the workhouses, many of them old and infirm themselves, who lived in the sick wards day and night and received as payment an extra allowance of food and beer, and sometimes a glass of gin a day as well. They were only occasionally visited by the workhouse matrons, sometimes but once a week, at most once a day. As a result the patients, as one lady described it, were "absolutely and helplessly at the mercy of these women, of whom they dare not complain, knowing what treatment would be visited upon them in revenge if they did. From the complete equality of the pauper nurses and their patients, no respect is felt for them, and no authority can be exercised. Obedience, therefore, is obtained through fear and terror." To be sure, the patients were often disorderly and even violent, and in many infirmaries, as Florence Nightingale later put it, "the policeman might have almost been called the night nurse."[11]

If the poor suffered for lack of good nursing care, the middle and upper classes were not much better served. But at least when they fell ill, they enjoyed the advantage of being cared for at home with a doctor on call and with servants and members of the family at hand to wait upon them. When a private nurse was hired, it was chiefly in order to have an extra pair of helping hands for the domestic duties of the household, and not for any skilled aid which she could give to doctor or patient. Private nurses were sometimes quite respectable women in need of work, but many came from the same degraded class that furnished nurses for the poor. In her early days Florence Nightingale nursed a woman who made five guineas a week nursing ladies, and alternated this with prostitution.[12] In Dickens's *Martin Chuzzlewit* (1843), Sairey Gamp enters the story as a private nurse in the households of the wealthy, an occupation which she combines with midwifery among the poor and the laying-out of the dead, and she was "drawn from life." In time her name became a synonym for the bad old nurse, ignorant, drunken, brutal, of the bad old days.

Gradually, the progress of medical knowledge and science transformed the country's hospitals from pestilential dens into true havens of healing, and also made obvious the need for trained and skillful women to serve as nurses. The keeping of accurate charts and records, the use of even such simple appliances as the clinical thermometer and the hypodermic syringe, the conduct of laboratory tests, the provision of scientific diets, and the enforcement of antiseptic and later aseptic practices, to name but a few developments, would all have been quite beyond the abilities of Mrs. Gamp. In time, a nursing profession was created to stand beside and serve the medical profession and to minister in a new spirit to the sick.

The Growth of Professional Training

The first organized attempts to raise the standards of nursing in England stemmed directly from religious motives and were embodied in religious foundations with the revival of the ancient church order of deaconesses and the formation of religious sisterhoods.[13] The birthplace of the modern deaconess movement was the institution founded by Pastor Theodor Fliedner at Kaiserswerth in Germany. Here, inspired by the work in England of the noted Quaker philanthropist Mrs. Elizabeth Fry, Fliedner opened in 1833 a refuge for discharged prisoners, to which he later added an orphanage, a school, and a hospital, where his wife instructed and supervised the nurses. To help carry on his work, Fliedner organized a group of deaconesses, women who took no formal vows but agreed to remain in the service of the institution for five years, receiving small salaries and living a simple, communal life under the direction of the pastor. Kaiserswerth won considerable renown, and similar deaconess institutions soon sprang up elsewhere on the Continent.

In 1840 Elizabeth Fry visited Kaiserswerth, and returned home to London determined to begin a similar experiment in nursing. The first institution for the training of nurses in England was her non-sectarian Society of the Sisters of Charity, later called simply the Institution of Nursing Sisters in deference to Protestant prejudice. The members of the Institution, who lived together under the direction of a lady superintendent and subject to stringent rules, attended for several months first at Guy's Hospital and later at the London Hospital, picking up what knowledge they could from the doctors and nurses. They then went out as private nurses for paying patients, their free time being devoted to nursing the sick poor in their homes. (The Institution continued in existence until World War II, when its house was destroyed and its members dispersed.)

Meanwhile, the Kaiserswerth deaconesses had made their way to England, where, well supported by the Nonconformists, they established nursing institutions and sent out trained nurses to other hospitals. The deaconess movement also attracted widespread interest within the Church of England, and the founding of the first Anglican deaconesses' home in London in 1860 was followed by the establishment of a considerable number of others.

At the same time, leaders of the High Church party were holding up for emulation the example of the Sisters of Charity and other Catholic nursing orders. In 1845 the first Anglican order was founded, that of the Sisters of Mercy, who lived under a rule modelled after that of St.

Francis de Sales' Order of the Visitation and performed general mission work, including nursing, among the poor. Three years later the first Anglican order devoted exclusively to nursing work, St. John's House and Sisterhood, was organized in London. Members of this order spent two years attending the Middlesex, Westminster and King's College Hospitals, after which they went out as private nurses for paying patients and as missionaries among the sick poor. They also achieved notable success in the staffing of hospitals, both in London and in the provinces. The proved value of St. John's House led to the founding of a considerable number of other Anglican nursing orders.

The deaconesses and the nursing sisters performed a great service for nursing in their day, yet in their spirit and organization they looked to the past and not to the future. Too often they viewed their nursing work as only part of their more general mission activities and had little or no training in nursing. Even when they were trained and worked in hospitals, there was liable to be friction between the hospital authorities and the spiritual authorities, as the later history of St. John's House showed. The deaconesses and nursing sisters tended to foster the image of the nurse as ministering angel, for whom a spirit of self-sacrifice and religious dedication were the main requirements, an appealing picture but one being rendered outdated by the progress of medical science. It remained for others to make nursing not only a respectable calling for the dedicated but also a secular profession requiring special training and technical skill. This work fell to a woman whose achievements and fame overshadow those of any other in this field and raise her to a place among the greatest of her own or any time.

The story of Florence Nightingale (1820-1910) is, writ large, that of many other women of her time who strove to break through the conventional shackles binding them to idle, useless lives and to find fulfillment in careers of active service.[14] The daughter of wealthy, cultivated parents, Miss Nightingale enjoyed all the advantages which, it might seem, a young lady could desire—the fellowship of a large, close-knit family circle (Barbara Bodichon was Miss Nightingale's first cousin) and a host of congenial friends, an excellent education (dissatisfied with the competence of their governesses, Miss Nightingale's father undertook the instruction of his two daughters himself), the opportunity to travel extensively, and many chances to make a fashionable marriage. Yet all this was far from enough to satisy her restless spirit, and she felt stifled by her comfortable but aimless existence. Inspired by a deep and mystical religious faith, she believed, as she once wrote to her father, "to do that part of this world's work which harmonizes, accords with the idiosyncrasy of each of us, is the means by which we may . . . render this world the habitation of the Divine Spirit in Man . . . The Kingdom of Heaven is within us." The two ideas which, she said, God had given her all her life, were: "First, to infuse the mystical religion into the forms of others . . . especially women, to make them the 'handmaids of the Lord.' Secondly, to give them an organization for their activity in which they could be trained to be the 'handmaids of the

Lord.'" Nor was there ever any question in her mind as to what her career should be. "The first thought I can remember, and the last," she said, "was nursing work."[15]

But Miss Nightingale's ambition was long deterred. The mere mention of her wish to become a nurse sent her mother and sister into hysterics, and her father at first gave in to their insistence that her proper place was at home with them. Only very gradually was he won over to support her in preparing for her life's work. Miss Nightingale visited hospitals in London and Dublin, and in the course of travels abroad with family and friends she observed the work of the Catholic nursing orders in Italy and the Near East and of the deaconesses at Kaiserswerth. In 1851 she returned to Kaiserswerth to spend several months, and two years later took up residence in Paris, where she lived and worked with the Sisters of Charity, visiting the hospitals and observing the doctors. Returning to London, Miss Nightingale at last assumed her first post of full responsibility as lady superintendent of the Hospital for Gentlewomen in Harley Street, a small establishment originally connected with the Governesses' Benevolent Institution. Here she received the call from her friend Sidney Herbert, Secretary for War, to serve in the Crimea.

There is no need to recount here Miss Nightingale's magnificent achievements during the Crimean War. They have been summed up eloquently: "Never again would the picture of a nurse be a tipsy, promiscuous harridan. Miss Nightingale had stamped the profession of nurse with her own image . . . strong and pitiful, controlled in the face of suffering, unself-seeking, superior to considerations of class or sex . . . in the midst of the muddle and the filth, the agony and the defeats, she had brought about a revolution." In a speech in her honour, Lord Stanley placed Miss Nightingale's achievements in an even wider perspective, alluding to the force of her example on the position of women generally: "A claim for more extended freedom of action, based on proved public usefulness in the highest sense of the word, with the whole nation to look on and bear witness, is one which must be listened to, and cannot be easily refused."[16] She had demonstrated on the grand scale what the feminists always claimed—the great good that could be done in society by trained and dedicated women.

Miss Nightingale's accomplishments loom all the larger in view of the great difficulties under which she had laboured. The original plan had been for her to take out to the Crimea a party of forty nurses, but in all of Britain only thirty-eight suitable women could be found to go—ten Catholic nuns, fourteen Anglican sisters, and fourteen hospital nurses—of whom Miss Nightingale considered only sixteen really efficient. Later other nurses went out to join the original number, so that by the end of the war she had had 125 all together under her supervision. The members of the religious orders acquitted themselves well on the whole, but the hospital nurses, attracted only by the prospect of good pay, proved utterly unfit, and a considerable number had to be sent home for insubordination, drunkenness and immoral conduct. Here was dramatic proof of the great reform waiting to be carried out at home.

Miss Nightingale returned to England to find herself the heroine of the day. But she never enjoyed her fame, disliking the sentimental reverence which her name inspired, and the only testimonial she would accept was a fund, heavily subscribed to by the public and named in her honour, which she was to use to found a training school for nurses. Originally she hoped to establish an entirely new institution and direct its work personally, but ill health and the pressure of other business forced her instead to work through existing hospitals and through other persons. Accordingly, she entered into negotiations which led in 1860 to the founding of the Nightingale School at St. Thomas's Hospital in London, under the direction of a committee nominated by her.

Miss Nightingale had already, in her *Notes on Nursing* (1859) and in a number of papers submitted for the guidance of the government in sanitary reform, enunciated her philosophy of nursing and laid down the lines on which the institution bearing her name should run. She denounced the prevailing notion that any woman, or at least any good woman, could be a good nurse, writing on one occasion: "Nursing is an art; and if it is to be made an art, requires as exclusive a devotion, as hard a preparation, as any painter's or sculptor's; for what is the having to do with dead canvas or cold marble, compared with having to do with the living body—the temple of God's spirit?"[17] In the existing circumstances, Miss Nightingale's most revolutionary proposal was that nurses should not be subject to the hospital directors, nor to the doctors except in strictly medical questions. Instead, they should be under the absolute command and control of the hospital matron, who would both oversee their training and supervise their nursing work after they were trained. Nursing was women's work, and women must reform it.

Indeed, the choice of St. Thomas's Hospital as a training center for nurses had been finally determined by the character of its matron, the redoubtable Mrs. Wardroper. Left a widow with a young family to provide for, Mrs. Wardroper had obtained a post as sister at St. Thomas's, although she had had no previous experience of nursing. The Gamps were then in their heyday, but she managed to establish a surprising degree of order, cleanliness and sobriety in her ward. In 1854 she became matron, a position she was to hold for thirty-three years. Of her, Miss Nightingale wrote: "The Matron of that Hospital is the only one of *any existing* Hospital I would recommend to form 'a school of instruction' for Nurses." She described Mrs. Wardroper glowingly as a thorough gentlewoman, magnanimous and generous, and remarkable for her powers of organization and administration and for her courage, a woman eminently suited to be "the pioneer of hospital nursing."[18]

In Miss Nightingale's scheme of nursing reform, a primary requisite was that only women of the highest character should be chosen as nurses, and the life they led in hospital must be irreproachably respectable and as homelike as possible. Mrs. Wardroper carefully selected the first fifteen probationers who entered the school at St. Thomas's in 1860 for a year of training, and somewhat later Miss Nightingale herself undertook to interview all applicants. The probationers lived all together, under the supervision of the matron, in comfortable quarters in a separate section of the hospital, and later, when St. Thomas's was moved to its new site on the Thames opposite the Houses of Parliament, in a separate nurses' home under the charge of a "home sister." Strict rules governed the probationers' dress, which must be neat and somber, and their general conduct. One girl who corresponded and "walked out" with a medical student was quickly dismissed, for no breath of scandal must touch the Nightingale nurses.[19]

The probationers at the Nightingale School had to follow a rigourous daily schedule, from six in the morning until ten at night. They served as assistant nurses in the wards, receiving daily instruction from the resident medical officer and from the sisters and taking careful notes on the cases they observed. They also attended classes and took notes on lectures by other members of the medical staff, followed a prescribed course of reading, and passed regular and thorough examinations. The sisters drew up weekly reports, and the matron monthly reports, on each pupil's progress, and Miss Nightingale herself looked over the students' notes and examination papers and the reports about them. During their training the probationers were paid small salaries and provided with uniform by the Nightingale Fund.

In founding her school, Miss Nightingale had always in mind that its students would be the pioneers of nursing reform throughout the country. Never was a plan more triumphantly realized. In return for their training, the Nightingale nurses were bound to remain in the service of the school's council for three years, filling any nursing posts to which they were assigned, after which their names were entered on a register of qualified nurses kept at St. Thomas's and they could go where they chose. The Nightingale nurses went out as matrons and sisters to other hospitals, both to raise the standards of nursing and to institute programs for training other nurses on the lines laid down at St. Thomas's, and in the early days of the new era of nursing scarcely one important hospital post in the country was not filled by a Nightingale nurse. By the turn of the century all the leading hospitals in London and the provinces, and many smaller hospitals as well, had established training programs for nurses, modelled more or less directly on the Nightingale School. A trained profession was growing up.

Nursing, as Miss Nightingale was fond of saying, is a progressive calling, that is, nurses must continually progress in order to keep up with the new demands placed upon them with the advance of medical science, so their training must not be stereotyped and static but must continually improve. The greatest advance in this period was the gradual adoption by most schools of a two-year and then a three-year or even a four-year period of training, followed by the grant of a certificate. This lengthened training period not only gave probationers a more thorough schooling in their profession but also furnished the hospitals with a steady supply of competent workers at a very low cost, since probationers' salaries were considerably below those of staff nurses, and prevented a too-rapid turnover of nursing personnel. Another educational development was the institution by some hospitals of special courses to prepare nurses for the administrative duties of hospital matrons and the teaching duties of sisters, although the need for such advanced training was not fully met until after World War I, when the universities began to offer post-graduate courses and award diplomas in nursing.[20]

Meanwhile, the fraternity of medical men did not always look with favour upon the training of nurses, for any criticism of the nurses reflected discredit on the doctors who supervised them. J. F. South, the distinguished senior surgeon at St. Thomas's, for example, published a pamphlet in 1857 to rebut claims that hospital nurses were both incompetent and immoral and to prove that the projected training school at his hospital was unnecessary, and he rejoiced that of 173 doctors in seventeen London hospitals, only five, from two hospitals, had subscribed to the Nightingale Fund.[21] Also, many doctors expressed the fear that trained nurses would consider themselves no longer the servants of medical men but more nearly their equals. For example, the introduction of a trained matron and a staff of trained nurses at Guy's Hospital in 1879 aroused a great furor, amounting almost to a public scandal, the medical staff claiming that the new nurses were impossibly conceited and completely unwilling to heed the doctors' orders.[22] In time and inevitably, medical men came to appreciate the value of trained nurses who, events proved, did not in fact question the doctors' authority over them with regard to the treatment of patients, and who were much more capable and dependable than untrained women in carrying out the doctors' orders. Still, the medical men's early attitude augured ill for the time when nurses would demand recognition as professionals in their own right.

Miss Nightingale at first thought that her new-model nurses, like the Gamps before them, would come chiefly from the domestic-servant class, for she believed that few women of the higher classes would forgo their ladylike airs and submit to the strict discipline in hospitals.[23] But she soon realized that while women of the lower classes could furnish the disciplined rank and file, only women of superior background and education could supply the hospital matrons and sisters, the nursing leaders of the future. To attract such women, a special class of "lady pupils" was introduced at the Nightingale School and at other training schools. These women paid substantial fees for their maintenance, often having special living and dining accommodations, and also for their training, which was shorter than that of regular probationers, and during which they were usually exempted from night duty and the more routine and menial work in the wards and enjoyed longer periods off duty. Sometimes they alone were eligible for promotion to the positions of matrons and sisters. Gradually, however, the lady pupils disappeared and all probationers were placed on an equal footing. The regular probationers naturally resented the privileged treatment accorded the lady pupils, and special inducements did not, in fact, prove essential to draw women of the better classes into nursing.

The ranks of nurses came to represent a good cross-section of society. Women of the lower classes flocked into nursing, for they could obtain higher pay and do less menial work than if they had entered domestic service, and also, as in the case of elementary-school teachers, they now definitely moved upward in the social scale by becoming nurses. At the same time, women of the better classes entered the field in large numbers when they realized that they could lead a life in respectable company and that the work was no longer a menial occupation but involved the training and exercise of their intelligence. For them, a guide to nursing claimed, nursing represented "a more easily accessible opening, at less cost, than any other branch of women's work." By the turn of the century the eminent hospital matron Isla Stewart could report: "Nurses are recruited from all classes . . . in the hospitals a housemaid may be found sitting next to a baronet's daughter, and all the gradations of rank between these two may be found at the same table."[24]

The nursing profession never lacked for recruits, the number of applicants for training always greatly exceeding the number of places available. In becoming a respectable and skilled profession, nursing had become tremendously popular as well. This was fortunate, for with growing public concern for the health and welfare of the community there came an increasing demand for trained nurses. During this period the number of nurses in the country grew by some 210 per cent, compared with an increase of only a little more than 44 per cent for all working women. (See Appendix, Tables 2a, 2b, 6a and 6b.)

The Working Life of Hospital Nurses

Toward the end of the century, two women writing of the life of nurses had this to say: "Nurses are supposed to take it up in a missionary spirit for the good of the community, without regard to their own comfort or health. Now unfortunately the more 'noble' a profession is considered, the greater is the tendency to neglect the material well-being of those concerned in it; and nurses have reason to feel the full force of this misplaced sentiment."[25] Even more to the point, nurses, like elementary-school teachers, did not compete in a market where the free play of economic forces determined their working conditions, where the great demand for their services in the face of a limited supply worked to their advantage. Instead, they were employed by charitable institutions and by the government, and their conditions of service therefore depended upon charity from endowments and voluntary contributions and upon the state of the tax- and rate-payer's pocketbook.

The working conditions of nurses in voluntary hospitals were first brought forcefully to public attention by the investigations of a select committee of the House of Lords, appointed in 1890 to study the alleged maladministration of the metropolitan hospitals.[26] The nurses heard by the committee complained chiefly of their excessively long hours of work. Day nurses averaged fourteen or fifteen hours a day, although this did include the time allowed for meals and an average of two hours off duty. Night nurses were on duty continually for eleven or twelve hours, but their work was admittedly lighter than that of the day staff. The Lords' committee recommended for hospital nurses an eight-hour day exclusive of mealtimes, leave of at least two days a month, and a holiday of three weeks a year.[27]

In the years that followed, nurses' hours were gradually shortened considerably. By the end of this period complaints still were heard of overwork, of nurses serving as much as seventy-three to eighty hours a week or even more. However, few well-managed hospitals required more than eight and a half or nine hours a day, or a maximum of sixty-three hours a week including mealtimes and off-duty periods averaging three hours a day, and most hospitals allowed their nurses leave of one whole day or one weekend a month and three weeks' annual holiday. Generally, a guide to careers for women pointed out: "A nurse is not the unconsidered hardworked woman she used to be, but has ample time for rest and recreation, and is considered as much as is compatible with the welfare of the patients she is nursing."[28]

Nurses also complained to the Lords' committee of their low salaries. The matron of the London Hospital claimed that they had "not had their pay directly increased ever since the improved nursing, and the better class of women coming to it." The committee found that probationers received about £12 during their first year of training and then £18-20 a year for the remainder of their training period; staff nurses received £20-30 and sisters £35-60, while matrons might receive anything between £100 and £350. In addition, all received free room and board, and some received free uniform and laundry as well.[29]

Disappointingly, nurses' salaries rose little in the years following the report of the Lords' committee. By 1914 it was estimated that staff nurses averaged £24-30 in the provinces and a little higher in London, and sisters £30-40 in the provinces and somewhat more in London, while matrons in the larger hospitals averaged about £100 and in small hospitals only £40-50.[30]

Another complaint of nurses was that because of their low salaries, they could seldom make adequate provision for old age and disability, a problem more acute for them than for many other classes of workers because of their shorter working life. They began as fully qualified workers only after three or four years of training, for which they were not accepted until the age of twenty-one or twenty-two or even later, and most found it difficult to obtain work after the age of forty, and practically impossible after age fifty, when the best hospitals made retirement compulsory. Upon retirement, some nurses received small gratuities from their hospitals as an act of grace. Few hospitals provided pensions for their nurses, and even had they done so, few nurses would have been eligible to receive them, for the great majority left their hospitals after completing their training to enter other fields of nursing or migrated from one hospital to another. Statistics collected about 1913 showed that among 560 nurses the average length of service in one hospital was only a little over four years, and only nine nurses had served in one hospital twenty years or more.[31] However, an important effort had been made to help nurses to help themselves in this respect. In 1887 Henry Burdett (later Sir Henry), long an outstanding figure in hospital administration, organized the Royal National Pension Fund for Nurses.[32] He was inspired by the plight of a hospital nurse who contracted typhoid in the wards, became permanently disabled, and at length died penniless in the workhouse. The Fund enabled nurses to insure for pensions of any amount to begin at any age, and also to insure against sickness and accident.

The Lords' committee on the metropolitan hospitals recommended that hospitals provide pensions for their nurses, either by instituting their own individual plans or by affiliating with the Royal National Pension Fund and paying part of their nurses' premiums. Unfortunately, few hospitals could or did heed this recommendation. Meanwhile, the popularity of the Fund among nurses individually fluctuated greatly, depending often upon whether or not hospital authorities made the Fund known and encouraged their staffs to join, and also upon the nurses' ability to pay the premiums, which, even for pensions very moderate in amount, were rather large.[33] A satisfactory, country-wide pension scheme, contributed to jointly by nurses and hospitals and allowing nurses to migrate freely between different hospitals without losing their right to pensions at age fifty-five, was not inaugurated until after World War I. Until then, insecurity in old age, as well as low salaries, remained a great grievance of hospital nurses.

The Nursing Services of the Armed Forces

Miss Nightingale's role in the Crimean War, by catapulting her to fame, had not only enabled her to begin the reform of nursing in voluntary hospitals but had also proved the practicability and desirability of women nurses serving with the armed forces. In 1865 the War Office issued detailed regulations providing for the appointment of sisters in any military general hospital, regulations which closely followed the suggestions which Miss Nightingale had drawn up seven years before, although the Army Nursing Service was not officially inaugurated until 1881.[34] The lady superintendent at the Netley military hospital headed the Service, while superintendents of nurses, appointed in every military hospital where members of the Service were employed, were directly responsible for the work and discipline of the women. In this early stage of nursing reform, the only qualifications required of army nurses were testimonials of good character and the ability to read and write, but they did receive some training under the lady superintendent at Netley after their admission to the Service. Army nurses received salaries somewhat higher than those in voluntary hospitals, plus allowances for rations and regulation dress, and

GRATITUDE.

Patient (cured, and leaving the hospital—to Nurse). "I THANK YOU KINDLY, MISS, FOR ALL YOUR GOODNESS—I SHALL NEVER FORGET IT! IF EVER THERE WAS A FALLEN HANGEL, YOU'RE ONE!"

pensions at the compulsory retirement age of sixty or after ten years' service if they became disabled.

The real beginning of professional nursing in the armed services came after Lord Wolseley's Egyptian campaign of 1882. During this campaign Miss Nightingale supervised the sending out of twenty-four nurses under a Nightingale-trained matron, and later took an active part in the work of a committee of inquiry appointed to study army nursing. In 1884 the War Office issued a new code of regulations for the Army Nursing Service, under which nurses were to be appointed to every military hospital with a hundred or more beds. A candidate for the Service must now have had three years' training in a civilian general hospital, after which she would serve a six-month probationary period at the Netley military hospital, and she must produce testimonials to the effect that she had "the birth, breeding, and education to make her an acceptable member of a profession which is made up of ladies"! The new code, like the earlier regulations, also provided for good salaries, allowances for food, uniform and laundry, and pensions upon retirement. In 1886 the Army Nursing Service Reserve was organized through the efforts of Princess Christian, with the same qualifications for members as the regular Service. The date 1884 also marks the birth of the naval nursing service. In that year the Admiralty appointed eighteen trained sisters to serve in the naval hospitals at Haslar, Plymouth and Chatham, and so successful was the experiment that their numbers were gradually increased and their services extended to other hospitals as well. In 1888 a separate military nursing service for India was organized under the India Office, the qualifications for membership and the conditions of service being similar to those for the regular Army Nursing Service.[35]

The war in South Africa brought forcefully to official and public attention the need for further expansion and reform of the nursing services of the armed forces. The regular Army Nursing Service included only enough women to staff the permanent military hospitals, with no surplus for time of war or emergency, the entire Service at the outbreak of war consisting only of the lady superintendent at Netley, nineteen superintendents, and sixty-eight sisters. More than nine hundred other nurses, including one hundred already in the Reserve and eight hundred others quickly enrolled in it, were sent out to South Africa, sometimes at twenty-four hours' notice. Hastily gathered from all walks, from great London hospitals, small provincial hospitals, and private practice, these women varied greatly in their training and abilities, but they were lumped together on a basis of equality and dumped into field hospitals without adequate supervision or well-defined authority. Moreover, although the duty of the women was supposedly solely to supervise the nursing, the actual work being done by male orderlies, the men proved to know little or nothing of nursing duties, while many considered themselves "too good" to do the scrubbing and other routine and menial work, so that the women usually had to do it all. But despite all these difficulties, the nurses acquitted themselves admirably on the whole, and an eminent surgeon who served in the war declared: "Their ministrations to the wounded were invaluable and beyond all praise."[36]

Following the report of a War Office committee appointed largely through the influence of the Queen and of Lord Roberts, the Commander-in-Chief,[37] the Army Nursing Service and Reserve were reconstituted in 1902 as Queen Alexandra's Imperial Military Nursing Service and Reserve. The reformed Service was headed by a matron-in-chief, the first being Sidney Browne (later Dame Sidney), who had entered the Service in 1883 and served with distinction in Egypt, the Sudan, Malta and South Africa. The Service was supervised by the Nursing Board at the War Office, which included the Queen herself as president and two members nominated by her, the director-general of the army medical services, the matron-in-chief, and two civilian hospital matrons. The Nursing Board selected all members of the Service, their qualifications remaining the same as before with regard to training and satisfactory references. Below the rank of matron-in-chief were four grades of Service nurses: principal matrons, matrons, sisters, and staff nurses. The principal matrons, together with the Nursing Board and the matron-in-chief, conducted regular inspections of military hospitals where nurses were employed; the matrons were responsible for the nursing in the hospitals they headed; and the sisters were, with the abolition of the post of ward master, solely responsible for the management of their wards. In addition to the actual nursing work, the women were responsible for helping with the instruction of the men in the nursing section of the reformed Royal Army Medical Corps, who now received three years' training in large military hospitals and were awarded certificates after passing examinations conducted by a board of officers and the hospital matrons. Nurses were enrolled in the Reserve with the same qualifications as those in the regular Service, and could volunteer for short training periods of one or two weeks a year in a military hospital or field camp in order to gain experience which they could not obtain in a civilian hospital. In 1902 reforms along these lines were also carried out in the two other government services, now renamed Queen Alexandra's Royal Naval Nursing Service and Queen Alexandra's Indian Nursing Service.[38]

Improvements in the nurses' conditions of service also followed the South African war. Salaries were raised considerably and compared very favourably with those of nurses in the country's voluntary hospitals. The matron-in-chief received £300-350, principal matrons £175-205, and matrons £75-150, while sisters received £50-65 and staff nurses £40-45. In addition, matrons and sisters received extra "charge pay" of £15-30 depending upon the size of their hospitals, while all ranks received an extra allowance of 3-6s. a day when on active or foreign duty and, as before the war, allowances for food, uniform and laundry. Service nurses were entitled to extended sick leave, twelve months on full pay and a further six months on half pay for illness or injury resulting from their work, and to generous annual leave of four to six weeks depending upon their rank. On their retirement, which was optional at age fifty and compulsory at fifty-five, nurses received better pensions, by right after ten years' service and sometimes by special grant with less than ten years' service. Added attractions to women of the nursing services were the opportunities of travelling and seeing foreign countries and of entering into the social life of the stations to which they were posted.[39] Small wonder that positions in the services were considered the "plums" of the profession, and were always eagerly sought after and easily filled. How different the days when Florence Nightingale painfully gathered together thirty-eight women to go to the Crimea!

The Poor Law Nursing Service

The development of the British military and naval nursing services represented "the initial deliberate step toward bringing modern nurses into the regular services of national governments."[40] But of much wider scope and greater significance was the employment of trained nurses by local authorities in Poor Law institutions.

In the reform of workhouse nursing, Liverpool led the country, owing to the efforts of William Rathbone (1819-1902), a wealthy merchant and shipowner noted for his philanthropy.[41] Rathbone had made the acquaintance of Florence Nightingale in 1861, when with her advice and help he built a training school for nurses at the Liverpool Royal Infirmary, the first such institution in the provinces. Soon he conceived the idea of introducing trained nursing into workhouses as well. Conditions in the city's Brownlow Hill infirmary were notoriously bad. Two paid but untrained women were employed to care for 1,200 patients, most of the "nursing" was done by drunken pauper attendants, and policemen patrolled the wards at night to keep order, while those too sick and weak to make a disturbance were simply locked up and not visited all night. The parish authorities refused to improve conditions, fearing the increased burden on the rates, but they at last agreed to allow Rathbone to introduce reforms at his own expense for a trial period of three years. Again he sought Miss Nightingale's aid, and in 1865 twelve Nightingale nurses and seven probationers from St. Thomas's began work at Brownlow Hill. The successful experiment carried out there not only proved the value of trained nursing in workhouses but also gave another heroine to the nursing world.

Agnes Elizabeth Jones (1832-1868), the first superintendent of nurses at Brownlow Hill, was a woman after Miss Nightingale's own heart, and early won her admiration and even veneration.[42] The daughter of an army officer, Miss Jones was a devout Churchwoman who, like Miss Nightingale herself, early decided to spend her life in the service of the suffering. She began as a Scripture reader or missionary to the poor, teaching classes in a ragged school in Dublin and visiting the sick among the poor cottagers around her family home near Londonderry. In 1860 she went to study and work for a time with the deaconesses at Kaiserswerth. There she became convinced that nursing was her vocation, and in 1862 she entered St. Thomas's as a probationer. Of her Miss Nightingale said: "She was our best pupil; she went through all the work of a soldier; and she thereby fitted herself for being the best general we ever had."[43]

Soon the Nightingale nurses at Brownlow Hill had improved conditions beyond recognition. At first they had to contend with the pauper women whom the workhouse authorities had chosen to help with the nursing in return for small salaries and a more liberal diet, but their work proved completely unsatisfactory, most of the women using their first pay to get drunk, and was soon discontinued. In their place probationers were accepted to be trained by and work with the Nightingale nurses, the Liverpool workhouse infirmary being one of the first in the country to become a training institution. In addition to the best nursing care, Miss Jones sought to provide spiritual comfort for the inmates, holding Bible classes in the wards and distributing small gifts, such as flowers, pictures and books. She quickly gained a remarkable ascendancy over her patients and, as Miss Nightingale put it, "reduced one of the most disorderly hospital populations in the world to something like Christian discipline."[44]

Within two years the parish authorities declared that they would never revert to the old system of pauper nursing but would throw on the rates the whole cost of trained nursing in the workhouse. Humanitarian considerations aside, trained nursing had proved to be a sound investment, for with good care many patients quickly recovered and left the workhouse, ceasing to be charges on the rates. But the winning of this victory had taken a heavy toll. The nurses' work was hard and exhausting, and many fell ill. In 1868 Miss Jones herself contracted typhoid and died. In her memory Miss Nightingale wrote eloquently:

> Let her not merely "rest in peace," but let hers be the life which stirs [us] up to fight the good fight against vice and sin, and misery and wretchedness, as she did—the call to arms which she was ever obeying:
> "The Son of God goes forth to war, who follows in His train?"
> O daughters of God, are there so few to answer?[45]

Meanwhile, a campaign had long been under way to win legislative reform of conditions in workhouses.[46] A number of organizations and many influential individuals took up the cause, and numerous books and articles were published, public meetings held, deputations sent to the Poor Law Board, and investigations both official and unofficial undertaken. All this led to passage of the Metropolitan Poor Act of 1867, "the starting point of the modern development of Poor Law medical relief." This Act embodied the main principles of reform which Florence Nightingale had urged upon the Poor Law Board, and both houses of Parliament acknowledged her influence in obtaining its passage.[47] The Act created the Metropolitan Asylums Board as the central Poor Law authority for the whole London area, and established a Metropolitan Common Poor Fund, in order that Poor Law institutions might be operated more efficiently and economically by organization on a larger scale. The new Board was responsible for providing facilities separate from workhouses for the care of pauper children, the sick and the insane, since they were not appropriate subjects for the deterrent principles of the Poor Law.

Unfortunately, the Act of 1867 applied only to London. Some of the larger towns began to provide care for the sick poor in infirmaries separate from the workhouses, and in time these, like the infirmaries under the Metropolitan Asylums Board, came to approximate the great voluntary hospitals, with excellent buildings and equipment. But the majority of those receiving Poor Law medical relief continued to be treated in workhouse sick wards, which represented every degree of efficiency, from excellent, usually those in urban districts, to very poor, especially those in rural districts. By 1909, when a royal commission on the Poor Laws reported, separate infirmaries accommodated only about one-third of the sick poor receiving relief, the rest, about 60,000 persons in England and Wales, being cared for in workhouse wards. Still, the scandalous overcrowding, dirt, neglect and inhumanity revealed by earlier inquiries were no longer to be found.[48] Reform in the system of Poor Law medical relief for the whole country, on the lines laid down in London in 1867, came only in 1929, when the functions of the boards of guardians were transferred to the county and county borough councils, which were charged with transforming Poor Law infirmaries into general public health hospitals.

Miss Nightingale was irate because, despite her recommendations, the Metropolitan Poor Act contained no specific provisions with regard to nursing arrangements in Poor Law infirmaries, although it did recommend the employment of trained nurses. In the early days of the new legislation women were hired as nurses for the metropolitan infirmaries at salaries of £16-18, with allowances of up to £4 in lieu of beer, and were expected to "pick up" their duties on the job. The introduction of trained nursing in London infirmaries dates from 1869, when Miss Nightingale supplied to the newly built infirmary at Highgate a matron and nine nurses trained at the Nightingale School. Like those sent out from the School to voluntary hospitals, the trained nurses at Highgate not only improved the standard of nursing in the infirmary but also instituted a program for training other nurses. Soon many other metropolitan infirmaries, and separate infirmaries and workhouses throughout the country as well, were employing trained nurses and accepting probationers for training.[49]

A great impetus to progress along these lines was given by the "Nursing in Workhouses Order" promulgated in 1897 by the Local Government Board, which had taken over the functions of the Poor Law Board in 1871. This Order prohibited the employment of paupers in nursing work, although with the sanction of the workhouse medical officers they could be used to do the cleaning and to assist the nurses generally. The Order further provided that all nurses and "assistant nurses" (the term applied to paid but untrained women) must have had "practical experience" making them fit and proper persons to hold office. Finally, in every infirmary with a staff of three or more nurses and assistant nurses, there was to be appointed a superintendent nurse, who must have had three years' training in a recognized hospital school or in an infirmary having a resident medical officer.

Boards of guardians now found it a sound investment to offer nurses' training, for probationers could be used to replace both the pauper attendants and the paid but untrained women. In 1896 there were 2,719 nurses and 936 probationers employed in Poor Law infirmaries; within five years these numbers had grown to 3,154 nurses and 2,073 probationers. By 1914 the Local Government Board recognized seventy-eight Poor Law infirmaries as nurses' training schools. These were divided into two classes: major training schools, the larger ones which had resident medical officers and trained superintendent nurses or matrons, and which gave three years' training, preparing their students for all grades of the Poor Law nursing service; and minor training schools, the smaller ones which had no resident medical officers and which sometimes gave less than three years' training and did not qualify their students for the posts of superintendent nurse or matron. The training provided in many of the Poor Law major training schools was excellent, being surpassed only by a few of the larger general hospitals, and the number of applicants for probationers' posts always exceeded the number of vacancies.[50]

Unfortunately, a very large proportion of the nurses trained in Poor Law infirmaries left the Poor Law service as soon as their training was completed, and many infirmaries had difficulty in keeping up adequate staffs. An explanation frequently given for this was that nurses found the work monotonous and unrewarding. Infirmaries had to accept many chronic, incurable and senile cases, which voluntary general hospitals did not take, so that the nursing work was not only professionally uninteresting but also afforded women experience of only limited value in obtaining other nursing positions.[51]

The actual working conditions which nurses encountered in Poor Law infirmaries also helped to explain their distaste for this field of work. Separate infirmaries, which in 1901, for example, employed 2,151 nurses and probationers, generally approximated voluntary general hospitals in their organization and conditions of service; but the majority of Poor Law nurses, in 1901 a total of 3,076, were employed in workhouse sick wards, where conditions were often far from satisfactory. One great difficulty was that the position and duties of workhouse nurses were ill-defined. The Order of 1897 provided that the nurses were under the authority of the workhouse master and matron except insofar as they were subject to the direction of the workhouse medical officer. In consequence, the master and matron exercised control over pauper assistants in the sick wards and over nurses when they were not in the sick wards, while the superintendent nurse had control over members of the nursing staff only while they were actually in the sick wards, and no control over pauper assistants in the wards.[52]

In addition, many workhouse nurses felt that their responsibilities for the care of the sick were too great. A large number of workhouses had no resident medical officer, and the doctor who combined Poor Law work with private practice often devoted very little time to his pauper patients, only fifteen minutes a day in some instances. In any case, he was likely to be a young man just out of school who had taken the post merely to gain experience and who knew little of nursing.[53]

In their work, Poor Law nurses often had to contend with the niggardliness of boards of guardians. They could not obtain the medicines, foods and appliances needed for patients, and they had to cope with an inadequate staff—too few trained women for the nursing work, not enough paid assistants for the routine chores, and too many pauper assistants, "lazy idle creatures, the lowest class of women, and some quite imbecile," as one trained nurse in a country workhouse wrote. The accommodations provided for nurses in workhouses were often uncomfortable, and the food poor. Nurses also complained of their low salaries. The Local Government Board, which after 1888 paid to boards of guardians grants in aid of workhouse officers' salaries, put a limit on the maximum salaries that could be paid but did not set a minimum that must be paid. Finally, it would seem that Poor Law nurses at least enjoyed the advantage of security in old age, since they came under the Poor Law Officers' Superannuation Act of 1896, which made contribution to a pension scheme compulsory. But the amending act of the following year allowed nurses to contract out, and the majority did so, both because the minimum age of sixty for pensions was too high and because few expected to spend their lives in the Poor Law service.[54]

Another branch of the nursing profession which developed chiefly in connection with Poor Law medical relief was fever nursing. The Metropolitan Poor Act of 1867 and later legislation for the provinces empowered local authorities to establish special "fever hospitals" for infectious cases. Like voluntary hospitals and Poor Law infirmaries, fever hospitals undertook the training of nurses, and the Fever Nurses' Association, founded in 1908, worked to maintain a uniformly high standard of training and granted certificates to trained nurses, entering their names in a register. The organization and working conditions of nurses in fever hospitals approximated those in voluntary hospitals, and in addition fever nurses could obtain pensions under the Poor Law Officers' Superannuation Act. But fever nursing was not a very attractive field, probably because of the isolated lives which nurses had to lead owing to the danger of spreading infection, and because the work tended to be monotonous and to afford only limited experience to nurses.[55]

Yet another special field was that of mental or psychiatric nursing, which was stimulated by the provisions of the Metropolitan Poor Act and of later legislation for the provinces allowing the establishment of asylums for the mentally ill. The special training of mental nurses was encouraged by the Medico-Psychological Association, which had been founded by a group of doctors in 1841 to promote the study of mental disorders. In 1890 the Association instituted an examination for mental nurses trained in institutions recognized for the purpose by the Association, and began granting certificates to those so trained. Asylum staffs were represented by the Asylum Workers' Association, founded in 1895 chiefly to promote the better education of mental nurses, and by the National Asylum Workers' Union, organized in 1910 primarily to agitate for better working conditions. Conditions badly needed improving, for hours were longer, leave less adequate, and salaries lower here than in any other branch of the profession, although pensions were won with passage of the Asylum Officers' Superannuation Act of 1909. Mental nursing remained the least attractive of all fields for nurses.[56]

To sum up, the work of Poor Law nurses generally was exceptionally hard and their conditions of service relatively poor, and it is not surprising that the Poor Law service was not popular.[57] By 1914 much had been done to improve Poor Law nursing, but much remained to be done.

District Nursing

The development of district nursing, which marks the beginning of public health nursing in England, represented a logical extension of workhouse nursing reform, supplementing as it did the existing system of Poor Law medical relief. A special class of nurses was raised up to care for the sick poor who could not be accommodated in Poor Law infirmaries or who could be better treated in their own homes. At the same time, with the increasing emphasis upon preventive medicine, the idea grew that these nurses must not merely care for the sick poor but also serve, in Florence Nightingale's words, as "health missioners" to the people.

In district nursing as in workhouse nursing reform, Liverpool again led the country, and under the inspiration of the same man.[58] In 1859 William Rathbone engaged the nurse who had attended his wife in her last illness to care for the sick in the poorest quarters of the city at his expense. Hoping to see this work expanded but failing to find qualified nurses to undertake it, Rathbone at last arranged, with Miss Nightingale's help, that the training school at the Liverpool Royal Infirmary should supply nurses for district as well as for hospital and private work. So much support did Rathbone win for his project that within a few years the whole city was divided into districts, in each of which a trained nurse visited and cared for the sick poor at home—hence the name of this branch of the profession, which in other countries is usually called visiting nursing.

Soon voluntary organizations to provide district nursing sprang up in many other cities as well. The most important of these was the Metropolitan and National Association for Providing Trained Nurses for the Sick Poor, founded in London in 1874 with the aid and support of Rathbone and Miss Nightingale. A sub-committee of the Association, appointed to investigate the state of district nursing in the metropolis, discovered that there were some twenty unconnected organizations, the majority of them religious societies or sisterhoods, which provided for the care of the sick poor at home about a hundred nurses, of whom only about one-third could be said to be trained at all. There was little direction and control of their work, which led inevitably to slovenly care and neglect of patients, and little communication between the nurses and doctors, which led to the nurses' usurping the doctors' functions. The sub-committee's report concluded that district nurses must do nursing work only and not proselytize or engage in almsgiving or the distribution of relief; they must be thoroughly trained for their work; and they must work only under a responsible organization and under effective supervision.[59] By implementing these recommendations, the Metropolitan and National Association laid down the lines along which district nursing throughout the country would develop.

The Association established a central home for district nurses in Bloomsbury, headed by a superintendent-general responsible for the work of the Association throughout London. To fill this important post Miss Nightingale recommended Florence Lees, whom she called "a genius of nursing" and who enjoyed the reputation of being the most highly trained nurse of her day. A graduate of the Nightingale School, Miss Lees also studied nursing in Berlin, Dresden, Kaiserswerth and Paris, and visited hospitals in many European countries and in the United States and Canada. She served for a time as surgical sister at King's College Hospital and in two military hospitals in France with the Paulist Sisters of Charity. During the Franco-Prussian War she was in charge of a military hospital before Metz, and later, at the request of the Prussian crown princess, headed a home for wounded soldiers at Hamburg. She had also taken an active part in the work of the Metropolitan and National Association's sub-committee of inquiry. Miss Lees held the post of superintendent-general until her marriage to the Rev. Dacre Craven in 1880, and thereafter continued her connection with the Association by serving as honorary inspector of its district nurses.[60]

The Metropolitan and National Association also founded a number of branch homes in other parts of London and later in the provinces as well, each under a fully trained nurse as superintendent. These homes were designed to end the existing lack of coordination and to build up an *esprit de corps* among district nurses, and also to attract a better class of women to the work by providing them with respectable lodgings and relieving them of the cares of housework. The superintendents of the homes received applications for nursing services from doctors, clergymen and charitable workers, and then assigned to cases and supervised the work of the nurses, who acted only under the direction of medical men.

The Association insisted, as Miss Nightingale always did, that district nurses should ideally be drawn only from the ranks of ladies, who could command respect in the performance of their duties more easily than women of the same social class as their patients. Moreover, district nurses had to have the best training possible, since their responsibilities were much greater than those of hospital nurses. They must, as Miss Nightingale put it, often nurse the patient's room as well as the patient himself, insisting upon absolute cleanliness and neatness, improvising with the materials at hand in the absence of hospital appliances and supplies, and reporting to the public health officers any sanitary defects the correction of which lay within the public province. Also, they must teach the patient's family how to care for him in their absence and how to maintain sanitary and healthful conditions in the home. As superintendent-general of the Metropolitan and National Association, Miss Lees chose only gentlewomen for her staff of nurses, and could boast that all were eligible for presentation at court and several had been presented! These nurses had to have one year's training in general hospitals, later increased to two and then three years of training as this became the standard adopted by hospitals. In addition, they spent six months in the Association's branch homes and at the central home, doing supervised work in district nursing and receiving special instruction to supplement their general training.[61]

The organization of district nursing on a national basis dates from 1889, when Queen Victoria's Jubilee Institute was established with funds collected by the women of the Empire as a gift to their sovereign. (In 1928 the name was changed to the Queen's Institute of District Nursing.) With the advice of Miss Nightingale and under the direction of Rosalind Paget (later Dame Rosalind) as its first superintendent, the Jubilee Institute set to work to establish throughout the country district nursing associations modelled after the Metropolitan and National Association. To affiliate with the Jubilee Institute, local associations had to agree to employ only nurses with thorough general training and with special district training. This district training was at first provided by the central home of the Metropolitan and National Association in London and later at other central homes established in Edinburgh, Cardiff and Dublin and by some of the larger local associations, such as that in Liverpool. Women completing their special training and passing an examination in district nursing had their names submitted to the Queen for registration on the roll of Queen's Nurses. In return for their training they were bound to serve for a year wherever they were required by the Jubilee Institute or by their local district nursing associations, after which they were free to go wherever they liked. In large towns Queen's Nurses lived together in the district homes under the direction of a superintendent approved by the council of the Institute, and were visited annually by inspectors appointed by the Institute. In small towns and rural districts Queen's Nurses lived and worked alone, sending monthly reports of their activities to the Institute's inspectors, who visited each of them twice a year. Queen's Nurses were soon to be found throughout the country.[62]

Out of district nursing two other fields for nurses developed. School nursing, a very popular field, was begun on a charitable basis through voluntary efforts in London in 1893, and later was greatly encouraged by the Education Act of 1907, which authorized the creation by local education authorities of school medical and nursing services.[63] The practice of midwifery was by legislative action in 1902 given the status of a profession, with officially approved training and state registration for trained women. However, because of poor working conditions midwifery as a career attracted few women of the middle classes, although a good number of nurses, especially those in district work, were also trained and officially registered as midwives.[64]

The life of women in district nursing was arduous. Nominally, Queen's Nurses worked about eight hours a day between the hours of nine in the morning and eight at night. Actually, because of the varying numbers of their patients and the different kinds of cases to be treated, it was impossible to fix and keep a regular schedule of work. The problem was worse in country districts than in towns, since the area served was larger, the population scattered, and public transportation often non-existent. Here district nurses made their rounds on bicycles—indeed, excellence in cycling was practically a prerequisite for the work!—or kept a pony cart at their own expense. One conscientious nurse reported that she had to work more than fourteen hours a day, from six in the morning until eleven at night. District nurses usually received an annual holiday of one month, but during the year they were lucky to have even a half day of leave every three weeks.[65]

As for their salaries, in 1914 Queen's Nurses were receiving £30 when they began work, rising to £35 in their third year of service, with room, board and uniform, or £90-95 inclusive. In addition, they had good opportunities of promotion to more responsible and lucrative positions. In 1914 superintendents of district homes in the larger towns received £110-120, superintendents of county nursing associations about £120, and inspectors £180 with travelling expenses.[66]

Despite the hard work and the great responsibilities which it involved, district nursing was a very popular field. Here, perhaps more than in any other branch of the profession, educated women found wide opportunities to lead independent, interesting and useful lives. One distinguished Queen's Nurse later wrote of her early work in a crowded London district: "Here I realized for the first time the tremendous scope and power of a nurse's life. One went into those homes, not as 'my lady bountiful,' but as a fellow human being, a friend to give personal help, to teach and to serve."[67]

Private Nursing

Important as were nurses in voluntary hospitals, in the military and naval nursing services, in Poor Law institutions and in district nursing, they represented only a minority of the profession. An estimated two-thirds of all nurses completing their training went into private nursing, which was probably the most lucrative branch of the profession, and which was also the most disorganized and, with reason, the most maligned.[68]

Some nurses in this field worked in private hospitals and private nursing homes, which received paying patients and were usually operated for profit. (The voluntary hospitals long remained purely charitable institutions providing free care for the poor, and only very gradually began to open special wards for paying patients.) Only a limited number of these private institutions were managed and staffed by trained nurses and conducted satisfactorily, and even in these the staff nurses were liable to receive little consideration, working excessive hours with too little time off duty, provided with poor accommodations and food, and paid inadequate salaries. Most of these institutions were controlled by laymen, among whom the unscrupulous perpetrated a double fraud upon the public, employing untrained women on their staffs, and accepting as probationers women who did not want to undergo the long grind of a thorough hospital training and sending them out with nurses' certificates of training. The worst of these institutions were simply houses kept for immoral purposes and abortion mills.[69]

But the majority of private nurses went out to tend patients in their own homes. Many of the great voluntary hospitals, of which the London Hospital was the pioneer in 1886, established private nursing institutions to supply nurses for the well-to-do sick, since doctors often could not find for them nurses of caliber equal to those in hospitals tending the poor sick. The hospitals' private nursing staffs were usually separate from the hospital staffs proper, but sometimes nurses were sent out from the wards to private cases, and hospitals often required that their probationers serve on the private nursing staffs during their fourth year of training. (The Lords' committee on the metropolitan hospitals investigated charges, especially those against the London Hospital, that nurses who had not completed their training were sent out on private cases as being fully trained, and also that the wards were sometimes stripped of their best nurses to keep up the private nursing staff; but the committee believed the charges were not substantiated.) When they were not out on cases, these private nurses were lodged and boarded at hospital expense, usually in buildings near the hospitals which were under the charge of a sister specially detailed for the work, and were responsible to the hospital matron. They received fixed salaries from the hospitals, which collected the patients' fees themselves. There were obvious advantages in these conditions of work. Nurses were assured of regular employment, a steady income, a good home, definite holidays, and time off for rest between cases. But there were considerable disadvantages as well. The pay of these nurses was too low, especially in view of the large profits which hospitals derived from their services. In 1914 it was estimated that their salaries were about £30-40 a year, with sometimes a percentage on their earnings, from 5 per cent to as much as 25 per cent, or a fixed bonus, while they might earn for their hospitals as much as two to three guineas a week or about £109-164 yearly. As a result, many private nurses, like regular hospital nurses, could look forward only to a dependent old age, since they could not save enough to provide for themselves and since the hospitals could not undertake to support them.[70]

Many private hospitals, nursing homes and other institutions also supplied nurses to attend paying patients in their homes. Some of these deservedly enjoyed an excellent reputation, such as the pioneers in the field, Mrs. Fry's Institution of Nursing Sisters and St. John's House. But

Nurse (who has been many hours on duty—to patient's mother). "WHEN DO YOU THINK I SHALL BE ABLE TO GO TO BED?"

Patient's Mother. "GO TO BED? I THOUGHT YOU WERE A TRAINED NURSE!"

many, even when determined to send out only fully qualified nurses, had problems in selecting suitable women, owing to the lack of uniformity in the standards of training institutions and the resulting difficulty in evaluating certificates of training. One lady who ran a highly respected nursing institution reported that in one year 460 women applied to her for employment, but she found only sixty-five properly trained or likely to do her establishment credit. Some private institutions did not scruple to send out as qualified nurses women with few or no qualifications and sometimes of bad or indifferent character, especially if they were young and good-looking. These institutions ran no legal risk thereby; they were not legally responsible for the conduct or competence of the nurses they supplied, since not they but the patients themselves were considered to be the nurses' employers. While charging fees which fully qualified nurses commanded, many private institutions paid to the nurses they sent out on private cases very low salaries or, if the nurses themselves collected their earnings, charged them a large proportion as a commission, sometimes as much as 25 per cent.[71]

In these circumstances, many private nurses preferred to work independently. They obtained work through doctors of their acquaintance who referred cases to them, through newspaper advertisements of their services, or through commercial employment bureaus, which often charged very large commissions. Actually, however, few nurses of good standing followed this course, and the independent worker was usually "one whom no institution of repute would admit to its staff." Indeed, some women assumed the guise of private nurse as a cover for criminal and immoral practices. The newspapers carried numerous accounts of "nurses" convicted of offenses ranging from theft to murder, and prostitutes donned nurses' uniform to ply their trade freely.[72]

The conditions in the field of private nursing showed how badly action was needed to protect the public from untrained and unscrupulous women, and also to protect respectable, fully trained nurses both from "sweating" by unscrupulous employers and from the competition of the unqualified. Nurses themselves sought to improve existing conditions by forming co-operatives. The first of these was the London Nurses' Association, established in 1873 by Maria Firth, a trained midwife and private nurse who later became matron of the Endell Street Lying-in Hospital. The co-operatives protected the public by admitting only fully trained nurses to membership. They also secured to their members the advantages of independence and self-government, since the nurses themselves organized and managed them, and of good salaries, since the nurses received all their own earnings and paid to the co-operatives only a small proportion, usually 7 per cent or less, to cover operating expenses. Some co-operatives also established homes where their members could obtain board and lodging at reasonable rates when they were not engaged on cases.[73]

The growth and success of the nurses' co-operative movement showed both the need to maintain standards of efficiency in a woefully disorganized branch of the profession and the willingness and ability of nurses to manage their own professional affairs. Thus they foreshadowed the development of professional associations of a more comprehensive character which would launch the great campaign to obtain for nursing the legal status of a profession through a system of state registration.

The Battle for State Registration

The struggle for state registration was long and difficult. The "Thirty Years' War," it was called, "the second revolution, probably equal in its daring to Miss Nightingale's."[74] And leading the battle was a woman who was generally accorded the first place among her generation in the nursing profession, just as Miss Nightingale ranked among the older generation. Ethel Gordon Manson (1857-1947), later the wife of Dr. Bedford Fenwick, received her nursing training at the Nottingham Children's Hospital and the Manchester Royal Infirmary. She then served as sister at the London Hospital for nearly two years, and in 1881, at the early age of twenty-four, she became matron of St. Bartholomew's Hospital. During her tenure of office she greatly improved the system of nursing, doubling the staff and winning for them much better hours and accommodations. She also reformed the nursing school, inaugurating a three-year program of training with close supervision and careful examination of the probationers. Even her enemies admitted that it was largely because of her precept and example that the best hospitals began to adopt the three-year training period, and they expressed admiration for her organizing ability, tenacious will, professional enthusiasm and public spirit. Upon her marriage to Dr. Fenwick in 1887, she resigned her post as matron, and together with her husband turned her energies to wider work for the advancement of her profession.[75]

With the support of nine other hospital matrons, Mrs. Fenwick organized the British Nurses' Association, which was formally inaugurated in 1891 with Princess Christian as president, through whose influence the Association soon won the Queen's permission to add the prefix "Royal" to its name. The Association admitted as members women with three years' training in recognized schools. Medical men could also join, and they were heavily represented on the governing bodies of the Association. "It was the first time in modern history that nurses had asserted the right to associate together for self-government, and to have ignored the medical profession would have seemed too revolutionary." The Association's chief object was to secure a royal charter of incorporation authorizing it to maintain a register of qualified nurses who had either graduated from recognized training schools or passed examinations conducted by the Association, and whose names could be removed from the register if they later proved guilty of some misconduct.[76]

Unfortunately, the Royal British Nurses' Association quickly raised up powerful and highly vocal enemies, who long thwarted the establishment of an effective nurses' register. Pre-eminent among these was Miss Nightingale herself, and following her lead were the authorities and staff members of some of the greatest hospitals and training schools in the country, among the most important of them Eva Lückes, matron, and the Hon. Sydney Holland, chairman, of the London Hospital. The opposition was also represented by the Hospitals Association, an organization of doctors and of laymen interested in hospital administration which was founded in 1884 by Sir Henry Burdett, and by the Central Hospital Council for London, created in 1896 to speak for twenty of the most important metropolitan institutions.[77]

The arguments of the opponents of registration and the rebuttals of the registrationists fell under three main headings.[78] In the first place, the opposition disliked the proposal, inherent in any registration scheme, to lay down minimum standards of training for nursing schools. They pointed out that, like medicine itself, nursing was a continually developing and changing field requiring ever more knowledge and skill, so that the well-trained nurse of today would be but a poorly qualified nurse tomorrow. The establishment of minimum standards would, they argued, discourage progress in nursing because schools would train students only up to the minimum required instead of continuing their friendly rivalry to achieve ever higher standards.

In reply to this argument, Lord Ampthill, the leading supporter of the registration cause in Parliament, declared:

> I am quite aware that a considerable number of London hospital managers do not care for what they consider state interference . . . but you might just as well have stayed the whole course of reform in factory legislation because there were a few model employers who thought, perhaps with right and reason, that they could do better for their workmen if they were left to themselves. But legislation, surely, must be for the imperfect general mass, not for the perfect few.[79]

The registrationists argued that the setting of minimum standards would not end progress in training schools and reduce all those registered to the same low level, any more than the registration of doctors had done. Registration implied a limit on general inefficiency but not a ceiling on individual achievement. Even Miss Nightingale conceded that registration, although undesirable at that time, "might not be preposterous" some time in the future, "*providing* that the intermediate time be diligently and successfully employed in levelling up. That is, in making all nurses equal to the best trained nurses of this day; and in levelling up training schools in like manner."[80]

Secondly, the opponents of registration disliked any assertion of independence or attempt to organize on the part of nurses. Miss Nightingale, whose ideals were of the highest, wrote in this connection: "There is no magic in the word 'Association'. . . . What the Association *is* depends upon each of its members. . . . Rules may become a dead letter. It is the spirit that 'giveth life.' It is the individual, inside, that counts, the level she is upon which tells. . . . We hear a good deal nowadays about Nursing being made a 'profession.' Rather, is it not the question for *me: am I* living up to my 'profession'?" Less altruistic, perhaps, many other opponents of registration seemed to fear that nurses, "instead of devoting themselves entirely to its [nursing's] onerous duties and noble ends, [would] make for themselves a kind of Trade-Union by which they would seek to give as little time and energy to their work as possible, and to demand as large a remuneration and as pleasant a time as the general conditions of the market . . . will permit." Charges, continually hurled at the London Hospital, of "sweating" nurses and of opposing their attempts to organize to protect themselves stung Sydney Holland to say: "We are always supposed to be 'degrading' the profession . . . because we want to stop nurses thinking themselves anything more than they are, namely the faithful carriers out of the doctors' orders."[81]

On the other hand, the supporters of registration pointed out that hospital authorities could scarcely view matters from the nurses' point of view. The nurses' claim was simple: "As working women, nurses have a right to run on their own responsibility . . . as working women they ought to be free to make their own conditions and not be at the beck and call of institutions." Events proved that the anti-registrationists did not, in fact, oppose registration in itself but objected to a register kept by a body which was independent of hospitals and training schools and on which nurses would be largely represented. For a number of years Sir Henry Burdett published, in connection with the Hospitals Association, an "Official Nursing Directory" containing the names of nurses with hospital certificates of training, but at length he gave up the venture as a failure. In 1905 seven prominent laymen tried to obtain from the Board of Trade a license to form an incorporated society which would grant certificates to nurses, but this "City Financiers' Scheme" was thwarted by Mrs. Fenwick and her supporters. In 1908 the Central Hospital Council for London sponsored an Official Directory of Nurses Bill, which would have included neither doctors nor nurses on the central registration authority which it proposed to create, but this bill was easily defeated through the efforts of Lord Ampthill when introduced in Parliament.[82]

Finally, opponents argued that registration simply was not necessary, that hospital certificates of training provided a sufficient guarantee of the fitness of nurses and a much better guarantee than could a register. They maintained that the quality of a nurse depended not so much upon technical skill as upon her personal character, which an examination for registration could not test, while a hospital certificate issued by those who knew their nurses personally attested both technical skill and character. The registrationists countered by demanding why there should be training schools at all, if good character rather than technical skill were the essential quality of a nurse. No one claimed that examinations could test character, but under every registration system which was proposed nurses would have to produce testimonials of good character from the authorities of their training schools, as well as pass examinations to prove their technical skill, in order to be registered.

The opponents of registration argued further that hospital authorities and the managing committees of district nursing associations guaranteed the efficiency of the nurses they employed, and that doctors would recommend nurses for private patients not because they were registered but because they were fully trained and efficient, a fact easily determined by making inquiries of the schools where they had trained. On the contrary, the registrationists claimed, owing to the absence of generally recognized minimum standards of training, schools varied so greatly in efficiency that it was difficult even for doctors to judge the value of the certificates which they issued, and how much more difficult it was for laymen. In any case, unscrupulous women could steal or forge hospital certificates, and in fact cases of this kind continually made news. Moreover, nurses were often wanted for emergency cases when there was no time to make inquiries about them, and hospital matrons were much too busy with the administration of hospitals and training schools to undertake besides the work of a great employment office by answering inquiries about nurses.

The anti-registrationists also claimed that while hospital certificates merely stated that nurses had satisfactorily completed their training, a register would imply that the state guaranteed the nurses' continuing efficiency long after their training was over and when their character was likely to deteriorate without adequate supervision. In reply, the supporters of registration pointed out that training schools did not have the power to revoke their certificates of training no matter what the later career of their nurses might be, and that therefore their certificates were in effect a continuing guarantee of their nurses' ability and respectability. A registration body, on the other hand, could act as a disciplinary organ, supervising the conduct of registered nurses and removing from the register the names of those proved guilty of unprofessional or criminal conduct.

Despite the powerful opposition to registration, the Royal British Nurses' Association in 1893 won its royal charter of incorporation, the first ever granted to an organization of professional women. However, the charter merely empowered the Association to keep "a list of persons who may have applied to have their names entered therein as nurses," and did not give those listed by the Association the right to call themselves "registered" or "chartered" nurses. An even greater blow to the Association came when its medical members finally succeeded in wresting all power away from the nurse members and placed the Association on record as opposing registration, the promotion of which had been its chief object from the beginning! At the annual meeting of the Association in 1897, Mrs. Fenwick and a number of other matrons denounced this action and resigned from membership.[83]

The early history of the Royal British Nurses' Association taught its members two great lessons. First, an effective registration system could not be established by a privately organized association but must be established by the state. (Actually, Mrs. Fenwick always favoured establishment of a register by act of Parliament, but she believed that this was not immediately possible and that the Association's register would represent both a definite improvement in existing circumstances and a basis for future Parliamentary action.) Secondly, the organization of nurses together with members of the medical profession could lead only to "disastrous results," as one eminent hospital matron declared, adding: "We must be free to organize ourselves; the relation of man to woman complicates the situation; the relative position of doctor and nurse makes it impossible . . . though we do not claim independence of the medical profession, we claim freedom to discuss our own affairs, to make our own laws, to decide on common principles of work."[84] In future, independent associations of nurses would have to lead the fight for registration by the state.

The first of these associations was the Matrons' Council, organized in 1894 by Isla Stewart, who served as president until her death in 1910. Miss Stewart had trained at St. Thomas's, where the authorities informed Florence Nightingale that she was the most promising probationer of her class, and then had remained at St. Thomas's for four years as a ward sister. Next she became head of the Darenth Smallpox Hospital, where, responsible for a large nursing staff and a thousand patients, she won her reputation in the nursing world. In 1887 she succeeded Mrs. Fenwick as matron of St. Bartholomew's, a post she held for the remainder of her life. Under her regime the high standards of nursing set by Mrs. Fenwick were maintained, and St. Bartholomew's became noted for its stand, almost unique among the great London hospitals, in favour of registration and the professional emancipation of nurses. The Matrons' Council admitted as members all trained nurses who were or had been hospital matrons or superintendents of nursing institutions. They conferred together on all matters affecting their profession, and from the first committed themselves to work for a system of state registration.[85]

Members of the Matrons' Council soon set to work to organize their profession at the grass roots level by forming "nurses' leagues" or alumnae associations at their respective institutions, the first being established by Miss Stewart at St. Bartholomew's in 1899. These leagues were primarily social organizations, but some also maintained registers of their members and dedicated themselves to work for state registration. At length, under the aegis of the Matrons' Council, a National League of Certificated Nurses was organized, representing nurses' leagues whose members were graduates of recognized general hospital schools or of Poor Law major training schools.[86]

In 1899 the International Council of Women met in London and, urged by the Matrons' Council, included in its program a session on nursing, the first international meeting of nurses in history. Here Mrs. Fenwick proposed the creation of an international organization for nurses, and the following year the International Council of Nurses was officially inaugurated. Mrs. Fenwick was elected its first president, and four years later became honorary president for life. At first, membership in the International Council was on an individual basis, but in 1904 the Council decided that national associations of nurses should constitute its membership, this being in line with its avowed policy of developing and strengthening professional self-government among nurses. To meet the new membership requirement, the National Council of Nurses of Great Britain and Ireland was founded in 1908, with Mrs. Fenwick as president (later the National Council of Great Britain, after Scotland and Ireland developed their own nurses' councils). Originally a federation of the Matrons' Council and the National League of Certificated Nurses, the National Council soon came to represent thirteen other affiliated associations as well.[87]

Meanwhile, professional and public interest in nurses' registration was growing. Although the opposition of some doctors had thwarted the original aim of the Royal British Nurses' Association, the real spokesmen for the medical profession looked favourably upon nurses' registration. As early as 1889 the General Medical Council, the central registration authority for doctors, had passed unanimously a resolution in favour of nurses' registration, and the British Medical Association in 1895, and again in 1904 and 1906, passed similar resolutions, moved by Dr. Bedford Fenwick. Concern for registration increased greatly as a result of the South African war, for in the absence of an official register of trained nurses it was difficult to judge the qualifications of those who volunteered to go out to South Africa when the supply of regular army nurses and the reserve were exhausted, and some inefficient nurses were accepted and good ones rejected.[88]

In 1902, at Mrs. Fenwick's suggestion, the Society for the State Registration of Trained Nurses was organized, with Louisa Stevenson of Edinburgh, long active in women's causes, as president, Isla Stewart as vice-president, and Mrs. Fenwick as secretary. The Society's sole purpose was to work for registration, and it included not nurses only but others interested in their cause as well. In 1904 the Society sponsored in Parliament a registration bill drafted by Mrs. Fenwick. At the same time another registration bill was sponsored by the Royal British Nurses' Association, in which the nurse members had at last regained control and reaffirmed their support of registration. The select committee appointed to study these bills heartily recommended a system of state registration, but a bill had still to be passed, "as difficult a process," one writer wryly remarked, "as the passage of the needle to the proverbial camel."[89]

Every year thereafter until 1914 registration bills were introduced in Parliament. The Society for State Registration and the Royal British Nurses' Association sponsored separate bills until 1910, when, on Mrs. Fenwick's initiative, the Central Committee for the State Registration of Nurses was organized, with Lord Ampthill as chairman and Mrs. Fenwick as secretary. This Committee, which included delegates from the Society for State Registration, the Royal British Nurses' Association, the Matrons' Council, the Fever Nurses' Association, the British Medical Association, and associations of nurses in Scotland and Ireland, coordinated the efforts of its affiliates and sponsored a single registration bill.[90] Unfortunately, the government refused facilities for the registration bills, and the press of other Parliamentary business prevented their passage.

It took another and a much greater war to demonstrate even more forcefully the need for registration and to persuade the government to take up the cause. In 1919 a government-sponsored bill embodying the principles for which the nurses' organizations had fought so long finally became law. It created a General Nursing Council for England and Wales (supplementary legislation created separate councils for Scotland and Ireland), including sixteen nurses' representatives, eventually to be elected by the general body of registered nurses, and nine representatives of the state. The Council was responsible for drawing up a syllabus of instruction for nurses' training schools, and only those schools conforming to it were allowed to present students for the Council's examinations for registration. The Council kept a general register of trained nurses who passed its examinations, and also supplementary registers for fever nurses, mental nurses, male nurses, and children's nurses, who had to pass special examinations. These nurses alone could call themselves "R.N.'s" and wear uniform and badges implying that they were registered. The General Nursing Council also served as a professional court of justice, with the power to remove from the registers the names of nurses proved guilty of unprofessional or criminal conduct. At long last nursing had won the full status of a profession.

V

WOMEN BEHIND THE COUNTER:
THE DISTRIBUTIVE TRADES

The ladies of Langham Place, those mid-Victorian feminists interested in increasing the opportunities of employment for middle-class women, seized upon work in shops as a most desirable occupation and complained that it was practically closed to women. The *English Woman's Journal* advised its readers that ladies could exercise a great influence in promoting the employment of saleswomen in shops simply by insisting that they be served by women, and an address to this effect to London tradesmen was signed by some two hundred influential women and published in the newspapers. In response, the proprietor of an old established lace shop declared: "You may be sure tradesmen employ as many women as they can, for their wages are half those of men." The clear implication was that women generally were too poorly educated to be suitable shop workers. Acting upon this assumption, Jessie Boucherett began, in connection with the Society for Promoting the Employment of Women, her special classes to prepare girls for commercial careers. In Parliament Viscount Raynham, treasurer of the S.P.E.W., even asked the Chancellor of the Exchequer whether, in order to encourage the employment of women as shop assistants, a tax might be levied on all men employed in shops.[1]

A tax was not, in fact, imposed upon male shop assistants, and Miss Boucherett's classes could never train a large number of women to be shop workers. Still there was in this period a tremendous increase in the number of women employed in shops. The absence of women workers in shops in mid-Victorian times was not, after all, due primarily to women's generally poor education, nor due at all, it seems, to prejudice against their employment, but resulted rather from the conditions of shopkeeping at the time. These conditions altered drastically in the later years of this period, and the woman shop assistant made her appearance upon the scene. Basically, the lace-shop proprietor seems to have hit upon the key to this development when he cited the low wages of women compared to men, for in the new conditions obtaining in the distributive trades women represented a welcome source of cheap but efficient labour. By 1914 women shop assistants numbered close to half a million, and were by far the largest single group of middle-class women workers in the country.

A Nation of Shopkeepers and Shop Assistants

To understand, then, the scarcity of women shop workers in the mid-nineteenth century it is necessary to understand the conditions of shopkeeping at the time, and to understand the rise of the woman shop-assistant class it is necessary to see how these conditions changed in the later years of the century. In the first place, there was not even a large body of male shop assistants in mid-Victorian times. The characteristic figure in retail distribution was the small-scale trader in business on his own account, controlling usually only one shop which he ran with the aid of members of his family and perhaps one or two helpers. Secondly, the retail trader was a skilled craftsman. Dealing in a very specialized and narrow line of goods, he had to know intimately the quality of the products available from his various suppliers, chiefly those in his immediate neighbourhood, and to handle the purchasing and storing of goods in large quantities. He also had to do much of the processing of the goods he sold, the grocer, for example, blending his own tea, grinding his sugar, roasting his coffee. The skilled nature of the retail trades entailed a system of apprenticeship. Youths paid premiums of £30-50 and bound themselves to serve a master for periods of three to seven years, during which time they lived as members of the master's family, often in accommodations behind or above the shops, learning the trade and helping with the business, and receiving only nominal wages if any. The goal of all apprentices was, of course, to set up in business on their own. Finally, retail traders worked in a relatively non-competitive atmosphere. Reputable dealers frowned upon open advertisement or "puffery," and made little attempt to display their goods to advantage, either inside their shops or in the shop windows in order to attract casual passers-by as customers. Instead, they served a regular clientele who sought them out for their skill and the quality of their wares, their reputation for honesty, and their readiness to take a personal interest in all transactions. Indeed, the prevailing practices of giving long credit, a necessity in the days when buying for large families was often done in bulk, and of bargaining and haggling over the prices of goods, made necessary an intimate knowledge of customers and close personal attention to them.

In these circumstances few women could be employed. There was no great demand for shop assistants. Parents were unwilling even if able to provide their daughters with the long and expensive training necessary to enter retail trade and to start in business for themselves afterward. And since shopkeepers relied for labour mainly upon apprentices whom they paid little or nothing, they saw no advantage in employing women with their traditionally lower wages.

But the later nineteenth century saw a revolution in the distributive trades which paralleled the contemporary trend in industry toward large-scale organization, specialization and division of labour.[2] An enormous increase in both the quantity and variety of goods to be channeled to the public by retail traders followed naturally upon industrialization with its mass production and new inventions and processes, upon improved methods of transportation, and upon British dominance in and dependence upon a world market, accompanied as it was by a policy of free trade. Retail traders also had to cope with the problem of distributing goods to new centers of population, with increasing urbanization and the movement of urban dwellers from the centers of towns to the suburbs. These developments also revolutionized the character of retailing by helping to destroy its craft tradition. Expanding factory production tended to standardize the kinds of goods available, and better transportation made these goods available more speedily and over a much wider area than previously. This enhanced the importance in the distributive process of the wholesaler and the large-scale manufacturer, who now performed work previously undertaken by the retailer, such as the holding of large stocks of goods, the processing of goods—grading and sorting, weighing and cutting, packaging—and even the advertisement of goods by "branding" and the setting of prices by the system of "price maintenance." At the same time, the development of industry served both to broaden and consolidate the middle classes and greatly to expand the wage-earning working classes. Throughout society there was a general and rapid rise in real income per capita, and consequently an increasingly effective demand for the goods of production.

Important results of all these changes were a great increase in the number of retail shops in the country and also an increase in the size of shops. In 1875 there were an estimated 295,000 shops in the country and in 1907, 459,592, an increase of 56 per cent, compared with an increase in the population of the country between 1871 and 1901 of 43 per cent. Moreover, the small independent shopkeeper of the past simply could not handle all the goods flooding into the market, nor could he serve the larger shopping public. Small one-man or one-family shops have never disappeared, but in this period they steadily lost ground, and many contemporaries, drawing often upon the analogy of the handloom weavers, confidently predicted their eventual extinction. Retailers, like industrialists, were quick to grasp the economic advantages of large-scale operation, now facilitated by the new principle of limited liability; and large firms, frequently joint-stock companies, sought to reach a wider public and increase their profits by adding to the lines of goods they sold and enlarging their premises or by opening branch shops. This trend toward large-scale retail organization was epitomized in the growth of co-operative retail societies, multiple shops, and department stores.[3]

With the increasing number and size of shops in the country, there arose a large body of shop assistants as distinct from shopkeepers, and by 1914 they were estimated to number about a million. (See Appendix, Tables 3a and 3d.) Apparently only a small proportion of this number were employed in very small shops, the great majority working in medium-sized shops employing ten or more, although some employers had hundreds and even thousands of assistants.[4]

At the same time, the decline of the craft tradition tended to transform shop assistants from skilled into unskilled workers. The old system of apprenticeship broke down, and the use of formal indentures, the payment of premiums, and service for specified, lengthy periods of time gradually disappeared. "Apprentices" were still taken on in shops at low wages to learn the business "on their good behaviour," but they received no regular instruction and merely picked up knowledge of the trade as best they could.[5] In any case, the duties of most shop workers were fast becoming mainly those of keeping the stock tidy and of showing merchandise across the counters and receiving payment.

With increasing competition among the growing number of shops, especially the competition between large and small shops, retailers began to turn more attention to the problem of attracting customers. Once shopkeepers had existed to supply a demand, but now they sought to create a demand for their wares among the shopping public. They expended huge amounts on the decoration of their premises, being greatly aided by two important improvements of the time, the invention of plate glass used in shop windows and display cases, and the introduction of gas lighting. They now relied unabashedly upon open advertisement, invited shoppers to inspect their goods freely without the obligation of buying, which entailed a system of clear and open pricing of goods, and offered special inducements to customers with the institution of great semi-annual sales, held usually in January and July, and of periodic bargain sales. Small wonder that the shopping habits of the public changed radically! Once a stern necessity, shopping was fast becoming, for working classes and middle classes alike, a very popular pastime.

All of these developments made possible the advent of the woman shop assistant. There was now a large demand for shop workers. With the decline of apprenticeship shop work had become easy of access. Indeed, an elementary education alone was sufficient preparation, and it is significant that contemporaries dated the trend toward the employment of women as beginning in the 1870's following passage of the Elementary Education Act. In the early days some people maintained that lady customers preferred to be waited upon by men, but this proved not to be the case. In an amusing article on shopkeeping past and present, a lady cited the employment of women assistants as one of the most important among the increasing temptations for the public to buy, for many claimed that women were more industrious and conscientious and quicker to appreciate their customers' needs than were men, and that a better type of women than of men were attracted to shop work. But of far greater importance to shopkeepers was the fact that the employment of women represented a distinct economic advantage in the now fiercely competitive atmosphere, because, as the London lace-shop proprietor had said, women's wages were only half those of men.[6] The number of women shop assistants increased, therefore, at a much more rapid rate than did the number of men, by more than 319 per cent compared with an increase of 118 per cent for men. (See Appendix, Table 3b.) And this pattern of employment has continued in the twentieth century, so that today women workers outnumber men in the distributive trades.

Still, women were not moving into all branches of retail trade and replacing men. Where a long and expensive training continued to be necessary, as for chemists and druggists, few women were employed. Where the expense of the stock in trade rather than the cost of labour was the main concern of shopkeepers, as among jewellers, wine merchants and good-class booksellers, there were few women assistants. The work of butchers, fishmongers, grocers, ironmongers, furnishers and the like was considered to be too rough and heavy for women. And in trades catering to a male clientele, such as gentlemen's outfitters, hatters, bootmakers and barbers, customers preferred service by members of their own sex. Women shop assistants were concentrated in those trades where no great degree of training was necessary, where the wages bill was highly important to the shopkeeper, where the work was considered light and suitable for them, and where the customers were chiefly women. Such, for example, were shops dealing in drapery, millinery, underwear, hosiery, baked goods and confectionery, dairy products, flowers, stationery and tobacco.[7] (For the distribution of retailers by "trade," see Appendix, Table 3c.)

Shopkeepers never lacked a plentiful supply of workers, both men and women. Not only did shop work offer a wide field of now easily accessible employment, but also there clung to it an aura of middle-class respectability, or so shop assistants themselves believed. (Some writers on the subject assign shop assistants to the working classes and shopkeepers to the middle classes; others consider shop assistants also as belonging to the middle classes.) To many young people of the working classes, becoming a shop assistant represented a definite step upward in the social scale, while for those of the middle classes it opened the way to a life of supposedly respectable work. Girls from every stratum of society were found serving behind counters, "the daughters of artisans, of agricultural labourers, of skilled mechanics, of struggling and of prosperous shopkeepers, of clerks and of professional men."[8]

But with good reason the public at large failed to share the shop assistants' own estimate of their social position. The upper and middle classes considered shop workers to be about on a level with the servant class, while the working classes sneered at their pretensions to respectability, derisively calling them "counter-jumpers." In fact, sympathetic observers were at a loss to explain the supposed "gentility" of employment in shops which attracted so many workers. "Is it," asked one, "because they do not like to dirty their hands or double up their sleeves?" And, he added: "In these days . . . clean hands often mean starvation." Perhaps, as was frequently claimed, many shop assistants would have been better off working in other occupations of supposedly lower social rank. For example, it was suggested that shop girls could often do better for themselves as domestic servants or factory workers. In any case, to describe the working life of shop assistants is but to present a long catalog of grievances.[9]

The Working Life of Shop Assistants

Whether the working conditions of shop assistants were actually growing worse in the later nineteenth century is a debatable question. Some
writers of the time, looking back nostalgically to supposedly happier days,
contrasted the sad lot of shop assistants with that of shop workers in the
earlier part of the century. Shopkeepers and their assistants and apprentices were remembered as having once lived together in close contact and
friendly camaraderie. Their work had been hard but not exceptionally so.
Their working day was said to have begun at eight in the morning with
nine at night the latest hour of closing, the customary working day being
twelve hours long and including two hours off duty for meals and rest.
Shop assistants as well as shopkeepers allegedly enjoyed a respected position in society, and the assistants and apprentices of London, for example,
were said to have been noted for their vigour, health and independence. On
the other hand, there is considerable evidence that in the earlier nineteenth
century shop assistants were an overworked and depressed group. Beginning in the 1820's there are accounts of shop assistants joining to petition
their masters for earlier closing of shops and shorter working hours. The
anonymous author of a pamphlet entitled *The Linen Draper's Magna
Charta,* published in 1839, inveighed against the usual sixteen to eighteen
hours of work required of assistants daily and demanded enactment of a
law compelling shops to close at a reasonable hour. The abortive Grand
National Consolidated Trades Union of 1834 had attracted as members
shop assistants as well as manual workers seeking to improve their working conditions.[10]

Whatever the truth of this matter, two things seem certain. In the first
place, the relative positions of shopkeepers and their assistants were being
radically transformed. Because of the increasing number and size of shops,
the decline of apprenticeship, and the fierce competition among shopkeepers, the close personal bonds or contacts between assistants and their
masters gave way to an impersonal relationship between employees and
employers, and the latter were able to drive hard bargains with the large
numbers of unskilled workers who now clamoured for employment in
shops and who found ever more illusive the goal of going into business on
their own. Secondly, the increasing employment of women in shops, itself
a result of changing conditions in the distributive trades and perhaps also
a result of increasingly poor working conditions, first aroused sympathetic
public concern at the conditions of shop workers and led to numerous
legislative attempts to improve those conditions, just as earlier the increasing employment of women in factories and workshops had attracted public
interest and resulted in passage of the Factory and Workshops Acts.

By far the greatest grievance of shop assistants was their excessively
long hours of work. There was no common understanding among shopkeepers as to a general hour of closing, and each sought to attract more
customers and do more business by staying open later and later into the
night, a practice now possible with the introduction of gas lighting.

Margaret Bondfield, a shop assistant who later achieved prominence in trade-union affairs and in politics, recalled that in one shop in London where she had worked, her employer found that the amount of money he took in after 8 P.M. did not even pay for the gas he used, but he did not dare to close then because his competitors did not. At another shop where she worked, her employer would send her out at night "to scout around and see if the shops over the way showed any signs of closing; if they did we, too, would hastily and gladly put up the shutters."[11]

Actually, however, the practice of keeping open very long hours was not universal. Shops varied widely in this respect, depending upon their location, their size, the kind of trade, and the class of customer. Shop hours in London were supposed to be the worst, but in other large cities they were equally bad, while the hours of shops in the smaller towns and in rural districts were considerably better. Within the towns, shops in the central business districts tended to close earlier than those in outlying residential districts. In 1886 the factory inspector for the Sheffield district reported that in the center of the city shops closed at 7:00 on weekdays and at 9:00 or 9:30 on Saturdays, while in the suburbs the closing hours were 8:00 on weekdays and 10:00 or 11:00 on Saturdays. Within the same districts, however, small shops stayed open later than the larger ones, presumably because they could compete effectively only by offering customers longer hours during which to buy. In 1886 a general dealer of Kensington estimated that large shops there were open nine and a half hours a day in winter and as long as eleven hours in summer, while small shops in the same district were open twelve and a half hours on weekdays and as long as fifteen hours on Saturdays. Shops dealing in goods for immediate consumption naturally often stayed open later than others. For example, in 1886 butchers in London were said to work an average of ninety-seven hours a week, grocers a maximum of eighty-nine hours, fruiterers and greengrocers a maximum of ninety-eight hours, and provision dealers about ninety-two hours. Finally, in upper- and middle-class districts shops closed early simply because their customers did not go out shopping late at night, but in working-class districts shops stayed open late so that customers could buy after their own working day was over. In 1886 the proprietors of several fashionable department stores in the West End of London reported their hours as about fifty-six a week (they allowed their assistants a half-holiday on Saturday beginning at 2 P.M.), while shopkeepers and assistants from poorer districts of the metropolis reported weekly hours ranging from seventy-six to ninety-four.[12]

In view of these facts, it is extremely difficult to generalize about the average working hours of shop assistants. In 1884 a champion of their cause estimated that most of them worked between seventy-five and ninety hours a week, one-fourth of them working ninety hours, one-half working eighty hours, and one-fourth working seventy-five. This claim was substantially borne out by the various official investigations of the subject during this period. The Factory and Workshops Acts Commission reported in 1876 that shop hours ranged as high as eighty-five, and the select committee of the House of Lords in 1901 cited the same figure.[13] Obviously the length of shop hours had not been exaggerated, nor had there been any general improvement in a quarter of a century.

Another major grievance of shop assistants was the insufficient time allowed them for meals. In the largest and best establishments assistants went out in shifts to eat at definite times, being allowed usually thirty minutes for dinner at midday and fifteen to twenty minutes for tea during the afternoon. Yet even these short periods represented not the actual mealtimes but merely the total amount of time assistants could be absent from their counters. In smaller shops, assistants took time to eat when and if they could, and if they ate on the shop premises were liable to be called from their meals to wait upon customers. Understandably, digestive troubles and anaemia were common complaints among shop assistants.[14]

Still another hardship for shop assistants was that they had to be on their feet constantly, even when not serving customers or tidying the stock. There was usually little room behind the counters for seats, and in any case shopkeepers generally disliked to see their workers sitting about idle, fearing that it would give their establishments the reputation of doing little business and that customers would consider it lacking in respect to themselves. The father of two girls employed in large drapery establishments in London stated that he knew of only three such firms which furnished their assistants with seats, and added: "The young ladies had better not use them if they wish to retain their situations."[15]

With regard to their physical surroundings at work, shop assistants did not enjoy the protection afforded many manual workers, for shop premises were excluded from the operation of the Factory and Workshops Acts and were not open to the factory inspectors. Retail establishments were often faulty in construction, being draughty and badly ventilated, and were rendered worse, as the long hours passed, by the flaring gaslight and the continual going and coming of customers. A particular grievance was that of the sanitary conveniences, which were frequently small and noisome and sometimes not separate for the sexes, and which in some small shops were simply non-existent.[16]

Despite these poor conditions in shops, many people contended that the work itself was not so hard and continuous as work in other occupations, in factories, for instance. Yet, one sympathetic observer pointed out:

> when young women are hanging on in shops, they are more tired than when they are at work actively. Then there is, in connexion with selling in shops, the anxiety to make sales and the anxiety for fear of losing sales and displeasing their employers, and so on; and the mental effort necessary in order to make exact calculations and prevent mistakes, all this leads me to believe that it is more exhaustive labour [than factory work] mentally and equally exhaustive physically.[17]

For their hard work shop assistants often received very poor pay. Competition among them for positions beat down the level of the compensation they received, and this competition was rendered exceptionally severe by the employment of a very large proportion of ill-paid young persons and by the increasing employment of women. One observer estimated in 1884 that one-half to two-thirds of all shop assistants were between the ages of twelve and twenty-one, although another estimate of about the same time was that workers in this age range represented only 40 to 48 per cent of the total. As for the employment of women, their salaries were generally estimated to be only 50 to 70 per cent of men's salaries, the figures most frequently quoted as an average range of pay toward the end of the century being £20-60 a year for men and £15 to £40 or £50 for women. However, this estimate included only the cash payments received by shop assistants, and if the value of the room and board they received from their employers under the living-in system, discussed below, were taken into consideration, the difference between men's and women's salaries might be only about 20 per cent. (In better-class shops, salaries were reckoned at so much per year and paid monthly to distinguish them from the weekly wages of the working classes. In this connection Margaret Bondfield later wrote that "industrial workers . . . used to say that 'counter-jumpers are paid by the year because their wages are too small to divide by the week.'")[18]

Actually, as in the case of working hours, it is difficult to generalize about the pay of shop assistants because of several complicating factors. In the first place, the level of salaries varied greatly with the location and class of shops. For example, a study made in London at the end of this period showed that women in fashionable shops in the West End might receive as much as 18s. to £1 a week, while in lower-class shops 10-14s. a week and even 7-8s. a week for women was common. Secondly, even in the same class of shops, and in the very same shops, there was a great range in salaries, depending upon the assistants' position. The same study of shop assistants' pay in London cited the following typical salaries: junior assistants, the younger and less experienced workers, £10-12; senior assistants supervising four or five other workers, £20-50; head salespeople, shopwalkers and window dressers in fashionable shops, £100-200; buyers and department managers in good stores, anywhere from £100 to over £1,000. However, these last highly paid positions were relatively few in number, and men rather than women usually filled them. Much also depended upon the individual assistant. "False pride," a feeling that it was "unbecoming a lady" to discuss the amount of pay received, a feeling which employers openly encouraged, sometimes resulted in a wide difference in pay between women of equal abilities, experience and position simply because one was forward enough to ask for a rise and another was not. Finally, in addition to their salaries shop workers sometimes received commissions and premiums upon the sales they made. A commission was a fixed sum or percentage of the total sales, and a premium usually a smaller amount or percentage which was paid on certain classes of goods only, such as those damaged or otherwise hard to sell, new goods to be "pushed," and expensive articles carrying a large profit for the retailer. Under these arrangements shop assistants might do very well financially, and one estimate was that a woman receiving an annual salary of £26 could actually earn £42 with commissions and premiums. Yet much depended upon the class of shop, the kind of goods sold, the general state of business and, of course, the temperament of the individual salesperson. Besides, employers never guaranteed their workers definite amounts of extra pay in this form, and they could change the amounts of commissions and premiums or abolish them completely at any time.[19]

The greatest difficulty in calculating the average salaries of shop assistants stems from the system of living-in, which next to long hours was their worst grievance. Under this system they received only an estimated half of their nominal pay in cash (so that figures on salaries cited above should presumably be doubled), taking the remainder in the form of room and board provided by their employers. By general agreement living-in traced its origin back to the days of apprenticeship, when apprentices lived with their masters while learning the trade.[20] Now, although apprenticeship itself was dying out, employers still clung to living-in, supposedly as a convenience and protection for their workers, but also undeniably as a source of profit.

Living-in was not universal, however. It was unknown in Scotland but widespread in England and Wales, common in the Midlands, general in the south, less prevalent in the north. The system seemed more common in cities than in smaller towns and rural areas, but even the cities varied greatly among themselves. In London living-in was said to be general and at its worst, in Liverpool and Bradford living-out prevailed, while in Manchester both systems existed together. Wherever living-in was found, it affected shops of all kinds, the large and the small and those of poor and of good class, and it was made a condition of employment, that is, shop assistants had no option but to live in. In 1908 it was estimated that the system affected perhaps 400,000 out of some 750,000 shop assistants. Even when assistants lived out, they frequently had to take part of their pay in the form of meals provided by their employers.[21]

Shop assistants often had good cause to complain of the accommodations and food furnished them. As one of them declared: "Our paupers [in workhouses] are in many instances better fed and better housed." In many small shops and even in some large establishments, the assistants slept in quarters over the business premises. More often, employers took over blocks of houses near their shops and converted them into sleeping accommodations. These might be small rooms shared by two or more assistants, who generally had no choice of roommates, or barrack-like halls for a dozen or more, the space for each sometimes separated by matchboard partitions. Water closets were provided, but adequate washing facilities often were not, in which case assistants had to resort to the public baths.[22]

At best these living-in accommodations were comfortable, if not luxurious; at worst they were overcrowded, dirty, unhealthful and dangerous. One girl who had gone into a shop in Baker Street in London left after two days, because there were only three bedrooms for twenty-two assistants and she had to sleep in a tiny room with eight others and in a bed with two other girls. The beds were sometimes vermin-infested, and one girl apprenticed to a draper stated that her sheets had been changed only once in three months. In one establishment typhoid broke out because of faulty drainage, and a tenth of the nearly six hundred employees fell ill and several died. Shop assistants also lived in constant fear of fire, especially those with accommodations above a draper's shop, a veritable tinder box. Conflagrations in which assistants died made news periodically, and questions on the subject were asked in Parliament, while many more workers lost their meager possessions and were left homeless when living-in premises burned.[23]

As for the meals provided, these were taken on the business premises. In the worst cases the dining rooms were located in the basements of the buildings, damp, poorly ventilated, overcrowded, infested with insects, permeated by odours from the kitchens, and further rendered unbearable by the rush and clatter. Sometimes the employers themselves provided the food; in other cases, caterers furnished meals at a fixed rate per head and often realized neat profits by cutting down on quantity and quality. At best the food was plentiful and good if not fancy; at worst it was insufficient, of poor quality, and badly cooked. Meat and vegetables were usually served only at midday dinner. Breakfast, tea, and even supper at the end of a long day's work consisted almost entirely of bread and butter. To supplement these rations shop assistants usually spent a considerable proportion of their pay on extra food, which the caterers or housekeepers sometimes displayed temptingly before them in the dining rooms.[24]

In short, many shop assistants felt that with regard to their salaries the living-in system cheated them doubly. They never saw a large part of their pay in cash, while the value of the accommodations and food provided them was not nearly equivalent to the amount which employers calculated them to be worth, so that salaries were actually considerably lower than the amounts for which assistants had agreed to work.

Besides the deduction for food and lodging, the pay of shop assistants was liable to further heavy exactions. One major expense was that of clothing. To obtain good positions, assistants had to make a very neat and prosperous appearance and, as one observer put it, "dress as well as their customers on half the wages of a cook." Young women working in drapers' shops faced a special temptation in this respect, for their employers often encouraged them to "book their wages," that is, to take their pay in the form of goods from the shop.[25]

Especially onerous were the fines to which assistants were liable for offenses committed on the job. Some shops had few official offenses, some a hundred or more. Some graduated the fine to fit the seriousness of the deed, from 1d. or 2d. to 2s. or 3s.; some levied a fixed amount, such as 1s., for each. Shop offenses fell into four general categories. The first and commonest was unpunctuality, arriving late for work in the morning and taking more than the allotted time for meals. Second, there were "business errors," such as incorrectly dating a bill, putting a wrong address, adding a bill wrong, taking or giving the wrong change, when the assistant also had to make good any deficit, and even failure to refer a dissatisfied customer to the shopwalker and allowing a customer to leave without making a purchase! Next came alleged breaches of manners, including talking or laughing with other workers, particularly between men and women assistants, sitting down, standing out of their place, and even failing to address members of the firm as "sir." Finally, there were fines for breakages and damage to goods. Employers claimed that fines were essential to maintain discipline among their workers, especially in large establishments where they could not supervise the assistants personally and department managers and shopwalkers exercised authority in their stead. But shop assistants themselves were convinced that fines simply represented a welcome addition to the shopkeepers' income, for although the money was supposedly used for the workers' benefit, as in the purchase of books for the house library, no account was ever given as to how it actually was spent.[26]

In addition to shop fines, the system of living-in made assistants liable to another series of exactions. They had to pay fines for such offenses as leaving their bedrooms untidy, failing to turn off the gas, unnecessary talking and noise in the bedrooms, bringing in visitors, and loitering near the house. They also had sums deducted from their pay for such items as provident and hospital funds, medical attendance, subscriptions to athletic and recreation clubs, use of the house piano and library, bootblacking and laundry.[27]

Yet another disability imposed upon shop assistants by the living-in system was political disfranchisement, since living-in premises did not qualify their occupiers to vote under any of the existing property franchises. Consequently, male assistants were deprived of the vote in both national and local elections, while female assistants were barred from municipal elections, in which qualified women were allowed to vote beginning in 1869, and from the elections for the new county councils and other councils created by the Local Government Act of 1888, in which qualified women were also eligible to vote.[28]

Besides all these burdens, the shop assistant, to a greater degree than the average worker, faced the constant threat of unemployment. Between 1895 and 1909 the average rate of unemployment for all trades was 4.6 per cent; during this period the average rate for members of the shop assistants' union in private trade was 7.3 per cent, but since the union's members represented the aristocracy of their trade and only a small proportion of the total number of assistants, the unemployment rate for all shop assistants was probably much higher. Many assistants, owing to the long hours, poor working and living conditions and meager pay, broke down in

ALL THE DIFFERENCE!

Haberdasher (to Assistant who has had the "snoop"). "WHY HAS THAT LADY GONE WITHOUT BUYING?"

Assistant. "WE HAVEN'T GOT WHAT SHE WANTS."

Haberdasher. "I 'LL SOON LET YOU KNOW, MISS, THAT I KEEP YOU TO SELL WHAT I 'VE GOT, AND NOT WHAT PEOPLE WANT!"

health and had to leave work temporarily. A large-scale employer in London stated that of the more than two thousand young women whom he interviewed annually for positions, some 20 per cent gave ill health as the reason for leaving their last jobs. And, he added, although many of these were very well qualified, he could not hire them because of their delicate health. Another threat to the employment of shop assistants was the competition of young persons with their low wages. Many businesses actually kept going by employing chiefly junior assistants, dismissing their senior workers when they demanded more pay. A worker in the shop assistants' cause reported: "Men and women between 30 and 40 years of age have the greatest difficulty in securing a re-engagement." "Too old at twenty-one" even was a familiar phrase. Finally, there was a great deal of seasonal unemployment in the distributive trades. Many firms kept only a small permanent staff of assistants, hiring large numbers of temporary workers during their busy times. Others adopted the practice of "laying off" workers without pay during slack seasons or of forcing them to take vacation without pay at these times. Some shops allowed their assistants a fortnight's holiday with pay after one year's service, but apparently this was not a general practice.[29]

When unemployment came, it came swiftly. A few shops allowed their assistants perhaps a week's notice, but the general rule was instantaneous dismissal, usually without wages in lieu of notice. This bore especially heavily upon shop assistants living in, for they lost homes as well as jobs at one blow.[30]

In the difficult task of finding employment when dismissed from their positions, shop assistants had to rely heavily upon written references from their former employers. Since references were secret and private documents, assistants had no chance to defend themselves if these were drawn up unjustly or carelessly, and one worker declared: "Any employer can close the doors of all other employers against you tomorrow."[31]

Another obstacle to shop assistants seeking new positions was the practice, especially of large company firms, of exacting from their senior workers "radius agreements." These were agreements not to take positions during a certain period of time, anywhere from one to ten years, in any shop within a certain radius, from one to thirty miles, of their former place of employment. Since many large companies had numerous branches throughout the country, such agreements might exclude a shop assistant from his trade altogether. The legality of the agreements was dealt with by the courts under the common law. In some cases, companies won substantial damages from assistants who had broken their agreements; in others, the courts held that such restrictive covenants were not necessary for the protection of the companies' business.[32]

Contemporaries seemed mystified as to what became of shop assistants, especially the older ones, who could not find work. Some suggested that the men might wend their way into other unskilled occupations, becoming, for example, cab drivers and tram or omnibus conductors, and that the women, unless they had money or friends to help them, drifted to the workhouse. But most women assistants naturally hoped to end their lives of hardship and insecurity in shops by marrying. An official investigator pointed out: "It is a significant fact that whereas large numbers of factory girls cannot be prevailed upon to give up their factory work after marriage, the majority of shop assistants look upon marriage as their one hope of release, and would, as one girl expressed it, 'marry anybody to get out of the drapery business.'"[33]

But the marital prospects of women shop assistants were not particularly bright. Because of their long hours and low pay, they had little opportunity for social life outside the shop. Assistants in living-in establishments were rigorously segregated by sex and often given no facilities for entertaining visitors. Moreover, employers generally frowned upon any display of friendliness between their men and women workers on the job. Indeed, if a man and woman showed a special interest in each other, one or both might be dismissed. In any case, the male shop assistant hardly represented a good matrimonial risk. The manager of a large London department store stated flatly that employers generally disapproved of the marriage of their men because they did not earn enough to support their families comfortably, which tended "to make them—well, certainly not honest . . .". Assistants usually had to obtain their employers' consent to their marriage, or at least to their living out and receiving the money equivalent of their lodging and food, since living-in establishments had no accommodations for married couples. Many cases were reported of married men who continued to live in, visiting their families only on weekends and fearing dismissal if their marriages were discovered. In these circumstances a weighty charge against living-in was that by making marriage nearly impossible it encouraged immorality among shop assistants.[34]

To sum up, shop assistants generally represented a depressed and pitiable class of workers. Help for their plight could come, it seemed, only from effective combination among them to protect their interests, although the obstacles to effective trade unionism in the distributive trades seemed almost insurmountable.

Trade Unionism among Shop Assistants

One great problem in establishing trade unions among shop assistants was their general attitude toward organization. Priding themselves on their middle-class status, they felt it "quite beneath them to belong to a common Trade Union like navvies and bricklayers" and "looked upon Trade Unionism as a high-caste Brahmin would look upon untouchables." Moreover, the persistent feeling that they were "employers in embryo" deterred many shop assistants from organizing. As one of them put it: "He would not join in any combination of a character which might ultimately become a weapon against himself." Finally, the shop-assistant class included those in many different trades and grades, "each insisting upon recognition of its own special privileges and position" and feeling little sympathy with others. The draper's assistant, for instance, considered himself superior to the grocer's assistant, the chemist's assistant looked down on all other assistants, and so on.[35]

There were also many practical obstacles to trade unionism. Even among shop assistants in the same trade there was little feeling of unity to serve as a basis for organization. Despite the growth of very large-scale retail establishments, the majority of assistants worked in medium-sized shops and, unlike workers in great industrial enterprises, came into contact with relatively few others of their class. In addition, there was always a great turnover of personnel in shops. Men especially sought to gain wider experience and obtain better positions by changing jobs frequently, while assistants forced by ill health to leave work often did not return to their former employers. The competition for positions, combined with the competition on the job which was fostered by the payment of commissions and premiums upon sales, encouraged a spirit of rivalry rather than of cooperation among shop assistants. At the same time, the strict discipline in shops enforced by fines, the threat of unemployment, and the system of secret references all deterred shop assistants from antagonizing their employers by attempts to organize. The employment of large numbers of young persons and of women posed additional problems, for youth militates against effective organization and the backwardness of women in trade unionism is likewise proverbial. Finally, even those assistants who favoured trade unionism had little money or leisure to devote to the cause.[36]

In these circumstances, trade unionism was slow to develop among shop assistants. Their first effective organization dates from 1891, when seventeen men representing eleven local associations of shop assistants met in conference at Birmingham. Of these eleven associations only two, those of London and Manchester, frankly styled themselves trade unions, the others calling themselves early-closing associations or half-holiday associations and being essentially philanthropic organizations. At Birmingham their representatives agreed to form a country-wide organization for the distributive trades, and so began the National Union of Shop Assistants, later named the National Amalgamated Union of Shop Assistants, Warehousemen and Clerks, one of the earliest and most successful examples of the "New Unionism" among unskilled workers. Indeed, the inspiration for its founding was said to have been the London dockers' strike of 1889.[37]

From its beginning, the N.A.U.S.A. was distinguished by its policy of admitting women to membership and by the equality of status accorded them. This was much more than a chivalrous gesture, for it was obvious that in order to be effective any shop assistants' union must cater for the large numbers of women employed in the distributive trades. The union was fortunate in starting with a clean slate, unhampered by the rivalries between men and women which plagued the older unions organized on a craft basis. "The woman . . . shop assistant had always had the free entry of her trade. Men were almost as backward as women in organization, and

there were no barriers to keep up or to break down except those of trade
or social tradition." The N.A.U.S.A. admitted as members any workers
of good character employed in any retail or wholesale establishment or
warehouse, regardless of "craft" or sex. Men and women members were
organized together in the local branches of the union, not separately as in
some other unions, and women were equally eligible with men for election
to all the union's official positions. Women enjoyed the same union benefits as men, the usual trade benefits, including free legal advice and aid in
disputes with employers, and provident benefits, including payments during unemployment, sickness and disability. In addition, the union made a
special appeal to women by giving them a dowry upon marriage. Any
woman who had belonged to the union two years and in that time had received no sickness or unemployment pay was refunded half her contributions when she married.[38]

But despite the union's official attitude, many of its male members at
first remained indifferent at best to the organization of women, and the
union appointed few women organizers. There was, in fact, considerable
justification for the men's attitude. Most women members took little interest in the union, merely paying their contributions and, although attending the meetings, rarely expressing their views. Even more important, women proved to be an extra drain on the union's resources, for
because of their lower wages they paid smaller contributions for provident
benefits than did men, but their demands for benefits exceeded those of
men.[39]

In the later years of this period, however, women began to play an increasingly important role in union affairs. This was largely due to the
creation of women's district councils or advisory committees composed
of women representatives from the local branches of the union. The first
of these councils was formed for the Manchester district in 1909, and such
was its success that within five years similar groups had been organized
in twelve other districts of the country and a women's advisory committee
had been appointed in connection with the national executive of the union.
In addition, beginning in 1910 a separate women shop assistants' conference was held yearly in conjunction with the annual general conference
of the union. The object of these groups was to educate women in trade
unionism and to encourage them to take an active part in union affairs so
that eventually they would be represented on all the governing bodies of
the union. But these groups never went to the extreme of demanding official positions for women as women, except, of course, the positions of
women organizers. They disliked the practice adopted by other unions of
reserving places on their committees of management to women elected
separately by women members only. They feared that the number of reserved positions would become the maximum number to which women
could aspire, and that women in reserved positions would lack the status
and influence they would have had if they had been elected by both men
and women in open competition, and would represent not trade interests
but the narrower interests of their sex. Other unions speedily recog-

nized the value of the N.A.U.S.A.'s system of women's councils and adopted a similar plan of organization, for it seemed the best way of affording a real means of expression to women members.[40]

The number of women in the shop assistants' union grew steadily. From only about 8 per cent of the union's membership in 1910, some 2,000 out of a total of 22,426, the number of women grew to represent by 1914 about 27 per cent of the union's members, 22,289 out of a total of 81,250. Their influence as well as their numbers grew. It became usual for one or two women to win places on the union's national executive committee at every election. In 1913 the T.U.C.'s badge for the best work done for women's trade unionism during the preceding year went to Isa Davidson of the N.A.U.S.A. In the same year Margaret Spencer Jones was appointed assistant editor of *The Shop Assistant,* the union's official organ. Also in 1913, Mabel Talbot attended an international conference of shop workers as the union's official delegate, and in 1919 she won the distinction of being the first woman elected president of the union.[41]

Here special mention should be made of the N.A.U.S.A.'s most outstanding woman member, Margaret Bondfield (1873-1953), who was to become the first woman cabinet minister in Britain.[42] The daughter of a lace factory worker of Somerset, Miss Bondfield began her career at the age of fourteen as a draper's apprentice in Brighton. Shortly after her arrival in London, where she had gone to seek work, she joined the union and, with the encouragement of its editor, began writing reports and stories for *The Shop Assistant.* Soon she was elected to the London district council of the union, and twice she represented London at the union's annual conference. She worked briefly as woman organizer and then served as assistant secretary of the union for ten years. She represented the union several times at the T.U.C., in some years being the only woman delegate present, and later she served on the general council of the T.U.C. In 1908 Miss Bondfield gave up her connection with the shop assistants' union to devote her energies to the Labour Party. She lectured extensively for the Party, actively supported the Parliamentary campaigns of several Labour candidates, and in 1913 was elected to the Party's national administrative council. Returned to Parliament first in 1923, she served for a time as Parliamentary Secretary for the Ministry of Labour and then as Minister of Labour in the MacDonald government of 1929-31, when she was also the first woman to be named a Privy Councillor.

Four years after the founding of the N.A.U.S.A., another union catering for shop assistants was organized. A number of local groups had been formed among the employees of various co-operative retail societies to provide sickness and unemployment benefits, and after several years of successful operation the associations at Manchester and Bolton joined forces in 1895 to form the Amalgamated Union of Co-operative Employees. Like the N.A.U.S.A., the co-operative employees' union was notable for the equality of status accorded its women members. There was no trade-union restriction on the type of work in which women members could be employed, men and women were organized together in the union's local branches, women were eligible for election to all official positions, and they received the same trade union and provident benefits as men, plus a dowry upon marriage. But unlike the N.A.U.S.A. the co-operative employees' union did not, before World War I, appoint women organizers or set up a special women's department, and no women won election to the union's national executive committee.[43]

The avowed aims of the A.U.C.E. were conciliatory, as being more in harmony with the spirit of the co-operative movement than the more forceful or strictly trade-union policy of the N.A.U.S.A. Also, a reflection of its origins, the A.U.C.E.'s provident benefits overshadowed its trade-union benefits in the minds of many of its members. It was true that the working conditions of co-operative employees were in general considerably better than those of shop assistants employed by private traders and organized in the N.A.U.S.A., for many co-operative societies, considering themselves in the vanguard of the working-class movement, prided themselves on being model employers. As an example, an investigation of the working conditions of women co-operative workers, undertaken by the Women's Co-operative Guild in 1895, revealed that although there was room for improvement in certain respects, very long hours, insufficient mealtimes, fines and dismissal without notice were practically unknown, and that many assistants enjoyed a weekly half-holiday beginning at noon and a week's annual holiday with pay. Still, many other co-operative societies did not measure up to these high standards, their committees of management proving just as obdurate as any private tradesmen or company board of directors in the face of their workers' demands for better conditions. So there was ample room for trade-union activities, and the major internal issue facing the A.U.C.E. in its second decade of existence was whether or not to establish a strike fund, as the N.A.U.S.A. had already done. The question was finally settled when the union's executive proposed to amplify the rules so as to provide support for members who lost their jobs as a result of strikes, lockouts or dismissals because of union activities.[44]

Meanwhile, the N.A.U.S.A. was also enrolling co-operative employees in addition to shop assistants in private trade, since all distributive workers were eligible to join its ranks. The union claimed not to make special efforts to attract co-operative employees, but the A.U.C.E. occasionally accused the other union of the "poaching" of its members, and relations between the two were sometimes far from harmonious. As a result, proposals for their amalgamation came to nothing in this period. After World War I the A.U.C.E. began to enlist shop assistants engaged in private trade as well as co-operative employees, and changed its name to the National Union of Distributive and Allied Workers. In 1947 this union and the N.A.U.S.A. amalgamated to form the Union of Shop, Distributive and Allied Workers, with some 374,000 members, nearly half of them women. This new union was at the time and is still today one of the "Big Six" of the trade-union movement. These are the country's six largest unions which together account for more than half of the union membership affiliated with the T.U.C., the others besides the distributive workers' union being the Transport and General Workers' Union, the National Union of General and Municipal Workers, and the unions of engineers, of miners, and of railwaymen (until 1964, when N.A.L.G.O., the National Association of Local Government Officers, supplanted the National Union of Railwaymen in sixth place).[45]

Between the time of their founding and the outbreak of war in 1914, the two shop assistants' unions grew dramatically in size. In 1910 there were an estimated 466,000 shops in the country employing about one million assistants, including 6,000 co-operative stores with about 63,000 employees. By this time the co-operative assistants' union could boast some 30,000 members, nearly half the workers eligible to join, and a 100 per cent increase in membership since 1905. In 1910 membership in the N.A.U.S.A. was 22,426, only a tiny fraction of those eligible to join but a remarkable increase in absolute numbers over the mere 1,618 members in 1895. In the next four years the union's growth was spectacular, membership rising to 81,250 by 1914. This great increase reflects two important developments. Following passage of the National Insurance Act of 1911, which compelled all workers earning less than £160 a year to join an "approved society" for the payment of insurance benefits, the union decided to become an approved society under the provisions of the Act. This also helps to explain the proportionately much greater enlistment of women than of men in the union during these years, for because of their lower salaries many more women than men were compulsorily insured under the Act. In 1913, further swelling its ranks, the union decided to admit as members workers engaged in the production of goods, such as dressmakers and milliners, if they were employed directly by distributive firms.[46]

Still, members of the N.A.U.S.A. and of the co-operative employees' union continued to represent only a very small proportion of the total number of shop assistants in the country. Indeed, this picture is little changed today, for only about 13 per cent of all distributive workers, 16 per cent of the men and 11 per cent of the women, are union members. Nevertheless, as one authority on the subject declared: "In the case of shop assistants . . . trade unionism has exerted an influence out of all proportion to the numerical strength of its adherents."[47] Both unions did outstanding work on behalf of the workers they represented. They succeeded in bringing before Parliament legislation to reform shop conditions, and the agreements which they won from employers benefited not their members only but many other shop assistants as well.

The Struggle for Shorter Hours in Shops

The reform which stood at the head of the shop assistants' list of demands was the limitation of their working hours. Actually, the movement to shorten shop hours had begun half a century before the appearance of the shop assistants' unions, with the organization in London in 1842 of the Early Closing Association. For decades this Association enjoyed considerable popularity, and the voluntary agreements among shopkeepers which it sponsored helped to win earlier closing of shops at night and also a weekly half-holiday. For example, in 1876 a Dundee draper testified that since about 1850 voluntary action had shortened hours from 9 P.M. on weekdays and 11 P.M. or midnight on Saturdays to 7:30 or 8:00 on weekdays and on Saturdays to 8:00 or 8:30, and even in some cases to 5:00 or 6:00. Some of the leading shops of London's West End pioneered with a Saturday half-holiday, and so many others followed their example that by the last decade of the century it was the exception for a first-class business in London to be open on Saturday afternoon. Other shops, whose busiest day was Saturday, instituted a mid-weekly half-holiday, and early closing on Wednesdays or Thursdays, at 2 P.M. in better-class shops and at 5:00 in poorer-class shops, became common throughout the country.[48]

Nevertheless, shop assistants themselves apparently took little interest in the Early Closing Association. Many belonged to it simply because their employers forced them to join and contribute to its funds. Indeed, it is ironic that an organization sponsored mainly by employers was so largely financed by their workers! In 1886 an estimated one-third of the Association's funds came from shopkeepers and two-thirds from assistants. Many other shop assistants feared to join the Association because of possible retaliation by employers who opposed early closing. Still others felt, and with reason, that the efforts of the Association were proving ineffectual. Voluntary early-closing agreements had touched only shops of the better class, presumably because they simply could afford to close early, while shops of the poorer class continued to stay open excessively long hours. Moreover, even where early-closing agreements obtained, there was always the danger of backsliding, and if one tradesman broke away from his agreement and began to stay open longer, all his competitors felt that they must follow suit. Finally, even when they gave their assistants a weekly half-holiday, many employers made up for the hours lost on that day by working their assistants longer and longer on every other day of the week, and some even claimed that the total number of weekly hours was greater after the early-closing agreements than before them![49] The work of the Early Closing Association was eventually largely discredited, and shop assistants looked to protective legislation as the only remedy for their ills.

The subject of legislation for shops first came before Parliament in 1873, when a bill was sponsored by the National Early Closing League, an offshoot of the Early Closing Association. Organized in 1870, the League was centered first in Yorkshire, but branches were soon established throughout the country and were supported by the philanthropic-minded nobility and gentry and important groups of shopkeepers, and apparently also by large numbers of shop assistants. The League's bill was introduced by Sir John Lubbock (1834-1913), who was to be the shop assistants' most prominent Parliamentary champion for three decades. Equally distinguished as a financier, a naturalist and a parliamentarian, Lubbock was best known and loved for his efforts to improve the conditions of the working classes. He was responsible for passage of the Bank Holiday Act of 1871, and bank holidays were long popularly dubbed "St. Lubbock's Days."[50]

The Shops Bill of 1873 would have extended to children, young persons and women employed in shops the provisions of the Factory and Workshops Acts relating to working hours. Impressed by the effect of these Acts on the conditions of industrial workers, supporters of the Shops Bill obviously believed that it would indirectly limit the hours of men in shops as well. This was an attractive piece of logic but fallacious. The cost of running a factory was large, and employers had found it uneconomical to keep their men working late at night after women and young persons, a large proportion of the labour force, had quit work for the day. On the other hand, the cost of running a shop was comparatively small, and even if it did not pay shopkeepers to work their male assistants into the night, at least they would suffer no great loss by keeping their shops open.

The royal commission on the Factory and Workshops Acts which was appointed shortly after the introduction of this first Shops Bill studied the question of shop hours thoroughly, hearing a great deal of evidence from interested witnesses and also requesting detailed information and opinions from the factory inspectors. Opinion as to whether shop hours could and should be legislated for seemed about evenly divided, with perhaps a slight preponderance in favour of legislation. Those who opposed extending the Factory and Workshops Acts to shops argued that this would hinder the employment of women and young persons. In rebuttal, those favouring legislation claimed that the work of women and young persons in shops was indispensable, and that because of their lower salaries employers would find it uneconomical to dismiss them and hire men in their place in order to keep their shops open later in the evening. Others argued that even if employers wanted to hire men in place of women, they would not find this easy to do. One witness pointed out that owing to long hours and other bad working conditions, it was becoming increasingly difficult to induce capable young men to enter shop work. "It looks," he said, "as if we were being fast driven into female labour instead of out of it, as things are." Some even argued that legislation would actually increase the number of women employed in shops, that with shops staying open shorter hours more women would be needed to carry on the business previously done by fewer women in a longer period of time.[51]

The final report of the royal commission was a great blow to the shop assistants' cause. The commissioners held that to restrict the hours of women would indeed hinder their employment, inducing employers to dismiss them and hire men instead, or that if shopkeepers continued to employ women they would find their customers drawn away by shops which employed men only and which therefore could stay open longer hours. In any event, despite the weighty evidence presented to the contrary, the commissioners denied that shop work was as hard as work in factories, holding that it "could hardly be considered fatiguing, much less unwholesome," and believed that no case for any legislation had been made out. Following this adverse report, the National Early Closing League, sponsor of the first Shops Bill, slowly dwindled away and died.[52]

Not until 1884 did Lubbock again bring forward in Parliament legislation for the benefit of shop assistants. In that year and in the two sessions following he introduced a measure sponsored by the new Shop Hours (Labour) League, a group organized in London and including employers and workers on an equal footing. Very comprehensive in scope, this Shop Hours Regulation Bill, which would be enforced by the factory inspectors, provided for limitation of the working hours of children and young persons but not of women employed in shops, restriction of the hours of overtime, regulation of the times allowed for meals, the grant of a weekly half-holiday to assistants, the right of assistants to obtain from employers written character references, and maintenance of sanitary conditions in shops. The select committee appointed in 1886 under the chairmanship of Lubbock to consider the measure recommended legislation favourably to the Commons.[53]

As amended by the committee and passed in final form, however, the Shop Hours Act of 1886 was completely inadequate, providing merely for an absurdly high maximum work week of seventy-four hours, including mealtimes, for young persons under eighteen. And even this limitation was honoured more in the breach than in the observance, for the Act contained no provision for its enforcement by inspectors or otherwise. Despite Lubbock's hopeful predictions, shopkeepers and shop assistants themselves did not see to the enforcement of the Act, perhaps because few of them even knew that it existed. The Early Closing Association and the Shop Hours (Labour) League undertook to publicize the Act and when offending shopkeepers failed to mend their ways, instituted legal proceedings against them. But the two organizations were hampered by the unwillingness of shop assistants to provoke the retaliation of their employers by reporting breaches of the law. Even when shopkeepers were successfully prosecuted, the fines imposed upon them were ridiculously small. For example, in the first two years after passage of the Act, a grand total of four convictions was obtained in the whole metropolitan area, and in a famous case in 1889 a London draper who had worked two boys, aged twelve and fourteen, from ninety to ninety-four hours a week was fined the great sum of £3 6s.[54]

To remedy this unsatisfactory state of affairs, A. D. Provand, another long-time Parliamentary champion of the shop assistants, introduced in 1892 a Shop Hours Bill which would amend the Act of 1886 in three ways: to make it permanent (the 1886 Act was originally passed for one year only but was renewed annually for the next six years); to apply to women as well as young persons the legal maximum of seventy-four hours of work per week; and to allow the appointment of inspectors to enforce the Act. Another select committee was appointed to study the problem of shop hours, and evidence was given by the Early Closing Association and by the National Union of Shop Assistants, which had appeared upon the scene as an interested group to be consulted since passage of the Act of 1886. By now the Early Closing Association had become convinced that the voluntary action of shopkeepers on which it had so long relied to effect reform was not enough, that legislation must supplement voluntary agreements, and it heartily endorsed Provand's Bill. The shop assistants' union had considered the Bill at its annual meeting in 1892 and again at a special conference to which it invited delegates from all associations connected with or interested in the distributive trades and which was claimed to represent directly or indirectly four-fifths of all the shop assistants in the country. As a result of these deliberations the shop assistants' representatives urged four points with regard to the Bill. First, it should apply to men as well as women: "no distinction should be made between the sexes such as would place any impediment to the employment of women, or would have a tendency to make women's labour cheaper than male labour." The N.A.U.S.A. was, in fact, one of the first unions to claim legal protection for its members regardless of sex. Secondly, the union felt that the proposed seventy-four hour weekly maximum was much too high and wanted instead a maximum of fifty hours weekly exclusive of daily mealtimes of one and a half hours. But in place of legal enactment of this maximum, the union preferred a fixed and compulsory closing hour for shops. Even if a maximum work week were enacted, shopkeepers could, by opening later in the day, continue to work their assistants late into the evening, and it was night work in itself almost as much as long hours to which the union objected. The union's third suggestion was that the Bill should provide for legal enforcement of a weekly half-holiday negotiated by shopkeepers and assistants and embodied in voluntary local agreements. Finally, the union held that the appointment of inspectors should be compulsory, not voluntary, and that the inspectors should include women as well as men.[55]

But the select committee of 1892 was in general much less favourably inclined to the shop assistants' cause than its predecessor in 1886. In particular, its members were convinced that any restrictions on women's hours would interfere with their employment in shops, and consequently they struck out the principal clause in the measure under consideration. As eventually passed, the Shop Hours Act of 1892 was as inadequate as the Act of 1886, merely making that Act permanent and allowing but not requiring local authorities to appoint inspectors to enforce it. Also, the Act of 1892 was so poorly drafted that two amending measures soon had to be passed. The Shops Act of 1893 allowed the salaries of local inspectors to be placed on the rates, while the Shops Act of 1895 set a fine of 40s. as a penalty for shopkeepers who failed to display conspicuously on their premises a notice stating the hours of work of young persons, as required by the Act of 1886. Legislation for shops continued to be largely a dead letter, for few local authorities appointed shops inspectors, although the N.A.U.S.A. laboured mightily to persuade them to do so. The Home Office returns for 1900 showed that in England and Wales 53 county councils and 218 town councils had made no provision for shop inspection; the few authorities which had taken action had appointed 288 inspectors, but only fourteen of these dealt with shops only, including nine appointed by the London County Council, the rest performing inspections under other legislation as well, such as the Public Health Acts and the Food and Drugs Act.[56]

Now another type of measure to limit the hours of shop assistants was introduced and held the Parliamentary stage for a decade. In 1894, on behalf of the Early Closing Association, Lubbock sponsored a Shops (Early Closing) Bill which would make legally binding on all shops in a particular district the hours of closing and the weekly half-holiday agreed to by three-fourths of the shopkeepers. Those who opposed this early-closing legislation argued that it would work a great hardship on small shopkeepers, who could compete successfully with larger shops only by staying open longer hours. But the opposition's chief argument was that late shopping was a necessity for the working classes, who, labouring all day, had only the evenings in which to shop, and therefore that it could not be legislated out of existence. In reply, Lubbock contended that many small shopkeepers wanted to close early but did not do so because of keen competition, and that his Bill would enable them to do legally what they now feared to do voluntarily. He claimed that early closing would actually benefit small shopkeepers, for with a shorter time in which to make their purchases customers would have to go to the smaller shops nearer their homes. Finally, he maintained, late shopping was not a necessity for the working classes but a bad habit. Although men worked late during the week, most of the shopping was actually done by their wives or other members of their families, who were usually free to shop at any time during the day. It had become the custom for working men and their families to make holiday on Saturday afternoons and then return to shop as late as midnight simply because they knew the shops would be open. In this connection, it was frequently pointed out that the hours of co-operative retail societies, which catered for the working classes, were considerably shorter than those of private tradesmen. Indeed, by the end of this period a forty-eight hour week had become reality for many employees of co-operatives, and if these shops could close early without inconvenience to their customers, other shops could do likewise.[57]

At first the N.A.U.S.A. staunchly supported Lubbock and the principle of early-closing legislation, but soon the union concluded that Lubbock's Bill contained serious defects and proposed a number of alterations and additions. The union wanted it to be compulsory rather than optional for local authorities to make early-closing orders upon petition of two-thirds rather than three-fourths of the shopkeepers. The orders should apply to all shops and businesses in an entire local government area, not to different classes of shops in certain districts only, and there should be one half-holiday for all shops, not different holidays for different classes of shops. The union also urged inclusion of a provision that shop assistants could not work longer than thirty minutes after shops closed, and that they must be paid for overtime work after closing, for it was estimated that assistants might be kept as long as six hours after closing time and that one to three hours of overtime after closing was general.[58] But Lubbock refused to consider the union's proposals, and the breach between the two gradually widened.

At length the N.A.U.S.A. repudiated the whole principle of Lubbock's Bill, that is, legal enforcement of voluntary closing agreements. Instead, it now demanded compulsory early closing enacted by Parliament, together with legal provisions to regulate Sunday trading, which it claimed had been on the increase for some time, to limit the overtime work of shop assistants after closing, and to insure inspection to enforce the law. Lubbock continued to maintain that his Bill provided all that a reasonable person could desire, more especially since its principle was approved by a select committee of the Commons in 1895 and by a select committee of the Lords in 1901. (Lubbock was elevated to the peerage as Lord Avebury in 1900.) He also claimed that the union was a mere upstart group, not representing shop assistants as a class at all.[59]

In 1904 the Early Closing Bill became law, but as the N.A.U.S.A. had predicted it proved ineffective. Few local authorities took advantage of its provisions to enact closing orders, and these were often not observed because of the failure to appoint inspectors to enforce them. By 1907 only 112 closing orders had been made. These included ninety-two orders applying to one type of business only, most often to hairdressers and barbers, who were particularly active in winning enactment of orders, and they affected only an estimated 9,000 shops and 15,000 persons out of some 800,000 shopkeepers and assistants. In 1907 David Shackleton (later Sir David), M.P. for Clitheroe and an important figure in the early days of the Labour Party, moved a resolution in the Commons to the effect that "more drastic legislation with regard to the closing of shops and the hours of shop assistants is required." Herbert Gladstone, the Home Secretary, freely admitted this on behalf of the government, and the resolution passed unanimously.[60]

Meanwhile, yet another ineffective piece of legislation for the benefit of shop workers had, with government support, been placed on the statute book, the Seats for Shop Assistants Act of 1899. The evils resulting from the long hours which women assistants had to stand up while at work aroused a great deal of sentimental public interest, and the Act required that shops must provide a seat for every three women employed. Unfortunately, the Act did not include provisions for fining employers for breach of the law or for insuring that women workers might use the seats provided without fear of dismissal.[61]

Having failed to win over Lord Avebury to its views, the N.A.U.S.A. looked about for help elsewhere. Sir Charles Dilke now came to the shop assistants' aid, and until his death in 1911 he was their most important

TAKING THE LAW IN ONE'S OWN HANDS.

Fair but Considerate Customer. "Pray sit down. You look so tired. I've been ridin' all the afternoon in a Carriage, and don't require a Chair."

Parliamentary spokesman. (In appreciation of his efforts the N.A.U.S.A. christened its new London headquarters Dilke House.) The N.A.U.S.A. also drew strength from the growing power of Labour. At the T.U.C. of 1899 Margaret Bondfield had spoken in favour of a Labour Representation Committee, pointing out that small unions such as hers could hardly hope for Parliamentary representation except by co-operation with other unions, and the N.A.U.S.A. was later one of the sixty-five unions affiliated with the L.R.C., the nucleus of the Labour Party.[62] In 1906 the shop assistants' union even succeeded in electing to Parliament its own representative, J. A. Seddon, a former grocer's assistant and a long-time union member who later, in 1915, served as president of the T.U.C. With the proven failure of existing legislation and with effective spokesmen in Parliament, the way was now clear for consideration of the shop assistants' comprehensive scheme of reform.

In 1908 Dilke at last won a hearing for the Bill called the "Shop Assistants' Charter" which had been drafted by the N.A.U.S.A. with the aid and support of the Parliamentary Committee of the T.U.C. and of the Amalgamated Union of Co-operative Employees, and which he had introduced in almost every Parliamentary session since 1896. This six-point measure provided that local authorities must issue orders setting hours of closing no later than 1 P.M. on one day a week, 7 P.M. on three days a week, 9 P.M. on one day, and 10 P.M. on one day. These closing hours were to apply to all shops except those specifically exempted, such as those selling certain kinds of food, tobacco, newspapers and magazines, and medicine and medical appliances. All shops were to be closed on Sundays. Shop assistants were to be employed for no longer than half an hour after shops closed except for seventy-two hours of legal overtime annually. The Bill also provided for a maximum work week for shop assistants of sixty hours, including daily mealtimes of at least one hour for dinner and half an hour for tea. No one under the age of fourteen was to be employed in shops. Shop premises were to be kept in a clean and healthful state, with seats provided which assistants were to be allowed to use without fear of penalty, and with sufficient sanitary conveniences separate for the sexes. (This last provision supplemented the Public Health Acts of 1875-1907, which by their definition of the term "workplace" included shops, warehouses and offices under their provisions.) The factory inspectors and the police were to enforce this measure, the powers of the local authorities to appoint inspectors under the Act of 1892 being repealed. On behalf of the government Gladstone, the Home Secretary, expressed approval of the principles of Dilke's Bill, although he objected to a number of its details, and there the matter rested for another year.[63]

In 1909 the government, in the speech from the throne, promised that a bill to amend the law regulating shop hours would be forthcoming, and several months later Gladstone introduced a Shops Bill which dealt with the same problems as Dilke's measure although differing from it substantially in details. However, owing to the conflict between the Lords and the Commons over the Lloyd George budget, the government could not proceed with its Bill for another two years. The N.A.U.S.A. used this time to carry on a campaign throughout the country to call public attention to the measure, and as a result gained a considerable number of new members.[64] But the shop assistants' supporters in Parliament were weakened by the defeat of Seddon in the second general election of 1910, and especially by the death of Dilke the following year. (During his days in Parliament Seddon had also worked, but unsuccessfully, to obtain legal prohibition of radius agreements and to win passage of a law compelling employers to give just and public character references for their workers. He also hoped to win the vote for shop assistants by including them under the service franchise, but he was opposed on this point by Dilke, who wanted to enfranchise everybody rather than to perpetuate and extend the system of special franchises.)

At last, in 1911, the government's Shops Bill had its day, now under the sponsorship of the new Home Secretary, Winston Churchill. Unfortunately, Parliamentary time was short, much of the session being devoted to consideration of the National Insurance Bill, and the Shops Bill was so pulled to shreds and patched together again in debate and in committee that Churchill at last declared that most of its provisions must be dropped in order to obtain its passage. The shop assistants' supporters bitterly resented Churchill's failure to fight for the whole Bill, and some actually threatened to vote against it on the third reading. But the N.A.U.S.A. pointed out that the Bill's provisions would be useful and urged its passage.[65] This Shops Act of 1911 guaranteed to workers a weekly half-holiday beginning at 1 P.M., and reasonable mealtimes with no more than six hours of work at a stretch without a break for a meal (three-quarters of an hour for dinner if it was taken on the business premises and one hour if it was eaten out, between the hours of 11:30 and 2:30, and half an hour for tea between 4 and 7 P.M.).

In 1912 the Liberal government sponsored yet another Shops Bill, but this was merely a consolidating measure, designed to incorporate into one Act all previous legislation applying to shops (the Acts of 1886, 1892, 1893, 1895, 1899, 1904 and 1911), and it passed easily. Under its provisions some 400 early-closing orders were made by local authorities before the outbreak of the war, but enforcement still depended upon local inspectors who, as experience had already shown, were neither very numerous nor very effective. For example, in London in 1912 only seventy-two legal proceedings were initiated against shopkeepers for failure to observe the weekly half-holiday, fifty-two convictions were obtained, and fines totalling the magnificent sum of £38 were imposed.[66]

Another government measure, the so-called Shops Act of 1913, applied only to employees in restaurants and other eating places, for whom some of the provisions of the 1912 Act had been found inappropriate and for whom alternative provisions were now made with regard to the compulsory half-holiday and mealtimes. However, waiters and waitresses were not considered "shop assistants" by the N.A.U.S.A. and were not admitted as members, a number of other small unions catering for them instead. Still, the Act of 1913 provided for a maximum work week of sixty-four hours exclusive of mealtimes, and thereby an important principle for which shop assistants had long fought finally received legal recognition.[67]

Thereafter the government consistently declined to sponsor further legislation for the benefit of shop assistants, who in vain continued to demand a legal limitation on their hours of work and other improvements in their working conditions. During the war compulsory closing hours for shops were enforced as an emergency measure, and these wartime regulations were made permanent by the Shops Acts of 1920 and 1928. The Shops Act of 1932 first regulated workers', hours, restricting those of young persons under age eighteen to forty-eight per week, and also limiting the amount of overtime work which they could perform. Another act of 1936 regulated Sunday trading. The provisions of these measures gave support to the shop assistants' unions in negotiating with employers agreements under which, in the inter-war period, a forty-eight hour week became common if not universal in the distributive trades. The Shops Act of 1932 also contained regulations for shop premises relating to cleanliness, ventilation, sanitary conveniences and washing facilities, facilities for meals on the premises and the like. The Act further provided that women shop assistants must be allowed without fear of penalty to use the seats which were provided for them under the terms of earlier legislation.[68] Still, it was allegedly not until 1963 and passage of the Offices, Shops and Railway Premises Act, the so-called "white-collar workers' charter," that shop assistants were guaranteed the same standards of comfort and safety in their workplaces as were those employees protected by the Factory Acts.

The Campaign against Fines and Living-in

While the battle for regulation of shop assistants' hours was being waged in Parliament, the N.A.U.S.A. had also turned its attention to the problem of fines and deductions from wages, which involved the whole question of living-in. To improve the lot of its members in this respect, the union now sought to extend to shop assistants the provisions of the Truck Acts which required that workers be paid their wages in full in the coin of the realm and not in kind.

At the urging of Dilke and others of the union's supporters, the government-sponsored Truck Bill of 1896 was amended to apply to shop assistants, the recent decision in the case of *Jackson v. Hill* (13 Q.B.D. 618) having held that a shop assistant was not included in the definition of the term "workman" in the Truck Acts. As finally passed, the new Truck Act included shop assistants under three of its sections. Section 1 provided that employers could impose fines only for acts causing or likely to cause damage or loss to them. These acts and the fines for each, which were to be "fair and reasonable" in view of the circumstances, must be specified in contracts agreed to and signed by employees or in public notices posted on the business premises; and employees must receive full particulars in writing of each offense for which they were fined. Section 5 of the Act provided for the recovery by employees of fines illegally imposed, and Section 6 required employers to keep, for the scrutiny of the inspectors enforcing the Act, registers of all offenses committed and all fines imposed. It was hoped that this last provision would encourage the complete abolition of fines because of the difficulty of keeping detailed records on large numbers of workers.[69]

Apparently shop assistants had scored a considerable victory. But the new Truck Act had one glaring defect: shop assistants were not mentioned in Section 10, which provided for enforcement of the Act by inspectors, the factory or mines inspectors as the case might be. It was suggested that the inspectors appointed by local authorities under the Shops Acts could also enforce the Truck Act in shops, but this raised the nice legal question of whether these inspectors possessed the authority, since they were not mentioned in the Truck Act. The bills which Dilke introduced on behalf of the N.A.U.S.A. in the years from 1896 on provided that the factory inspectors must enforce the Truck Acts in shops. Meanwhile, the Act was not a total loss to shop assistants. The N.A.U.S.A. took up the matter of its enforcement, and although it actually carried no cases of breach of the law to court, it did in some instances persuade employers by the threat of legal proceedings to remit fines which they had imposed illegally. With the moral backing of the Act, the union also won the voluntary abolition of fines by many of the best employers.[70]

The N.A.U.S.A. next concentrated its attention upon the question of living-in, at first seeking merely to mend and not to end the system. The earliest bills which Dilke introduced in Parliament at the union's behest provided simply that living-in accommodations, like shop premises, must be kept in a clean and healthful state, while Seddon suggested the extension to living-in premises of the system of inspection applied to lodging houses. At the same time, representatives of the N.A.U.S.A. approached employers in hundreds of cases at the request and on behalf of shop assistants all over the country, winning complete abolition of living-in in many instances or at least winning better accommodations and food, although these improvements often continued only so long as members of the union were employed. When employers refused to make improvements, the union permitted its members to give up their jobs and supported them until they could find new positions.[71]

The N.A.U.S.A. also embarked on a campaign to attract public attention to the evils of living-in. In 1898 the *Daily Chronicle* carried a series of articles on "Life in the Shop," based on material gathered in a wide variety of London shops by Margaret Bondfield, who thus deliberately sacrificed for the cause her own future as a shop worker. In 1906 T. Spencer Jones, the grocer-editor of *The Shop Assistant,* wrote a series of articles on "The Moral Side of Living-in," which, reprinted in a pamphlet that sold hundreds of copies, was credited with having profoundly affected public opinion, especially in religious circles. About this time also H. G. Wells published *Kipps,* for which, to depict shop life, he drew upon his own early experience as a draper's assistant. (Wells was a nearly life-long member of the N.A.U.S.A.) Cicely Hamilton's play *Diana of Dobson's,* produced in London's West End, also portrayed the lives of shop assistants, and Margaret Bondfield served as technical adviser on the living-in setting for the production. In every large city in the kingdom the N.A.U.S.A. sponsored public meetings, all of which, advertised as meetings of protest against living-in and attended not by union members only but by shop assistants generally, unanimously carried resolutions condemning the system.[72]

Gradually the attitude of the N.A.U.S.A. toward living-in hardened, and by 1907 it stood committed to complete abolition of the system. In that year, feeling strong enough at last to begin a direct attack, the union waged the first of several successful strikes to force employers to abolish living-in, this one ending with the closing down of the shop concerned. At the same time the union demanded legislative reform, specifically, that shop workers be included under the provisions of the Truck Acts which required the payment of wages in full in the coin of the realm.[73]

When a departmental committee of the Home Office was appointed in 1908 to consider further reform of the Truck Acts, the N.A.U.S.A. persuaded the Home Secretary, Herbert Gladstone, to extend the committee's terms of reference so as to include shop assistants in the scope of its inquiries.[74] The Truck Committee heard the evidence of four representatives of the N.A.U.S.A., who were also authorized to speak for the Amalgamated Union of Co-operative Employees—Margaret Bondfield, J. A. Seddon, Frank Tilley, and P. C. Hoffman, who was later a Labour M.P. and the union's historian. The Committee also heard the testimony of various employers of shop assistants and of a number of assistants speaking independently. In addition, Lucy Deane, a senior lady factory inspector, made an independent investigation and submitted a report on her findings. The Truck Committee's final report contained a separate special report on shop assistants.

In presenting their case to the Truck Committee, the shop assistants' representatives sought to counter the argument of employers that living-in represented a pecuniary convenience for their workers. They denied that the system provided assistants with homes and meals at a cost much lower than that at which they could obtain lodging and food if they lived out, and claimed that the accommodations and meals provided were often very inferior and by no means worth the amounts at which employers usually valued them. Employers heard by the Truck Committee estimated that they spent on room and board 9-14s. a week for each assistant, and in one case as much as 17s. 6d., that is, £21-36 a year and as high as £45. On the other hand, Margaret Bondfield presented evidence from several establishments to prove that the cost to employers actually ranged from 4s. 6d. a week, or about £12 a year, where accommodations and food were bad, up to 6s. 6d. or 7s. a week, or about £17-18 a year. The N.A.U.S.A. claimed that if shop assistants received the same wages as at present, plus £25 representing the supposed cost of their lodging and food, they could live just as well or even better out than in. Miss Bondfield even reported cases where assistants who were allowed only £10 a year in lieu of room and board lived better off their employers' premises. Lucy Deane's report seemed to confirm the shop assistants' evidence. In the course of her investigations she was allowed to visit the bedrooms and kitchens only of those establishments which prided themselves on their good conditions, and she found employers generally very reticent both about the supposed equivalent in money of the lodging and food provided and about how much of this amount they actually spent. In short, the shop assistants claimed that living-in simply represented a welcome source of profit to employers at their workers' expense. Indeed, some employers themselves did not deny this. For example, A. E. Derry of the famous London firm of Derry and Toms, who disapproved of living-in and gave evidence to support the shop assistants' case, admitted that he had abolished the system only for his male employees and not for the women because, he said, "financial considerations at present stand in the way."[75]

The shop assistants' representatives also rebutted the employers' claim that living-in represented a "moral safeguard to young people in the modern Babylon," that the system enabled employers to exercise a benevolent supervision over the lives and conduct of their workers, while communal living stimulated healthy camaraderie and *esprit de corps*. Owing to the large numbers accommodated in living-in establishments, assistants received no individual attention or supervision, and the only "moral control" on them was that they had to be in their lodgings by a certain hour at night, after which the door was locked and they were fined for returning late. No check was made to see whether all the occupants were in, and if roommates did not tell tales an assistant who stayed out all night would never by discovered. Margaret Bondfield told the story of a girl who, returning to her lodgings too late one night and fearing to arouse the housekeeper to admit her and to be reported and punished the next day, "ran the streets all night; she was terrified; she had no money, and she simply kept running; the next morning when she came back she was absolutely ill from sheer exhaustion." In certain establishments, however, assistants could obtain their own latchkeys by paying a deposit, and this inspired a bitter joke: "A girl asking for a rise is told, 'No, miss, we cannot give you a rise, but we can give you a latchkey.'" That is, she could turn part-time prostitute. Assistants also were often expected to be absent from their lodgings all day on Sundays, when no meals were provided for them. Miss Bondfield pointed out that employers never mentioned the fact that when dismissed, assistants lost homes as well as jobs at a moment's notice. The shop assistants' spokesmen also stressed the possible bad influence of certain workers on their fellows in living-in establishments. For example, Miss Bondfield testified that at the age of fourteen, in her first situation at Brighton, she had to share a room, the window of which faced the street and afforded an easy and secret exit, with "a woman of mature age who led a life of a most undesirable kind."[76]

More generally, the shop assistants' representatives denied angrily that they needed "moral supervision" more than any other class of workers. Miss Bondfield declared that working girls who did live in their own lodgings, "girls such as women clerks, typists, civil servants, post office employees, school teachers, and so on . . . are very largely drawn from the same type of homes as are shop assistants, and the assumption that these girls are less moral than girls who live in is never thought of." Further, the shop assistants' spokesmen argued: "The whole thing is against the development of character of the assistants. They seem to lose all individuality. . . . An assistant who lives in never handles part of his wages, everything is done for him, he is treated like a child, and it discourages the growth of all manly and womanly characteristics in shop workers." In particular, women workers gained no experience in housekeeping and domestic management as they would do if they lived in their own lodgings. In this connection Ernest Debenham, of the renowned London firm of Debenham and Freebody, reported that during the past fifteen years he had gradually abolished living-in almost completely since he believed it tended to diminish the workers' independence of character, a trait he considered most desirable, and as a result he found his business better conducted and his assistants brighter, more energetic and thoroughly pleased with the change.[77]

But despite the vigourous presentation of the shop assistants' case, the majority of the Truck Committee remained unconvinced. With regard to complaints about the accommodations and food, the Committee's report concluded: "It has not . . . been proved to our satisfaction that the evils alleged to exist are either so serious or so widespread as has been represented." Members of the Committee had personally visited some of the living-in establishments in London about which the N.A.U.S.A. specifically complained, and found the complaints not substantiated. The Committee believed, they said, "that the colour of the individual experience of many of the witnesses has been applied to the system as a whole," and that much of the evidence heard against living-in "related to the past, not to the present time . . . conditions had improved considerably and were improving." Indeed, P. C. Hoffman of the N.A.U.S.A. later commented on the "flutter" among employers caused by the appointment of the Truck Committee; sudden refurbishing of living-in premises went on everywhere, and was exceeded only during World War I, when employers spent huge amounts on improvements in order to avoid paying excess-profits taxes. The Truck Committee was greatly impressed by the evidence of employers and of individual shop assistants, most of them from good-class London houses, who testified in favour of living-in as they knew it, and believed that the accommodations provided were at least as good as shop assistants could obtain for themselves living out. Also, the Committee believed that the system did afford valuable protection to workers, especially the younger ones and those coming to towns from the country, and that the danger of being thrown with undesirable associates was no greater in living-in establishments than in lodgings outside.[78]

Feeling that a sufficiently strong case against living-in had not been presented, the majority of the Truck Committee did not recommend that shop assistants be included under the Truck Act provisions requiring the payment of wages in full. Instead, the majority report merely recommended that the Home Office make regulations for living-in premises concerning sanitation, ventilation, cubic space, bath and lavatory accommodation and the like. Equally disappointing were the majority's recommendations regarding fines and deductions, these recommendations applying to all workers and not to shop assistants only. Fearing that if fines and deductions were legally abolished employers would resort to severer disciplinary measures, such as reduction of wages and suspension or even dismissal of workers, the majority recommended simply that the amounts of fines and deductions should not exceed 5 per cent of the total weekly wages. These provisions should be enforced for shop workers by the local shops inspectors. But the government was slow to act, and not until 1914 did the Home Secretary propose a new Truck Bill to give effect to the recommendations of the majority report, and this was soon shelved because of the war.[79]

Meanwhile, the N.A.U.S.A. had continued to agitate for passage of new legislation along the lines laid down by the minority report of the Truck Committee, which was signed by Stephen Walsh, M.P., and by Mrs. H. J. Tennant, formerly chief of the women factory inspectors at the Home Office. This report recommended the complete legal abolition of fines and deductions from wages and of living-in, the law to be enforced in shops as elsewhere by the factory inspectors. At the same time the N.A.U.S.A. continued its efforts to persuade employers to abolish living-in voluntarily. Fortunately, time and events were on the shop assistants' side, and in the years immediately before World War I and especially during the war years living-in showed signs of dying a natural death. With the rising level of rents and prices in general, employers were finding the system increasingly uneconomical. During the war, price controls and food shortages and rationing further increased the employers' difficulties, and those employers who abolished living-in often discovered that the premises vacated by their assistants were so valuable for business purposes that they did not want to return to the old system.[80] Amendment of the Truck Acts in the shop assistants' interests was never, in fact, carried through, as living-in ceased to be an important issue.

When persuasion failed to induce employers to abolish living-in or at least to provide better accommodations and food, the N.A.U.S.A. resorted to more drastic action. The union discovered a particularly effective weapon in the stringent enforcement of local building acts and codes, especially the clauses relating to the provision of fire escapes. Tradesmen's associations frequently opposed such regulations on the ground of the "unnecessary" expense imposed on employers, but where these regulations existed the N.A.U.S.A. helped to bring violations to light, thereby forcing employers to improve their premises or to abolish living-in entirely in order to avoid the expense of making improvements. For example, the Drapers' Chamber of Trade and the London Chamber of Commerce raised £1,000 in an unsuccessful attempt to oppose certain clauses in the London County Council Building Act Amendment Bill of 1905. The N.A.U.S.A. sent a deputation to the London County Council to demonstrate that of some 50,000 buildings coming under the provisions of the 1905 Act, only 527 had been put in order, and with the prodding of the union and of the Council hundreds of living-in establishments were corrected. P. C. Hoffman later boasted: "It cost those short-sighted, close-fisted, hard-hearted drapers hundreds of thousands of pounds. It touched them in the tenderest part of their anatomy—their pocketbooks. It was one more smashing blow at 'living-in.'"[81]

As a last resort, the N.A.U.S.A. could still use the weapon of the strike, although in fact it seldom did so, waging only about a dozen strikes against living-in before the war. Especially notable, however, was a strike waged by the union at Hanley in 1912, as a result of which the shop assistants won the abolition of meals in (there was no living-in) and the establishment of minimum-wage rates, a settlement which furnished the pattern for many later agreements. By 1914 the union was claiming payments in place of lodging and food of 13s. a week for men and 10s. for women in the provinces, and 15s. weekly for men and 12s. for women in London.[82] Emphasis on the abolition of living-in was now giving way before the demand for minimum wages, including allowances in lieu of room and board.

The Fight for Minimum Wages

The Amalgamated Union of Co-operative Employees was, in 1896, the first of the shop assistants' unions to embark upon a minimum-wage campaign. At first the union set a single minimum wage for all trades throughout the country, 24s. a week at age twenty-one, which applied to men only and not to women. The union succeeded in bringing several hundred co-operative societies into line on the basis of this minimum wage, but the societies tended to make this wage the standard rate of pay rather than the minimum. Consequently the union drew up additional wage scales providing for higher pay in London and some other parts of the country, higher pay for managerial positions, and annual increases.[83]

The question of minimum-wage scales for women co-operative employees did not receive attention until 1906. In that year the Women's Co-operative Guild presented and carried a resolution at the Co-operative Congress demanding minimum wages for women as well as men, a resolution reaffirmed at each annual Congress for the next six years. In 1907 the Women's Co-operative Guild and the co-operative employees' union formed a joint central committee to draw up minimum-wage scales for women and to urge their adoption by the co-operative societies. Under these scales women were to receive 5s. a week at age fourteen to 17s. at age twenty, compared with the rates for men of 6s. at age fourteen to 24s. at age twenty-one. Women in managerial positions were to receive 21s., whereas men in these positions received 30s. Before the war the union succeeded in getting these scales adopted by 240 co-operative societies with some 12,000 women employees. In especially well-organized districts, such as South Wales and Monmouthshire, women won higher wages than the minimum, thereby narrowing the gap between their pay and men's, and also obtained together with men supplementary wage scales providing for annual increases.[84]

Meanwhile, as the first step in its minimum-wage campaign, the N.A.U.S.A. had set up in 1908 a special committee charged with collecting information on prevailing rates of pay and with making recommendations for a union wages policy. The committee found that among union members the average earnings of men were 5d. to 9-3/4d. an hour, or about 25-49s. weekly if calculated on the basis of a sixty-hour week, while women earned only 3-3/4d. to 5-1/4d. an hour, or roughly 19-26s. a week, about half to three-fourths the pay of men. Yet even these low figures represented fairly well-paid cases, for many shop workers were known to earn as little as 5-10s. for a seventy- to eighty-hour week.[85]

At its annual conference in 1910 the union adopted the recommendations of the wages committee and to publicize its policy soon published a booklet, *The Case for Minimum Wages in the Distributive Trades,* which went through several editions. In line with the committee's recommendations and in contrast with the initial policy of the co-operative employees' union, the N.A.U.S.A. set different minimum rates of pay for different trades rather than a single minimum for all trades, and different rates for different age levels. It also provided that, with the approval of the union's national committee, local committees could set for their areas rates different from the national minimum rates. At the same time, rejecting the principle of equal pay, the union set different minimum rates for men and women, women's pay to be three-fourths that of men in the provinces and four-fifths that of men in London, although women doing "equal work" with men, such as those in managerial positions, were to receive equal pay. As set by the union, the minimum wages for workers at age twenty-one ranged between a low for hairdressers and for workers in the boot trade of 24s. a week for men and 18s. for women in the provinces, and 29s. and 22s. respectively in London, to a high for jewellers of 30s. for men and 22s. 6d. for women in the provinces to 35s. and 27s. 6d. respectively in London.[86]

In 1911 the N.A.U.S.A. began its campaign to enforce minimum-wage rates. In the years before the war the union negotiated with many employers on the subject of wages, sometimes reinforcing its arguments with strikes and winning considerably higher pay in a number of cases. For example, in 1911 the union concluded with a drapery firm in Hanley an agreement under which girls previously receiving wages of 2-8s. a week obtained minimum rates of 7s. 6d. at age seventeen or with three years' experience to 17s. at age twenty-one or with seven years' experience. Gradually the union scale of wages came to be used as a guide to employers offering and assistants accepting work.[87]

Although their pay was often substantially improved by the winning of minimum-wage rates, women shop assistants long continued to have a real grievance in the policy of unequal pay which both unions had adopted. This policy was justified by the usual time-worn arguments—that women's labour was intrinsically less valuable than men's because they were not equal to men in physical strength, because there was a greater supply of women workers than of men, and because many women were "pin money workers" not wholly dependent upon their wages for subsistence. Of greater importance than such arguments, however, was the general feeling of men that equality of pay was impracticable, and that for them to insist upon it would jeopardize their own chances of obtaining higher wages.[88] Eventually both unions and their successor, the Union of Shop, Distributive and Allied Workers, adopted the policy of equal pay for women which the trade-union movement as a whole had long endorsed. But the policy was not very actively or successfully pursued, and unequal pay for women continued to be the rule. Only in 1970, with passage of the Equal Pay Act, could women shop assistants, and many other women as well, see an end at last to wage discrimination against them.

Meanwhile, in addition to their efforts to establish minimum-wage rates by collective bargaining, both of the shop assistants' unions hoped to secure a legally enacted minimum wage. This would be done by bringing the distributive trades under the Trade Boards Act of 1909, which was passed largely through the efforts of Sir Charles Dilke and which established for certain "sweated industries" boards responsible for setting minimum rates of pay. Such minimum wages would, the unions felt, serve as a "floor" under the wage agreements which they were negotiating with employers. However, as in the case of hours and truck legislation, shop assistants failed to achieve this reform before the outbreak of the war. No trade board was set up for wholesale and retail distribution after the war, although separate boards for the grocery trade and for dressmaking were established in 1920. Thereafter the hostility of employers in the midst of the post-war depression prevented the creation of other trade boards. Not until 1945 and passage of the Wages Councils Act did the protection which shop workers had so long demanded become law.[89]

By 1914 shop assistants were far indeed from having won all the reforms they desired. They were still demanding in vain a legal limitation of their hours of work, the legal abolition of fines and deductions from wages and of the living-in system, and the setting of minimum wages by a trade board for the distributive trades. However, with the rise of their small but vigorous unions, with the growth of public opinion in their favour, and with the winning of Parliamentary attention for their claims, shop assistants, women as well as men, could hope for a brighter future.

VI
WOMEN IN OFFICES:
THE CLERICAL OCCUPATIONS

As in the case of shop work, mid-Victorian feminists who were concerned to increase the employment of middle-class women believed that clerical work was a field eminently suitable for them, and complained that women behind desks in offices were even more rare than those behind counters in shops. "Dickens, who died in 1870, had not known the woman clerk. We should have met her if he had. David Copperfield's Dora could only hold the pens and Caddy Jellyby was an inky amateur." The census of 1871, the year after Dickens's death, showed that there were only a few hundred women clerks in the country, although even this small number represented a substantial increase over the mere 279 women clerks employed ten years before. Here, too, the ladies of Langham Place took up the cause actively. That women were quite capable of doing clerical work was proved by Maria Rye's experience at the law stationer's office begun by the Society for Promoting the Employment of Women, and by the success in business offices afterwards of the young women trained for commercial careers in Jessie Boucherett's special classes.[1]

Yet, again as in the case of shop work, the absence of women in offices was not entirely due to their generally poor education. Much the same general conditions which prevailed in the distributive trades in the mid-nineteenth century and which discouraged the employment of women also obtained in the clerical occupations, while the later nineteenth and early twentieth centuries saw a revolution in clerical as in shop work, a revolution which made possible the advent of women clerks as a new class of cheap but efficient workers. The increase in their numbers in this period was tremendous, far greater even than the increase in the numbers of women shop assistants, and by 1914 women clerks had become, after shop assistants and teachers, the most numerous and important group of middle-class working women in the country.

A Nation of Clerks

To understand the absence of women clerks as of shop assistants in the mid-nineteenth century, it is necessary to understand the conditions of work at the time. The typical business establishment then was a small-scale affair, either an individual enterprise or a partnership, conducted with the aid of only a few clerks and also, often, of premium-paying, indentured apprentices who were learning the business. Both clerks and apprentices were drawn from among men of the middle classes, who alone possessed the education necessary for the work, their chief qualifications being simply the ability to read and write and do simple accounts accurately and rapidly, and the social background fitting them to work in close contact with their employers. And both clerks and apprentices were imbued with "the idea that . . . they themselves might one day become employers, and that there was 'plenty of room at the top,'" that they might set up in business on their own or at least become partners in their firms.[2]

In these circumstances, not surprisingly, women clerks were unknown. There was no great demand for clerical labour, but even if there had been, middle-class women could hardly have supplied it. Believing that their daughters would marry and be taken care of, parents of the middle classes generally provided girls with an education notably inferior to that of boys, and they naturally saw no point in preparing them for life in the business world by a long and expensive apprenticeship and in helping them to set up in their own businesses afterward.

But in the later part of this period clerical work, like shop work, began to be affected by the revolution in industry and commerce and to exhibit some of the characteristic features of that revolution. In the first place, with the expanding scope of industrial and commercial enterprises, independent proprietors and partnership firms gave way before large joint-stock companies, which in turn tended to be replaced by large-scale amalgamations, representing huge agglomerations of capital. All this led naturally to a growth in the size of business offices. Secondly, there was a tremendous increase in the amount of clerical work to be done. Such work, always necessary and present where industry and trade are found, naturally grew in volume as the country's production and commerce expanded. Also, with the progress of industrialization the number of clerical workers increases more rapidly than does the number of manual workers directly engaged in the work of production. At the same time, enterprises closely allied with industry and trade in which clerical workers formed the major part of the labour force, such as banking, insurance, publishing and advertising, greatly expanded the volume of their business. Finally, the growing size of business concerns and the increasing amount of clerical labour required made possible the rationalization and mechanization of office work, now necessary as, with increasing industrial production, widening commerce and improved transportation, there came a demand for greater speed and accuracy in business transactions.[3]

In this connection, special mention must be made of two major improvements of the time, the introduction of shorthand into the business world and the invention of the typewriter. Known since antiquity, shorthand had been used in England for centuries, chiefly in the transcription of legal proceedings and of Parliamentary and other public speeches. In the middle decades of the nineteenth century there developed an amazingly widespread public interest in the use of shorthand, largely owing to the inspiration of that remarkable gentleman Isaac (later Sir Isaac) Pitman (1813-1897). A sometime clerk and elementary-school master, Pitman became interested in shorthand as an aid in the teaching of reading and writing. "Phonography," the system of shorthand which he developed and made public first in 1837, used signs to represent sounds and thus represented a great improvement upon earlier systems, most of which had used signs in place of letters of the alphabet. Pitman actually hoped that his system would eventually replace longhand writing and conventional printing altogether, and to this end he worked with all the energy and dedication of an evangelist, establishing a publishing house to churn out propaganda and instruction material, founding societies to work for the cause, and sending lecturers and teachers throughout the country. In his work Pitman had numerous successors and also rivals, many of whom developed and propagated new systems of "script shorthand" as distinguished from his "geometric shorthand." The most important of these was the system of John Robert Gregg, first published in 1888, which in time tended to supersede Pitman's.[4]

Sir Edward Watkin claimed the credit for first using shorthand in business practice. In 1853, as general manager of the Manchester, Sheffield and Lincolnshire Railway, he required that all his apprentice clerks learn Pitman's shorthand. Watkin pointed out that whereas he had once half killed himself with work, writing his own business correspondence in longhand or dictating to clerks who took down his words in longhand, he could now get through the same amount of work in a fraction of the time by having his clerks write in shorthand. This innovation quickly spread, as businessmen everywhere discovered that shorthand "was to writing what the jenny was to the loom and the train to the coach." By the last decade of the century there was "hardly an office of any standing—no matter in what line of business"—which did not employ shorthand-clerks.[5]

The invention of the typewriter carried forward the revolution which the introduction of shorthand had begun. Attempts to perfect writing machines can be traced back to the early eighteenth century, and the first half of the nineteenth saw a number of workable models produced, both in Europe and in the United States. All of these possessed the merit of greater legibility than handwriting, but none could exhibit greater speed as well until the work of the American Christopher L. Sholes of Wisconsin. A printer and publisher by trade and a sometime newspaper editor, state legislator and public official, Sholes patented his writing machine in 1868. (For his machine, Sholes coined the word "typewriter," but in the early days it was used for both the machine itself and the woman who operated it.) Five years later the firm of E. Remington and Sons, makers of arms and of sewing and agricultural machines, began the manufacture and marketing of Sholes's typewriter. Remington typewriters were sold in England as early as 1874, but their real impact on the world market dates from 1882, when a separate company was established as the international selling agency. Other manufacturing concerns quickly followed the Remingtons' lead, and new model American and European typewriters soon made their appearance.[6]

The typewriter was the natural companion of shorthand. The use of shorthand had speeded the dictation of business correspondence, but in the early days this correspondence had still to be written by hand, whereas now shorthand notes could be rapidly transcribed by machine. Later, transcription was further speeded as the "hunt and peck" system of the earliest "typewriters" gave way before "touch typing," a method apparently taught first by an American lady at a Cincinnati business school about 1882. By the turn of the century an entirely new kind of clerical workers was well-established in the business world, the shorthand-typists.

The introduction of the typewriter represented only the first step in that mechanization of office work which made steady if not very rapid progress in the later years of this period. Among the important new appliances perfected were calculating machines, addressing machines, duplicating machines, dictating machines, and machines for sorting, stamping and sealing.[7] Obviously the operation of such machines would become an increasingly important part of clerical work.

The growing size of business enterprises and the increasing mechanization of clerical work led to considerable specialization and division of labour within offices. The "general clerk" has never disappeared, but in the largest offices the trend was toward the setting up of separate departments or groups of workers, each dealing with a single aspect of the business, such as stenographic, filing, bookkeeping, records, machine operation.[8]

All of these developments had a profound effect upon clerical workers. In the first place, there was a great increase in their absolute and relative numbers, an increase which would have been impossible had not clerical work, once the preserve of men of the middle classes, become easier of access. (See Appendix, Tables 4a and 4b.) The growing size and complexity of business concerns and the increasing division and mechanization of office work rendered outmoded the old system of paid apprenticeship, under which youths were supposed to learn all the ramifications of a business in order eventually to become employers themselves. Also, these developments probably lowered the general standard of education necessary for clerical work.[9] A sound elementary education now seemed sufficient preparation for anyone aspiring to be a clerk, and with the creation of a national system of elementary schools, especially after 1870, this education became available to the whole community. Moreover, the special technical skills connected with routine clerical work were becoming easily attainable as a result of the increasing demand in this period for "commercial education."

Those advocating "commercial education" meant a sound general training preparing students for careers in the business world, and their interest reflected concern over the limited attainments of young people who entered commercial work directly from the elementary schools. For example, the Edinburgh Chamber of Commerce reported in 1902: "There is a consensus of opinion among the business men that elementary education is so imperfect that many boys entering offices or warehouses write in a slovenly way; that their arithmetic is deficient; and that they are unable to compose a letter properly, and in some cases even to spell correctly . . .".[10] Interest in commercial education also reflected a widespread feeling that secondary education must be systematized and that the secondary-school curriculum must be remodelled to meet the needs of a changing society. Just as "technical education" would help insure the continued industrial supremacy of the country, so "commercial education" would help the country to withstand the pressure of foreign commercial competition. In short, schools must now provide that general training for business which masters no longer gave their apprentices.

Unfortunately, the broad conception of commercial education as a sound general training for business was scarcely realized in this period, and in practice "commercial education" became almost synonymous with "clerical training." First in this field of education were private-venture "business colleges" or "commercial colleges," which sprang up all over the country to supply the training in such subjects as shorthand, typing and bookkeeping which was not readily available in existing schools. Not being subject to any public regulations or inspection, these colleges varied greatly among themselves with regard to the length and quality of the training offered and the fees charged. In conjunction with these private-venture schools there were sometimes established "copying offices" or "typewriting offices," a new kind of enterprise representing a modern and enlarged version of the old law stationers and law engrossers. These offices received all kinds of documents to be reproduced, and they afforded a wide field of employment for typists as well as a good practical training ground for students in the schools connected with them.[11]

The last decade of the nineteenth century saw a growing interest in commercial education among public education authorities. Taking advantage of government grants for commercial subjects of an elementary nature, many school boards began to offer such subjects in evening continuation schools, their aim being to provide young persons with knowledge of immediate practical use at no or only nominal cost. At the same time, the acts of 1889 and 1891 which made funds available to the county and county borough councils for technical education encouraged these authorities to provide training in commercial subjects in connection with the technical classes and schools under their jurisdiction, and sometimes to subsidize such training in secondary schools as well. Following passage of the Education Act of 1902 the development of evening continuation schools and of technical schools and classes continued under the new local education authorities. Some continuation schools developed into "commercial institutes" offering very advanced instruction, while nearly all of the technical schools came to have commercial departments, which in the largest cities developed into distinct "colleges."

By 1914, then, a commercial education, or at least clerical training, was easily accessible to all classes of the community, either in fee-charging private schools or in publicly supported schools charging no or very low fees. And these schools were always crowded with students, for, one observer remarked: "A knowledge of shorthand and typewriting is the only requisite deemed necessary to start on a career *ad Parnassum.*"[12]

In these changed circumstances, the woman clerk made her appearance. There was now a great demand for clerical labour, and with the decline of clerical apprenticeship and the general improvement in education in the country, including the provision of "commercial education," women could help to supply this demand. They could, and they did. Between 1861 and 1911 the number of male clerical workers increased fivefold, while the number of women clerks increased no less than four hundred times over. (See Appendix, Tables 4a and 4b.) Still, as in the case of shop assistants, women were not encroaching upon the work of men in all branches of clerical work. Most women clerks were found in the offices of commercial enterprises, relatively few working in banks or in insurance and railway offices. (See Appendix, Table 4c.)

Many writers on the subject of clerical work in this period attributed the entry of women clerks into the labour market, and the increase in their numbers at a rate much greater than the rate of increase for men, to the growing mechanization of office work, specifically, the introduction of the typewriter. In speaking of the new machine, contemporaries likened its operation to piano-playing, and noted that consequently it was an instrument especially suited to women's abilities! In any case, typewriting was from the beginning an almost exclusively feminine occupation.[13]

But there were other important reasons for the increasing employment of women. Many asserted that women were temperamentally better suited to routine clerical work than were men, and that women worked harder and with more interest in their work than "youths whose minds are still full of football and cricket." Moreover, women were probably much more easily reconciled than men to the lack of opportunity for advancement which was becoming characteristic of many clerical positions.[14]

Another interesting reason given for the growing numbers of female clerks at the turn of the century was the fact that a much better class of women were entering the work. According to one observer, these women possessed, besides the requisite technical knowledge and skills, the advantages of superior education and manner and tended to replace the board-school girl, "with her many limitations and her sometimes unprepossessing manner," who had been first in the field. Well-educated middle-class women naturally also began to replace men of lower social standing and more limited educational attainments. Sir John Clapham seems to be wrong when he says that the earliest women clerks were "recruited, or so

MR. PUNCH'S ILLUSTRATIONS TO THE POETS.

"So careful of the Type, she seems."—*Tennyson.*

memory and untested observation suggest, mainly from the families of clerks, shopkeepers, small tradesmen and poor professional men. Recruitment from families of skilled manual labourers was just beginning [by 1914] . . . These careers were still beyond the reach of girls from average rank-and-file wage-earning homes." On the contrary, as a conference on commercial education sponsored by the London Chamber of Commerce in 1898 reported, the great mass of clerks entered business directly from the elementary schools at about age fourteen.[15]

Finally, but almost certainly most important of all, women received lower pay than men. Indeed, the whole question of the increasing employment of women clerks can be neatly summarized by recounting an exchange between a clergyman giving evidence in 1909 before the royal commission on the Poor Laws, and the Fabian Socialist George Lansbury, one of the members of the commission:

LANSBURY: With regard to women, did I understand you that the employers tell you they are better adapted for the work of clerks, and that sort of thing?

WITNESS: I said that a great many employers I had consulted frankly said that they preferred them.

LANSBURY: And they paid them better wages than the men, I suppose?

WITNESS: I should not say that.

LANSBURY: You would rather think if they were so much more valuable that they would be paid better wages?

WITNESS: I do not think that follows at all.

LANSBURY: Then it follows that a woman can give so much better value to the employer than a man and she gets less wages?

WITNESS: Yes, I suppose that is . . . the only conclusion you can draw.

LANSBURY: Therefore the bottom fact of it is that the woman works cheaper?

WITNESS: Yes, decidedly.[16]

The woman clerk was obviously on the scene to stay.

The Working Life of Clerks

Clerical work was a very popular occupation. Not only had it become more accessible but also it was easy and light compared with manual labour, and it was traditionally associated with middle-class respectability. This work represented an expanding field of congenial employment for the existing middle classes, and at the same time it provided a ladder by which members of the working classes could clamber upward in society. Yet many observers deplored the ever increasing numbers of aspiring clerks. They suggested that many of the men could do better for themselves in skilled manual labour and that the women would often be better employed as domestic servants and in factories, for, they maintained, despite the traditional social superiority of clerical work the lot of clerks generally was steadily growing worse.[17]

As in the case of shop assistants, the question of whether the working conditions of clerks were deteriorating in this period is debatable, but certainly the economic and social position of clerks as of shop workers was being radically and irrevocably transformed. In the earlier nineteenth century, the day of limited literacy and of clerical apprenticeship, clerks ranked as highly skilled workers, and in the small family concerns and partnerships of the time there was "an almost feudal relationship" between clerks and their employers. "The clerk was more a family servant than a wage labourer."[18] Certainly this relationship was not necessarily a happy one (the example of Scrooge and Bob Cratchit immediately comes to mind), but at least the clerk enjoyed the confidence of his master, with whom he worked in close contact, and could hope to rise to become a master himself. The coming of universal education and the growth of large-scale joint-stock business enterprises changed all this. The great body of clerks were employed more and more on routine work of limited scope, for which little training was necessary and for which there were always large numbers of aspirants clamouring. Clerical work was becoming an unskilled and overcrowded occupation. At the same time, the old relationship of master and servant was "depersonalized and transformed into the modern relationship between capital . . . and wage labour," and clerks had little hope of rising into the capitalist ranks. One embittered worker declared: "The clerk who today allows himself to be deluded with The Bunch of Carrots Labelled 'Prospects,' dangled in front of his nose is an ass indeed." Clerks had become small cogs in large machines, and easily replaceable cogs at that.[19] In these circumstances they often had cause to complain of their poor working conditions.

One recurring complaint of clerks was that of their excessive hours of work. Clerks in railway service and many of those in commercial houses were said to work twelve to fourteen hours a day, while clerks employed in retail establishments worked the same long hours as the shop assistants. Still, since their hours were often determined by those kept by their superiors working in the same offices, many clerks enjoyed very short hours compared with other classes of workers. Indeed, one of the attractions of a clerical career was that business began at the genteel hour of nine in the morning, if not later, while artisans started work three hours before this. An inquiry conducted in London in 1906 by the Association of Shorthand Writers and Typists revealed that the majority of the women clerks questioned worked, between the hours of nine and six, only eight to nine hours a day, which included an interval of perhaps an hour for lunch.[20]

In connection with the subject of their hours, clerks also frequently complained of the amount of overtime work they were expected to perform during periods of pressure. One writer in the clerks' cause asserted that many of them worked hours overtime, night after night, and received no extra pay or very little, averaging perhaps 2d. an hour. On the other hand, the Association of Shorthand Writers and Typists reported, on the basis of its 1906 study, that of the women workers queried about 27 per cent worked no overtime and 61 per cent little overtime; only the remaining 12 per cent frequently worked overtime, often receiving no extra payment but sometimes being given "tea money."[21]

Another grievance of many clerks was that of unpleasant and unhealthful surroundings on the job. They worked in dirty, overcrowded rooms lacking in ventilation and natural light, and rendered deafening by the jangling of telephones and the clatter of typewriters. A particular complaint was that of the lack of sufficient sanitary accommodations separate for the sexes. In this connection, an inquiry into conditions for London typists conducted by the Women's Industrial Council in 1898 revealed that among the fifty-one business establishments studied, seven provided no sanitary accommodations for women workers; in ten cases the accommodations were shared with men; and in thirty-four establishments there were separate accommodations. It was often asserted that as a result of poor working conditions clerks as a class suffered in health, especially from consumption, nervous breakdown, and strained eyesight and hearing.[22] Actually, however, generalization on this subject is difficult, for obviously much depended upon the standards of decency of individual employers and upon the general condition of buildings in which offices were located.

By all accounts poor pay was the greatest grievance of clerks, and this resulted from the excessive competition for clerical positions. The board schools and the numerous business colleges turned out every week "dozens of young persons possessed of ambition, a little shorthand and typewriting, a few mistaken notions of bookkeeping and weird ideas of the mother tongue and its use," all of them ready to accept ridiculously low pay in order to get on a rung of the commercial ladder, "which oftener than not proves a treadmill." Proponents of "commercial education" also made much of the competition of foreign clerks working in England, especially the Germans, who, it was claimed, had received a much better education than most English clerks and accepted any salaries offered in order to gain experience and spy out the lay of the commercial land before returning home to enter business. In 1887 the London Chamber of Commerce questioned the leading City firms on this subject, and discovered that 35 per cent of them employed foreign clerks. Finally, it was alleged, the "entry of women into Clerkdom" tended to drag down the general salary level.[23]

As in the case of shop assistants, it is difficult to generalize about the pay of clerks owing to a variety of complicating factors. In the first place, wages varied considerably among the different branches of trade, banks and insurance companies paying the best, and transport service the worst, with industry and commerce falling somewhere between. For example, one writer estimated the average weekly wages of clerks in different lines of work in the period 1910-1914 as: insurance, men 53s. 6d. and

women 23s.; commerce and industry, men 40s. and women 15s. 6d.; men
in banks, 53s.; and men in transport service, 36s. He gave no figures on
women in banks or transport service, presumably because so few women
were employed; but for women clerks in the transport field another writer
estimated their pay as being about three-fifths of men's pay, varying with
the line and the district and ranging from 20-28s. to as low as 11s. 6d. In
the second place, wages naturally also depended upon the size and class
of firms and upon the clerk's general education and technical qualifications, position in the firm, and length of service. An official inquiry into
the working conditions of women clerks in London in 1910 revealed that
these workers were divided roughly into three classes. At the top were girls
of superior education and distinct proficiency in shorthand and typing and
often with knowledge of one or more foreign languages, who had usually
trained in typewriting offices. Some of these continued to work in typewriting offices after completing their training, forming part of the skilled
staff capable of doing the most difficult work and performing the higher
secretarial duties, but the majority left to enter good-class business houses
where they received wages of £2, £3 or even £4 a week. Next, there were
fairly intelligent and capable girls proficient in ordinary typing and copying, who were found in all the better-class typewriting offices and business houses and who earned £1 to 30s. a week. Finally, there were girls
of limited intelligence and education, who went into clerical work because
they considered it higher-class employment than domestic service or
factory work. Most of them had had some training in large commercial
schools, but had never become very proficient. They entered second-rate
typewriting offices and inferior business houses, where their pay was very
low, 10-15s. a week.[24]

In these circumstances there was a very wide range in the wages of
women clerical workers. Official statistics collected in London in 1914
showed a low of 8s. a week and a high of 78s. 6d. Women with less than
five years' experience averaged about 26s., and those with fifteen years'
experience or more about 45s. The average for all the women sampled
was a little more than 32s. a week, or about £83 a year. But according
to a later estimate, the average of all women clerks' salaries was only
£45 a year. Yet another later estimate emphasized the wage differential
between men and women clerks: in 1914 estimated average earnings were
for men, 55-85s. a week or £143-221 a year, and for women only 15-25s.
a week or £39-65 a year.[25]

With regard to clerical salaries, many women writers maintained that
it was not the competition of women as women which pulled down the
general level of pay, but rather the competition of the poorly educated
and poorly trained working classes with the better educated and better
trained classes, women as well as men. Such writers claimed that the competition of the unqualified so discouraged the best women that it was
almost impossible to find capable, cultured, well-trained gentlewomen
for clerical work and that there were always more well-paid positions
open than there were women to fill them.[26]

Others, however, advised well-educated women not to enter clerical work, claiming that such employment was suitable only for girls who received free lodging at least from their families, because otherwise they could not live on the small wages they would be able to earn. In this connection it was also pointed out that few higher positions in business were open to women. Employers felt that women could not handle more responsible work, or in any case would soon marry and quit work (apparently many employers insisted that their women workers retire upon marriage) and that it would be easier to replace them in subordinate positions than in higher ones. Women clerks generally could expect to obtain only routine and poorly paid work, with little prospect of rising to more interesting, responsible and well-paid posts. These claims are substantiated by statistics on clerks' salaries for the years 1909-1910: 54 per cent of all men in clerical work were earning over £100 a year, and the majority of these earned more than £160, while only 3 per cent of all women clerks earned over £100; 46 per cent of the men and 97 per cent of the women earned less than £100.[27]

Considering the problem of clerical salaries and the competition between men and women workers, an early trade-union leader declared: "It is no use men burying their heads in the sand and saying, Women's Place is not in the Office." That is, men had no right to complain of the employment of women, but only of the unfair competition of women who accepted lower salaries than men. He added that this unfair competition not only lowered salaries generally but also decreased young men's, and therefore young women's, chances of marrying, because few men would marry when earning a salary "that means certain misery," while many firms actually forbade their male clerks to marry until they reached a certain salary level. A woman echoed these sentiments, saying: "Friendship, not war, between the sexes would be the more excellent, as well as the more paying way." But, she added: "Friendship means equal chances, and a realization of the fact that women come into the labour market chiefly because they have to."[28] If clerical workers, women as well as men, could unite together, perhaps they would succeed in obtaining higher salaries and in winning other reforms which they desired.

Trade Unionism among Clerks

The outlook for effective trade unionism among clerks, as among shop assistants, was not very promising. Both groups of workers faced similar problems when it came to organizing, one of the greatest being the general attitude of workers themselves toward organization. George Bernard Shaw, who began his working life as an estate agent's clerk in the 1870's, explained why he would not have joined a union in his youth, had one existed: "Not only would it have been considered a most ungentlemanly thing to do—almost as outrageous as coming to the office in corduroy trousers, with a belcher handkerchief round my neck—but, snobbery apart, it would have been stupid, because I should not have intended to remain a clerk. I should have taken the employers' point of view from

Lady Clerk. "Yes, they actually complained in the office to-day because we were talking too much. They wouldn't do that if we were men!"

the first." Priding themselves on their middle-class respectability and identifying their interests with those of their employers, clerks generally felt themselves to be much superior to manual workers socially, and frowned upon any activity which savoured of working-class tactics and which might blight their own future prospects, an attitute which employers actively encouraged. As Shaw later wrote: "The clerks have tall hats and hymnbooks and keep up the social tone by refusing to associate on equal terms with anybody." The working classes in turn looked disdainfully upon clerks, regarding them as "boss's men," and claiming that since they often were no better paid than manual workers they were merely "snobs fancying themselves gents."[29]

In addition to social prejudice, there were also many practical obstacles to clerical trade unionism. In the first place, clerks were not concentrated in large numbers in well-defined sectors of the economy but worked in many different offices in many different lines of business with widely varying conditions of service, and there was little feeling of unity among them. One observer remarked: "The banker's clerk cultivates not the acquaintance of the lawyer's clerk; the draper's clerk prefers not to associate with the grocer's clerk," and so on. Moreover, even in the same establishment "the spirit of caste has often a prominent place; those who by chance sit at a mahogany table would seem to say by their demeanour that they are far removed from those who occupy a deal desk." Finally, there was a great deal of temporary employment in clerical work, for employees often considered their positions merely as stepping stones to better things. Like Shaw himself, who forsook clerking for literature and socialism, many young men "hated business and meant to get out of it and become a great man: poet, novelist, polar explorer, field marshal . . . prime minister." The large numbers of women workers obviously posed a great problem, for most of them intended to give up their jobs upon marriage. Statistics on the ages of clerical workers in 1911 illustrate the high proportion of temporary employees: nearly half of all male clerks were under the age of twenty-five, compared with only 29 per cent of the total male working population, while about two-thirds of all women clerks were under twenty-five, compared with about half of all working women.[30]

In these circumstances trade unionism was slow to develop. The first country-wide organization of clerks began to take form in London about 1889. (There were already numerous associations of clerks in existence, but most were purely local and organized on a friendly-society basis.) At first intended primarily for male clerks in London, this union soon decided to admit women as well and to expand its operations beyond the metropolis, and the name National Union of Clerks was adopted. In 1894 a second union, the National Clerks' Association, was founded in Leeds, and soon branches were established elsewhere in Yorkshire and in Lancashire. Three years later the London and Leeds organizations "discovered one another" and an amalgamation was arranged, the name National Union of Clerks being retained. (In 1920 the union added the

words "and Administrative Workers" to its title.) But progress in enrolling clerical workers in the early years was extremely slow. By 1900 the
union boasted only eighty-two members, and it surely would have disappeared but for the personal friendships among its few active leaders.[31]

From its beginning the N.U.C., like the unions of shop assistants, was
notable for admitting women to membership on equal terms with men.
As the union's secretary testified in 1912 before the royal commission
on the civil service: "We realise that if the status of the clerical profession is to be raised, men and women must go up together." Women
were organized together with men in the union's local branches, where
they played an active part, often serving as branch secretaries. They
paid the same trade-union contribution as men, and equally with men
they could contribute separately for unemployment, sickness and death
benefits, although comparatively few women actually chose to do so. (In
1923 the union's annual conference accepted the principle of contributions lower for women than for men because of their lower level of pay,
although the two women members who spoke on the question at the conference opposed this action.) Like the shop assistants' union, the N.U.C.
at one time sought to attract women members by allowing them dowries
upon marriage, but the women actually protested this preferential treatment and the practice was dropped. Women members were eligible for
election to all posts in the union, and although in this period none achieved
national office, it became common for at least one woman to be chosen for
the union's central executive council every year, being elected by all the
union members in open competition with men. The representation of
women on the executive council was not proportional to the number of
women members in the union, who by 1914 represented slightly less than
12 per cent of the total membership of over 12,000. Still, an attempt in
1911 to give women special representation by organizing a "women's
league" analogous to the women's councils of the National Amalgamated
Union of Shop Assistants failed, supposedly because the women themselves did not want it. One of the outstanding women who came to the
fore in the union was Dorothy ("Dolly") Lansbury, eldest daughter of
George Lansbury, described as "a vigourous and attractive personality,"
who married her fellow union member Ernest Thurtle, later Labour
M.P. for Shoreditch and a junior minister in Ramsay MacDonald's
administration. Another was Margaret Postgate, later Mrs. G. D. H.
Cole, of whom the union's historian later reminisced: "My first impression
of her was of an attractive young woman taking an intelligent part in
the branch meeting while rather ostentatiously smoking a clay pipe."[32]

Another organization catering for clerical workers was the Association
of Shorthand Writers and Typists, formed by a small group of women
in London in 1903. At first the Association admitted men to membership, but under a new constitution adopted in 1912 male members, already
a small and diminishing number, were excluded, and the name was
changed to the Association of Women Clerks and Secretaries. The Association acknowledged the theoretical advantages of joint organization

with men but preferred an independent course in practice, feeling that an all-female organization would serve as a nucleus for wider association among women clerical workers, and that here women could learn to hold their own before joining an organization dominated by men. Only in 1940, under the auspices of the T.U.C., did the women's Association and the National Union of Clerks and Administrative Workers merge to form the Clerical and Administrative Workers' Union. Earlier negotiations for amalgamation had failed, apparently because the women's Association insisted upon preferential treatment for women in any new organization, while the women members of the National Union of Clerks opposed such special treatment. Under the terms of the 1940 merger agreement, a woman was appointed as assistant general secretary of the new union; two seats, to be held by women, were added to the union's executive council; and at each annual election a woman was to be chosen as president or as one of the two vice-presidents of the union.[33] In 1972 the name of the union was changed to the Association of Professional, Executive, Clerical and Computer Staff, or A.P.E.X.

A third organization for clerical workers which appeared in this period was the Railway Clerks' Association, founded in 1897. By 1910 it had a membership of less than 10,000, but after the railway strike of 1911 it forged ahead, and by 1914 claimed some 30,000 members. Besides clerical workers, the Association admitted as members stationmasters, inspectors and superintendents, who were also eligible to join the National Union of Railwaymen. The Association always admitted women on equal terms with men. They were organized together with men in the local branches; they paid the same contributions as men and enjoyed the same benefits; and they were eligible for election to all offices. However, women's employment as railway clerks was only beginning by 1914, as was their employment in banks and in insurance offices. (See Appendix, Table 4c.) Their numbers in the union, only about a hundred in 1914, and consequently their role were small. After nationalization of the railways in 1950, the union's name was changed to the Transport Salaried Staffs' Association, and it began to enlist all clerks under the jurisdiction of the British Transport Commission, such as those employed in connection with road transport, docks, hotels and catering. This Association is today one of the largest "white-collar" trade unions in Britain. Meanwhile, clerks employed in banks remained unorganized as such until the founding in 1918 of the Bank Officers' Guild, later known as the National Union of Bank Employees. Clerks working for insurance companies first organized in the Guild of Insurance Officials in 1919.[34]

In addition to strictly clerical associations, a number of other unions also admitted clerks to membership. For example, the National Amalgamated Union of Shop Assistants and the Amalgamated Union of Co-operative Employees admitted clerical workers employed by distributive firms; the National Society of Operative Printers and Assistants organized clerks employed in the printing trades, chiefly those in London newspaper offices; the Amalgamated Engineering Union and the National

Union of Mineworkers admitted clerks employed in those industries. In addition to these industrial unions, the great general unions, the National Union of General and Municipal Workers and the Transport and General Workers' Union, formed special clerical sections within their ranks. (Inspired by the Guild Socialism preached by G. D. H. Cole, the National Union of Clerks between 1919 and 1932 experimented with the organization of clerical workers on an industrial rather than on a geographical basis, but unsuccessfully.)[35]

By 1914 trade unionism among clerks seemed to be off to a fairly good start. But the membership of the clerical unions, although increasing, remained relatively very small, and their record of achievement before the war was a disappointing one. This picture is little changed today, for although "there is a multitude of white-collar associations . . . very few have more than a handful of members or have any influence on the national scene."[36] And this lack of trade-union success is probably largely explained by the fact that today the great majority of clerical workers in Britain are women.

The Struggle for Better Working Conditions

By general agreement the excessive competition among clerks for positions was one of the greatest obstacles to improving their status, and both the National Union of Clerks and the Association of Women Clerks and Secretaries considered what might be done to solve this problem. The N.U.C. worked for legislation to raise the school-leaving age so as to postpone the entry into the labour market of large numbers of boys and girls, and also advocated better counselling in the schools for young people choosing jobs after the completion of their education, counselling which would point out the overcrowded state of the clerical occupations and suggest alternative careers.[37]

Both organizations also insisted upon the need to maintain a high standard of general education and of technical training for clerical work and thereby eliminate incompetent workers. The N.U.C. hoped to see the return of some sort of apprenticeship for clerks, and wanted to organize examinations and grant certificates of proficiency for clerks. The women's Association in 1913 sponsored an important conference on clerical training, held at the University of London and chaired by Elizabeth Haldane, then serving as a member of the royal commission on the civil service. The speakers at this conference emphasized the need for better and broader education for girls entering clerical work and the fact that their technical training should not begin before the age of sixteen. (The setting of this age limit represented more than an attempt to insure the sound education of girls entering clerical work, for the women's Association maintained that "no girl should be allowed to enter the profession until she is old enough and wise enough to protect herself, should need arise, from the undesirable employer, who may insult her with unwelcome attentions.")[38] Unfortunately, the clerks' associations were fighting an up-hill battle, and neither of them was able even to insist upon a minimum educational qualification for its own members.

Because of the keen competition among clerks, even the best-qualified found it difficult to discover and obtain positions. One observer declared that a clerk's chance of getting a post was "reduced to the merest accident—to seeing the advertisement an hour before his neighbour, to living near the place at which candidates are sent to ask for particulars, to having a pleasanter appearance than the rest of the applicants." Both the National Union of Clerks and the Women Clerks' Association sought to improve this situation by serving as employment bureaus for their members and suggesting to employers seeking well-qualified workers the appropriate rate of pay which they should offer. In connection with this work, the N.U.C. also maintained for its members an information index which set forth the standing of different employers and the working conditions in their offices, and was always ready to advise members whether to accept or refuse certain positions.[39]

The N.U.C. also concerned itself with employees' security of tenure. Clerks enjoyed the status of "contract servants" under the common law, and as such, in the absence of a definite agreement, they were presumed to be employed under a year's contract at a yearly salary and were entitled to three months' notice upon dismissal. Where they were engaged by the week or month at a weekly or monthly rate of pay, they were entitled to a week's or a month's notice respectively. In any case, however, employers could pay their clerks wages in lieu of notice. An employer did not have to state his reasons for dismissing a contract servant, but if a worker brought suit for wrongful dismissal the employer had to justify his action. When satisfied that a member dismissed from his position had a legitimate grievance, the union was prepared to take legal action to have him reinstated or to force his employer to pay wages in lieu of notice. But often the mere threat of legal proceedings was enough to persuade employers to come to terms.[40]

In connection with the question of tenure, the N.U.C. also had to deal with the problem of secret references. Employers were not legally bound to furnish character references for their clerks, but if they did so the statements had to be true or else they could be sued for libel. Like the National Amalgamated Union of Shop Assistants, the N.U.C. for years advocated establishment by law of the right of workers to obtain open references, but eventually dropped this demand in deference to the opinion of the trade-union movement as a whole. The union then concentrated upon legal action in cases of clerks suffering as a result of unjust references from employers, bringing its first libel suit on behalf of a woman member in 1912.[41]

Both the N.U.C. and the Women Clerks' Association were much exercised over the question of pensions and sickness benefits for clerks, which came to the fore during the discussions on the National Insurance Bill of 1911. The executive committee of the N.U.C. wanted to approve the Bill with reservations, but the annual conference of the union in 1911 "banned it (metaphorically) with bell, book and candle," apparently because of misgivings as to the possible effect on the right of clerks as contract servants to receive full payment of their salaries during absence from work because of illness. The Women Clerks' Association also opposed the inclusion of clerks under the Insurance Bill, sponsoring a large protest meeting in Hyde Park.[42]

When the Insurance Bill became law, however, both of the clerks' associations decided to form approved societies for those compulsorily insured under its provisions. As a result, the numbers of their members increased dramatically, the N.U.C. growing from a membership of 1,218 in 1910 to include 12,680 members by 1914. The women's approved society was not a complete success, but the Women Clerks' Association rejected a proposal to merge it with the N.U.C.'s society. Later the women's society amalgamated with that of the National Federation of Women Workers, an organization which subsequently merged with the National Union of General and Municipal Workers. As passed, the Insurance Act contained a clause, inserted by Lloyd George as a result of the clerks' representations, to safeguard their common-law right to receive salaries during sick leave, but this clause was omitted from a later amending act, and in practice the clerks' original misgivings proved justified. In 1914 the N.U.C. brought its first legal action to test the effect of the Insurance Act on the clerks' common-law right to receive their regular pay during sickness, and the county court judge decided in favour of the union, the member in question being awarded arrears of salary without any deduction. With this precedent established, many similar cases were later settled satisfactorily without going to court.[43]

Important as all these activities were, still more pressing matters engaged the attention of the clerks' associations. According to *The Clerks' Charter*, a little pamphlet by W. J. Read which was published by the N.U.C. in 1910, the three chief demands of clerical workers were: hours which would not leave them exhausted in body and mind at the end of the day but which would afford them leisure to develop their faculties and individuality; healthful and comfortable offices in which to work; and a wage that would enable them to live as educated citizens.[44]

The problem of enacting legal protection for clerical workers eventually came before Parliament. The N.U.C. affiliated with the Labour Party in 1906 and won a hearing for its claims largely through the efforts of Labour M.P.'s, although the union wanted and welcomed support from any party. Unlike the National Amalgamated Union of Shop Assistants, the N.U.C. did not, before World War I, seek to elect its own representatives to Parliament. In 1922 the union undertook its first Parliamentary candidature, but without success, although at this time the future prime minister Clement Attlee, a member of the N.U.C. since 1912, won election, as did several other union members.[45]

With regard to the hours and working conditions of clerks, Ramsay MacDonald twice during the Parliamentary session of 1909 asked the Home Secretary, Herbert Gladstone, whether he would institute a test prosecution to determine whether the Factory Acts applied to typewriting offices. On both occasions Gladstone replied that according to the official view, the processes for duplicating documents carried on in typewriting offices were not manufacturing processes within the meaning of the Factory Acts, and that if the Acts were amended to apply to such offices, they would also have to be extended to ordinary business offices, where similar duplicating processes were used and where enforcement would be nearly impossible.[46]

Nevertheless, in 1910 Gladstone commissioned a special inquiry to determine whether the Factory Acts should be extended to typewriting offices and what the effect of the Acts upon the work of such offices would be. The investigation was carried out by Adelaide Anderson, the chief lady factory inspector, and by one of the male inspectors, who visited offices and business houses and conferred with employers and workers in all branches of trade in London and in other large cities. As a result of their studies, the two inspectors concluded that the hours and conditions of employment in typewriting offices did not warrant the inclusion of these offices under the provisions of the Factory Acts. The hours of work and the amount of overtime required were not excessive and were certainly not enough to injure the health of the workers, and the overtime was generally paid for. As for sanitary conditions, typewriting offices were generally satisfactory, for they, like shop premises, came under the provisions of the Public Health Acts and were inspected by the local sanitary authorities. (A similar inquiry conducted in London in 1898 by the Women's Industrial Council had reached the same conclusion, that there was no reason for amending the Factory Acts so as to cover offices.) In any case, the two investigators reported, the number of women and girls employed in business houses so far exceeded the number working in typewriting offices that it would be unreasonable to place the latter under the Factory Acts without including the former as well. Still, they pointed out that the rapidly increasing employment of women clerks suggested that some regulation of offices might eventually be necessary, and they mentioned that future legislation for shops might be framed to cover clerical workers as well as shop assistants.[47] This, in fact, was done, for the Shops Act of 1911 applied to all workers employed by retail and wholesale establishments.

The government not being disposed to take action for the benefit of clerks, some of their friends in Parliament introduced private legislation on their behalf. The first measure presented was the Railway Clerks' Weekly Rest Bill of 1911. To be enforced by the Board of Trade, this measure would have guaranteed to railway stationmasters and clerical staffs a free and uninterrupted rest day of twenty-four hours every week, to fall on Sundays as far as practicable. No clerk would be employed on two successive Sundays, and Sunday work would be paid for at the rate of time and a quarter.[48]

A much more sweeping measure was the Railway Offices Bill, which was sponsored by the Railway Clerks' Association and introduced in

1911 and again in 1912 and 1913. It provided that no young person under the age of sixteen was to be employed, while other young persons aged sixteen to eighteen were not to work at night or on Sundays. Workers' hours would be limited to eight daily and a total of forty-two weekly for daytime work, and to seven nightly and a total of thirty-seven weekly for night work. Overtime work, restricted to four hours a day on not more than three days a week or thirty days a year, was to be paid for at the rate of time and a quarter. Railway clerks were to have a weekly rest day of twenty-four hours, on Sundays as far as possible, and an annual holiday of fourteen days with pay, as well as the usual public holidays. These provisions would be enforced by the factory inspectors.[49]

The National Union of Clerks drafted yet another bill, which Ramsay MacDonald introduced in 1911 and which C. W. Bowerman, secretary of the T.U.C., sponsored in 1912. Much less comprehensive than the railway clerks' bill, this Offices Regulation Bill would have extended to offices those provisions of the Factory Act of 1901 relating to sanitary conditions and overcrowding, and to the keeping of registers of children and young persons employed and of accidents. These provisions would be enforced by the local sanitary authorities or, in their default, by the factory inspectors acting at the special direction of the Home Secretary.[50]

One last piece of legislation that would have benefited clerks was the Underground Workrooms Bill, introduced in the House of Lords in 1912 and 1913 and in the Commons in 1914. This Bill would have extended to a number of specified trades, among them "typewriting and other clerical work," the provisions of the Factory Acts of 1901 and 1907 requiring that underground workplaces be certified as suitable and inspected by the local sanitary authorities, or in their default by the factory inspectors under special orders from the Home Secretary.[51]

Unfortunately, none of these measures ever attained a second reading, despite the vigourous publicity campaign waged by *The Clerk,* the official organ of the N.U.C. But the campaign did bring some improvement by influencing local sanitary authorities to exercise more effectively their powers under the Public Health Acts to inspect offices. Also, the N.U.C. won the extension to clerks of the Workmen's Compensation Acts by enlisting in their cause the powerful sympathies of Joseph Chamberlain, although few cases affecting clerks actually arose under these Acts, owing to the nature of clerical work.[52] Like shop assistants, clerks did not gain legal regulation of their working conditions equal to that enjoyed by manual workers under the Factory Acts until passage of the Offices, Shops and Railway Premises Act of 1963.

While fighting their unsuccessful Parliamentary battle for legislation insuring better hours and working conditions, the clerks' associations had also attacked the problem of obtaining higher wages in a campaign which the N.U.C. called "Killing the 'Pound-a-Week' Clerk." In 1909 the N.U.C. fixed as its immediate goal a minimum weekly wage of 35s. for clerks, women as well as men. The Railway Clerks' Association likewise claimed equal pay with men for its women members. Some men objected to this policy, presumably because, like male shop assistants, they feared that insistence on equal pay for women would jeopardize their own chances of success in wage disputes. But the unions' reason for adoption of this policy was obvious, that is, to prevent the lowering of men's standards by women's invasion of the clerical market. The Association of Women Clerks and Secretaries naturally supported the other associations' claims for equal pay, although its own standard was a minimum of only 30s. a week for women clerks in London.[53]

The N.U.C. waged a vigourous publicity campaign for adoption of its minimum wage, sending deputations to the Prime Minister and the Chancellor of the Exchequer. Beginning in 1910 the union persuaded a number of local government authorities to adopt the 35s. minimum wage for their clerical staffs, as a result of its drive to recruit members among those employed in government service. On the whole, however, the N.U.C. enjoyed little success, for it had no means of enforcing its claims owing to the great weight of unorganized clerical workers. Before the war the union waged only one strike, at Wolverhampton, which the outbreak of the war brought to an inconclusive end, and it achieved only one definite victory regarding pay in a struggle at Birmingham in 1914. In no case did the N.U.C. win equal pay for women. The Railway Clerks' Association likewise made little progress, and in transport service as in all other branches of clerkdom low pay for men and lower pay for women remained the rule.[54] This situation has continued unchanged to the present day, with women clerks receiving only about two-thirds to three-fourths of the pay of men. Not until 1970 and passage of the Equal Pay Act could women clerks and other workers look forward to the end of such discrimination against them.

By 1914 clerical work had become one of the most popular careers open to women. Despite its disadvantages, of which sympathetic observers and clerks themselves complained, the work was light and easily accessible and respectable, and the number of workers, especially of women, increased with astonishing rapidity. This popularity and the increase of workers continue unabated today, when no less than 40 per cent of girls under the age of eighteen obtaining employment for the first time take clerical positions, compared with slightly more than 8 per cent for boys, and when one worker in ten is a clerk. Napoleon called Britain a "nation of shopkeepers." Karl Marx labelled the country a "nation of clerks," a description even more apt now than in Marx's time. And since women represent the great majority of clerical workers in Britain today, it is simple truth that middle-class working women, albeit unorganized and underpaid still, are absolutely indispensable to the country's economy.

VII

WOMEN IN THE SERVICE OF THE STATE: THE CIVIL SERVICE

The employment of middle-class women in the civil service in the later nineteenth and early twentieth centuries was, in a sense, a microcosm of the employment of middle-class women generally in this period. In the earlier years of the period, owing to conditions prevailing in the service, few women civil servants were employed, just as there were few women shop assistants and few women clerks. But as the years passed, the nature and structure of the service changed, as did the character of the retail trades and of the clerical occupations, making possible and even essential the employment of middle-class women. In the case of the Post Office manipulative grades, as in teaching, middle-class women had always been employed, and they were simply absorbed into the civil service as the state took over their work. In the inspectorate, the government began to employ educated women in order to take advantage of their special abilities and qualifications, the motive which led middle-class women to enter nursing. The entry of women clerks into the civil service reflected the increasing demand for clerical labour, as for shop labour, throughout the community, and the fact that women could supply that demand as well as men. In all branches of the service, as in elementary-school teaching and in shop and clerical work, women represented a welcome supply of cheap but efficient labour, and their numbers in the service increased some twenty times over compared with a threefold increase in the number of men. (See Appendix, Tables 5a and 5b.) By 1914 women civil servants were a minority, but an important and essential minority, among the servants of the state.

The Changing Civil Service

In the mid-nineteenth century almost no women civil servants were employed in Britain, a fact which is easily understood in view of the state of the service at the time. In the first place, the civil service was a small organization, for according to the prevailing laissez-faire philosophy there was little for the government to do beyond maintaining law and order within the country and defending it from enemies without. In 1851 some 85 per cent of the persons employed by the central government were involved in defense work, while of the rest, about half were found in the ancient departments concerned with foreign affairs, internal order and justice, and revenue, the great majority of them tax collectors. In the second place, the relatively small number of civil service posts were filled by the nominees of political patrons, a practice reflecting the aristocratic social structure of the time. Finally, the work of the service was then regarded as "highly skilled and carried a considerable degree of prestige," for "the Civil Service represented part of a small market for a similarly small supply of educated men who were well paid for their ability to read and write."[1] It may be added that their work was far from arduous. Indeed, it had become proverbial that "civil servants, like the fountains in Trafalgar Square, play from ten to four." In these circumstances, middle-class women could hardly aspire to positions in the government service. There was little demand for workers, and this demand was fully supplied by educated men who were lucky enough to find patrons to support their claims to employment.

But the later nineteenth and the early twentieth centuries saw a great increase in the size of the civil service and a radical change in its functions and structure. In response to the needs of a rapidly expanding industrial and urban economy, the state was fast becoming both the servant of its citizens and the regulator of their activities. By far the most important of the government service departments was the Post Office, which reflected in its growth the great improvements in transportation and communication of the time and the progress of the economy generally. There was a great expansion in the postal service proper, the establishment of the penny post in 1840 being followed by the introduction of the book post in 1848, of postal cards in 1870, of postal orders in 1881, and of the parcel post in 1883. The Post Office also assumed control of other systems of communication, taking over the country's telegraphs in 1870 and completing its gradual takeover of the telephone system in 1911. Finally, the Post Office entered other fields of service, becoming a popular banker and investor through the establishment of the Savings Bank in 1861, and being a convenient organization for such official transactions as the payment of government pensions and the sale of health and unemployment insurance stamps. As a result of all these developments, the Post Office increased the number of its employees six times over between 1851 and 1891, and doubled them between 1891 and 1914. Other important services for which the state assumed responsibility in this period were the provision of elementary, technical and secondary education, especially as embodied in the landmark Education Acts of 1870, 1889 and 1902, and the provision of old-age pensions and of health and unemployment insurance under the National Insurance Act of 1911. At the same time, with the waning of the day of laissez-faire, a number of government departments expanded to enforce the new regulations upon industry, notably the Home Office, the Board of Trade, and the Local Government Board.[2]

The growth in size and the diversification of functions of the civil service coincided with the internal reform of the service. The beginning of the modern British civil service may be dated from 1854, when the Trevel-yan-Northcote report on its reorganization appeared, although not until the famous order-in-council of 1870 did the government officially de-nounce patronage and recommend in its stead recruitment through open competitive examinations conducted by the Civil Service Commission. No longer were government posts to be distributed by political patrons, although patronage did in fact linger on in patches. This reform in turn coincided with, indeed would have been impossible without, an increase in the number of qualified candidates for employment in the service. The coming of popular elementary education, especially after 1870, and the reforms in secondary education destroyed the monopoly of government employment which middle-class men had once enjoyed, as the only class sufficiently well-educated for the work. In fact, the supply of qualified workers, women as well as men, outstripped the demand, with some un-fortunate results for civil servants generally.

By 1914 the Post Office had grown to become the largest business or-ganization in England. It was also the greatest single employer of middle-class women in the country, and accounted for more than 90 per cent of the women employed by the central government. (See Appendix, Table 5c.) These women postal employees were divided into two large categories, "manipulative" workers and clerical workers.

Apparently women had been employed in telegraph work almost as soon as the new invention was perfected and put into commercial use. The story goes that about 1853 the chairman of the Electric and International Telegraph Company in London heard of the daughter of a railway station-master who for three years had ably carried on all of her father's tele-graph business, and this suggested to him the idea of the Company's train-ing and employing women for this work. Soon it could be said that the Company was "perfectly satisfied that the girls are not only more teach-able, more attentive, and quicker-eyed than the men clerks formerly employed, but . . . also . . . more trustworthy, more easily managed, and . . . sooner satisfied with lower wages."[3]

When the Post Office took over the work of the telegraph companies in 1870, the official decision was to continue to employ women, who would enter the service in the same manner as men and be employed together with men on the same duties, although supervised by their own women officers. At first, telegraphists obtained nominations for positions from the Postmaster-General or from local postmasters and then passed a qualifying examination, but later open competitive examinations were instituted. Workers then attended telegraph schools for several months of instruction, receiving no pay during this training until regular pay scales for them were introduced in 1905. From the schools telegraphists were drafted off as needed to fill positions in the Central Telegraph Office and in the branch offices in London, and in post offices throughout the country. In the Central Office and in the larger branch offices they were employed solely on telegraph work, while in smaller offices they did tele-graph work and also waited upon customers at the postal counters.[4] With regard to the policy of employing men and women telegraphists together, the Postmaster-General as early as 1871 declared:

> there has been no reason to regret the experiment. On the contrary, it has afforded ground for believing that, where large numbers of persons are employed, with full work and fair supervision, the admixture of the sexes involves no risk, but is highly beneficial. It raises the tone of the male staff by confining them during many hours of the day to a decency of conversation and demeanour which is not always to be found where men alone are employed. Further, it is a matter of experience that the male clerks are more willing to help the female clerks with their work than to help each other; and that on many occasions pressure of business is met and difficulties overcome through this willingness and cordial co-operation.[5]

As in telegraph work, women seem to have been employed as telephone operators almost as soon as the new instruments were first made available to the public in 1879. These workers were long divided into two groups, those employed by the commercial telephone companies licensed by the Post Office, and those employed by the Post Office itself, which established exchanges in certain areas to maintain a competitive atmosphere. Gradually the Post Office expanded its operations, and employees of the private companies were absorbed into the civil service, a process completed by 1911. The great majority of telephone operators were women, men being employed almost entirely on night duty. Workers were recruited for government telephone service by public advertisement, and then passed a qualifying examination to gain admission to telephone schools for training which usually lasted three months, during which time they received only nominal wages. They were then transferred to telephone exchanges, where they served a two-year probationary period before receiving appointments as established Post Office servants. Telephone operators were still a relatively small group of workers when the government completed its takeover of the service in 1911, but the years immediately before the war saw a very rapid expansion of the service under government control.[6]

The Post Office was also the first government department to employ women in clerical work. As early as 1871 a few women entered the Telegraph Clearing House Branch of the department, and four years later about thirty more women were introduced as clerks in the Savings Bank Department. All were "gentlewomen of limited means," such as the daughters of army and navy officers, of civil servants and of professional and literary men. They received nominations for their positions from the Postmaster-General, passed a qualifying examination conducted by the Civil Service Commission, and then served a six-month probationary period before their appointments were officially confirmed. In 1876 the women's clerical branch of the Post Office was formally organized and placed under the command of a lady superintendent, Maria Constance Smith. The daughter of a university professor, Miss Smith had had no

THE CENTRAL TELEGRAPH OFFICE: INSTRUMENT GALLERY.

regular work before she entered the Post Office at the age of twenty-one, but she soon demonstrated remarkable qualities of leadership, dedicating herself wholeheartedly to making the government's experiment in employing women clerks a great success. So well did the women workers perform their duties that their numbers were steadily added to and their employment was extended to other branches of the Post Office. In 1881 Henry Fawcett, the distinguished and popular Postmaster-General, created an established civil service grade of "women clerks," to be recruited no longer by nomination but by open competitive examinations. (Always a friend of women's causes, Fawcett encouraged his wife, the former Millicent Garrett, to take an active part in the women's suffrage campaign, which he promoted in Parliament.) At the time considerable concern was expressed at the idea of open competition for women clerks. One writer said: "We fear . . . that . . . friends of young gentlewomen will shrink from allowing them to work in offices that will practically be open to women of all classes." And Queen Victoria is said to have ordered written to Fawcett a strongly-worded letter of protest.[7]

Two more women's clerical grades soon made their appearance in the Post Office. In 1883 Fawcett introduced the grade of "women sorters," who, despite their name, were essentially file clerks and did not perform work done by male letter sorters. Like women clerks, the women sorters were recruited by open competitive examinations. In 1897 the grade of "girl clerks" was introduced. These workers entered the service by taking the same examinations as women clerks but at a younger age, sixteen to eighteen. After two years' service they automatically became women clerks or, if they proved incapable of handling the more responsible clerical duties, entered the women sorters' grade.[8]

Meanwhile, men in the Post Office had looked askance at the introduction of women clerical workers. *The Civilian,* the postal employees' journal, published numerous attacks on the innovation, speaking of "the grievous dangers, moral and official," likely to result, and generally making "allegations of favouritism and immorality only fit to appear in a gutter journal."[9] Certainly there was no ground for such comments, for Miss Smith and the department officials always insisted that the women be employed in strict segregation from men and that they perform different kinds of work from men under the supervision of women officers.

From the Post Office the employment of women clerks spread to other government departments. A few women in clerical positions were to be found at the Board of Education, in the Labour Department of the Board of Trade, in the Office of the Registrar-General, and at the Home Office. The largest employers of women clerks outside the Post Office were newly created branches of the government, such as the Office of the Public Trustee, established in 1908, and the National Health Insurance Commission and the Board of Trade Labour Exchanges, set up in 1911. The method of recruitment for these clerical positions varied among the departments. A considerable proportion of the women were transferred from the Post Office, while others received their appointments by nomination or, as in the case of the Labour Exchange clerks, by passing a special qualifying examination which was the same for them as for men. Still, by 1914 only a handful of women clerks were employed outside the Post Office.[10] (See Appendix, Table 5c.)

Just as the increasing use of the typewriter helped to open the doors of the business world, so it served to widen women's opportunities of employment in the civil service. Sir Algernon West, head of the Internal Revenue Department, pioneered in the employment of women typists in the early '80's, after "a battle royal with the Treasury," as he described it. Finally won over by West's recommendations, the Treasury tried to force all departments to follow his example in employing women, and in 1894, after presentation of a petition by the women requesting increased pay rates and permanent status, "women typists" became an established civil service grade. The recruitment of typists varied among the departments. Only in the Post Office and in the Internal Revenue Department was there an open competitive examination, the rest of the departments filling typists' positions by nomination, sometimes coupled with a qualifying examination conducted by the Civil Service Commission. Typists served a one-year probationary period before becoming permanent employees. After three years' service they could take the Civil Service Commission examination in shorthand and obtain promotion to the higher class of shorthand-typists if vacancies existed, the number of shorthand-typists being limited to half the total typing staff. Like women clerks, typists worked strictly segregated from men under the control of women supervisors. By 1914 a few hundred women typists were employed in about half of the government departments.[11]

The first woman to enter the state inspectorate was Mrs. Jane Elizabeth Senior, sister of the novelist Thomas Hughes and daughter-in-law of the noted economist, Nassau Senior. In 1874 Sir James Stansfeld, president of the Local Government Board and always a friend of women's causes, appointed Mrs. Senior as an inspector of workhouses and workhouse schools, following her special inquiry into and report upon the education of pauper girls. Her appointment was anathema to most of the officials at the Board, one of whom declared that she had found "faults, mostly imaginary, with what I am satisfied is the best system of pauper education yet invented," and accused her of bias, bad faith, sensationalism, and the like.[12] Unfortunately, Mrs. Senior soon had to resign her position because of failing health (she died in 1877), but her recommendations regarding Poor Law education were gradually put into effect. Not until 1885 was another woman appointed at the Local Government Board, as an inspector of boarded-out children, and in 1897 a second, as inspector of Poor Law infirmaries in the metropolitan district. Gradually a few other women were added, until by 1914 there were six all together.[13]

The Education Department also early made use of women inspectors, appointing a "directress of needlework" in elementary schools in 1883 and an "inspectress of cookery and laundry work" in 1890, and later adding a few other women. But the real beginning of the women's inspectorate in the field of education dates from 1904 and the reforms initiated by Sir Robert Morant, permanent secretary to the newly created Board of Education. Morant appointed as chief woman inspector the Hon. Maude Lawrence, a former student at Bedford College who had gained valuable experience by service on the last two London school boards and on the education committee of the London County Council. By 1914 the original group of seven women inspectors employed when Morant took charge had grown to number forty-three.[14]

In no government work were women more successful than as factory inspectors under the Home Office. Agitation for their appointment originated among working women, who felt that women inspectors would understand their problems more readily than male inspectors and could be confided in more easily. Significantly, the chief inspector of factories wrote in 1879: "It is seldom necessary to put a single question to a female." Beginning in 1878 the spokesmen for women at the T.U.C. succeeded in carrying annual resolutions demanding the appointment of women factory inspectors. Soon a number of middle- and upper-class organizations also took up the question, for they saw in factory inspection a new field of social usefulness for educated women. At last, in 1893, Herbert Asquith, then Home Secretary, appointed two women inspectors, although most of his officials considered the step "a terrible proposition," fearing that "the women would get their petticoats in the machines" and might even lose their lives, and feeling that "it would be unseemly that they should go about at night alone in the workshops." In 1897 a special women's branch of the Factory Department was formally constituted under the command of May Abraham, one of the first two women inspectors appointed. Miss Abraham became interested in labour problems through her association with Lady Dilke, for whom she worked as secretary, and had served as an officer of the Women's Trade Union League and done outstanding work as special investigator of women's industries for the royal commission on labour of 1892-94. However, she soon resigned from the service upon her marriage to H. J. Tennant, brother-in-law and formerly private secretary to Asquith, and later a Liberal M.P. and member of Asquith's cabinet. She was succeeded as the women's chief by Adelaide Anderson (later Dame Adelaide). A graduate of Girton, Miss Anderson had lectured on social questions for the Women's Co-operative Guild and had served on the staff of the royal commission on labour before her appointment as a factory inspector in 1894. For twenty-four years she headed the women's branch of the Factory Department, which by 1914 included twenty-one inspectors.[15]

The largest employers of women of inspectoral rank were the newly created National Health Insurance Commission and the Board of Trade Labour Exchanges. In addition, a few scattered women were serving at the Home Office as inspectors of prisons and reformatory schools, as inspectors in the Office of the Public Trustee, and at the Board of Trade as inspectors under the Trade Boards Act.[16]

All women inspectors obtained their positions as men did, being nominated by the heads of departments because of their educational attainments and their special knowledge of the problems with which they would have to deal. For example, those at the Board of Education were usually former teachers or others experienced in school administration, and many were university graduates, while those under the Local Government Board had to have training as doctors, nurses or midwives. Qualifying examinations after nomination were rarely demanded. The Home Office, for example, required that its factory inspectors pass a general qualifying examination on their appointment and, after a two-year probationary period, a special examination in factory law, sanitary science and allied subjects.[17]

Organized separately from men and working under their own officers, women inspectors generally were employed not on ordinary inspectoral duties but only on duties considered to lie within their special sphere of competence. Women employed at the Local Government Board dealt mainly with the care of pauper women and children and the condition of workhouse sick wards and Poor Law infirmaries. Those serving at the Board of Education were responsible for the inspection of girls' and infants' departments and the teaching of domestic subjects in the elementary schools, and for the supervision of girls' secondary schools and of women's teacher-training colleges. Women factory inspectors in theory had the authority to investigate any complaints and prosecute any violations of the Factory Acts and Truck Acts, but in practice they concentrated upon dealing with the complaints and investigating the conditions of women and children in industry. As a result of this policy of segregation, the effectiveness of the women inspectors often depended upon the extent to which their services were requested and utilized by the male inspectors who headed the inspectoral districts into which the country was divided for various administrative purposes. However, after 1908 women factory inspectors, the exception to this general rule, were no longer sent out from London to different parts of the country as needed, but were "planted out" in their own districts with headquarters at Manchester, Birmingham, Glasgow and Belfast. By 1914 only about two hundred women inspectors were employed by the government, but as the MacDonnell Commission on the civil service declared, their importance was out of all proportion to their numbers "by reason of the responsibility of their duties."[18]

For women of exceptional ability and education, the government inspectorate and, to a degree, the service clerical grades were attractive fields of work, while for women of average ability and attainments government positions as typists, telegraphists and telephone operators were equally appealing. There were, in fact, always many more applicants for positions than there were positions to be filled. This was so because of the increasing accessibility of the work, with the waning of patronage and the growth of popular education, and because of its tradition of middle-class respectability. Also, employment in the civil service, compared with employment outside the service, had a number of special advantages to recommend it.

The Working Life of Civil Servants

A great attraction of civil service employment for women, and for men as well, was the security which it offered. Unaffected by the fluctuations and vagaries of the business world outside, civil servants were assured of steady employment at regular rates of pay. Also, they enjoyed almost complete security of tenure unless they were proved guilty of gross misconduct or incompetence, for there was no "spoils system" in Britain.

Another decided advantage enjoyed by civil servants was that their working hours were fixed and relatively short. In the 1870's and '80's, the majority of government offices were open only six hours a day, and a Saturday half-holiday was common if not universal, so that government clerks worked only a thirty-six hour week at most, and even this included the time allowed for a midday meal. In 1890 a forty-two hour week, seven hours on six days including mealtimes, was prescribed for the service clerical grades generally, but in 1910 the Saturday half-holiday was restored, so that the clerks' standard became a thirty-nine hour week inclusive of mealtimes. On the other hand, owing to the nature of their work, the Post Office manipulative grades always worked longer hours than did the clerical grades. By 1913 the standard for the manipulative grades was a forty-eight hour week, eight hours on six days, although workers in supervisory positions sometimes enjoyed a forty-two hour week. Workers in these grades also had a number of special grievances with regard to their hours. They complained of "split duties" and long "covering periods," in extreme cases five spells of duty daily covering as much as fifteen hours, and of the excessive, poorly paid overtime, night duty and Sunday duty required of them. Still, these were largely men's grievances, for women were seldom called upon for long duties or overtime work and were not required to work at night, and women telegraphists did not work on Sundays, although telephone operators did. Naturally men resented the women's favoured position, since it meant worse hours for them.[19]

Civil servants also enjoyed generous provisions for sick leave and for annual holidays. All were entitled when ill to six months' leave on full pay and a further six months on half pay. In addition, Post Office workers could receive free treatment and medicines from the medical officers attached to the department. (The first woman doctor to enter the service of the central government was appointed by the Postmaster-General, Fawcett, as medical officer to the women on the Post Office staff.) Post Office manipulative workers enjoyed two weeks' annual leave during their first five years of service and three weeks yearly thereafter, while those in supervisory positions received twenty-seven days' leave. In the clerical grades of the service, girl clerks received leave of eighteen working days annually and women clerks one calendar month.[20]

Finally, under the Superannuation Act of 1859 civil servants, upon retirement at the age of sixty, received pensions calculated according to the length of their service of up to two-thirds of their final salary. Those who retired because of ill health after ten years' service received pensions calculated at a lower rate, while many of those who retired with less than ten years' service were given gratuities. The Superannuation Act of 1909 made changes in this system. Pensions were to be lower in amount, and the difference between the amounts of the old pensions and the new was to be made up either by cash payments at the time of retirement or by cash payments later to survivors. But women in the service disliked this scheme, feeling that their salaries were so low that they could not afford to accept reduced pensions. As a result of their protests they were excluded from the operation of the new Act, and not until the Superannuation Act of 1935 were they brought under the same pension provisions as men.[21]

Obvious as were the advantages enjoyed by civil servants, there were major disadvantages in their work as well. The most important of these was low pay, and in this connection the special nature of the service contrasted with the outside world of industry and commerce must be borne in mind. The service is a non-profit organization supported by the taxpayers and therefore its employees, unlike those outside, cannot hope to benefit by expanding production and increasing profits. Indeed, as the civil service expands, it is actually in the public interest for the government to restrain its expenditure on wages, which must be paid out of public moneys. In the later years of the nineteenth century, prices and the standard of living generally were rising, while the state was assuming new duties and increasing the number of its employees. "The Treasury found its wages bill swelling tremendously, and, quite naturally, it gasped." The government now began to concentrate upon keeping down the level of pay, with the result that the real wages of civil servants fell more rapidly than did real wages generally.[22]

One device which the government adopted to keep down wages was the "downgrading" of clerical work, that is, the introduction of new grades of workers to perform at lower pay some of the duties of higher grades. The plan of the Trevelyan-Northcote report of 1854, endorsed by the royal commission of 1875 under Lyon Playfair (later Lord Playfair) and by the royal commission of 1886 under Sir Matthew Ridley, was that administrative and clerical workers in the civil service would be divided into two grades. The upper grade, known successively as the Higher Division and then as the First Division, was to be recruited from among university graduates and perform the top-level duties of government. The second grade, the Lower Division or Second Division, was to be recruited from among men with an "ordinary commercial education" to perform the more routine and clerical duties. Unfortunately, this two-grade organization of the service lacked flexibility, and much of the work which should have been done by Second Division clerks was considered to be of too low quality for such a well-paid grade.

In these circumstances, new lower-paid clerical grades made their appearance in the service, among them the women's grades. For example, in 1896 a grade of male "assistant clerks" was introduced to do the more mechanical work of Second Division clerks, and a grade of male "sup-

plementary" or "intermediate" clerks to do work in the higher ranges
considered too good for Second Division clerks but not good enough for
the First Division. In like manner the grade of women clerks, established
in 1881, was employed on work previously performed by Second Division
clerks, and it was stated baldly in evidence before the Playfair Commission that by the employment of these women "the public gets a very cheap
service indeed." It certainly did, for while male Second Division clerks
received salaries of £80-350, women clerks, at the time of their establishment, received only £65-150. Also, women typists were paid at much
lower rates than the men and boy copyists they replaced. By 1914 women
typists received 20-26s. weekly or roughly £52-68 yearly, and shorthand-
typists 28-30s. a week or about £72-78 a year, compared with men typists
in one department receiving £3-4 a week, or £156-208 a year, at piece
rates, and men shorthand-writers in various departments earning £104-
300 yearly.[23]

While men complained of women's undercutting of their salaries,
women clerks had a grievance in the undercutting of their own grade.
Women sorters were introduced in the Post Office in 1883 to perform
such simple duties as sorting, folding and binding papers, but gradually
they assumed some of the clerical duties previously performed at much
higher salaries by women clerks and by men in comparable grades. By
1906 the women sorters' scale of pay was 14-30s. weekly or about £38-78
yearly. In comparison, first- and second-class women clerks were receiving
£55-130 yearly and the comparable grade of male paper-keepers were
receiving 18-45s. a week. The grade of girl clerks was established in
1897 to perform the simpler duties of women clerks, but despite their low
salaries, only £35-40 a year, the government actually effected little economy since after two years' service the girls could become women clerks
enjoying salaries appropriate to that grade. Women clerks were especially
irate when, in 1911, the Postmaster-General, Herbert Samuel, proposed
to create a new grade of "female assistant clerks" who would perform
work that according to one Post Office official "did not require any
judgment or thinking or anything else," who would be employed eight
hours a day instead of the clerks' seven-hour day, and who would receive
weekly wages amounting to only about three-fourths the pay of women
clerks. So fiercely did the women clerks oppose the proposal to create this
new grade that settlement of the matter was postponed until after the report of the Holt Committee on the Post Office in 1913.[24]

The introduction of new low-paid grades did not obtain among the
Post Office manipulative workers as among the service clerical grades,
but here too the undercutting of men's salaries by women was found. By
1906 the pay of telegraphists in London was 20-62s. for men and 18-38s.
for women, while in the provinces men received 18-56s. and women 15-35s.
Men claimed that in some places the Post Office was actually curtailing
the hours of business, since women did not work at night, in order to save
money by employing women in place of men. The pay of women telephone
operators was considerably below that of women telegraphists and also

that of male telephone operators. By 1906 women telephone operators in London received 7s. a week during their training, compared with the 20s. a week paid to men, and as established workers received 17-26s. weekly compared with 25-36s. for men.[25]

In the inspectorate the employment of women was traceable not to considerations of economy but to official recognition of new social problems and public pressure upon the government. But here too women's salaries were comparatively very low, often only about half those of men entrusted with similar duties. For example, by 1914 the "senior lady factory inspectors" at the Home Office received salaries of £300-400, while their duties corresponded to those of male superintending inspectors receiving £600-750.[26]

In short, women in nearly every grade of the civil service and in nearly every government department received less pay than men. There were, in fact, only three exceptions to this general rule: women clerks and male assistant clerks, men and women members of the four National Insurance Commissions, and men and women clerks employed by the Board of Trade Labour Exchanges received the same salaries. But in the last case men could rise automatically to a higher class and maximum salary, while women could rise to the higher class and maximum only if they were needed to fill supervisory positions.[27]

In addition to "downgrading" and "undercutting," the government also employed large numbers of "unestablished" workers as opposed to "established" civil servants in order to keep down its wages bill. Unestablished workers received lower salaries than established workers. For example, in 1906 men employed in London as unestablished telegraphists could rise to a maximum weekly wage of only 45s. compared with the 62s. maximum for established men, and unestablished women could rise to only 30s., compared with the 38s. maximum for established women. Also, unestablished workers did not receive the same sick leave and annual leave with pay as did established workers, and they were not entitled to pensions. Women clerks in the Post Office, women typists and some of the first women inspectors were first employed as unestablished workers, although they later attained permanent status. The Post Office employed large numbers of unestablished telegraphists, while many clerks in departments other than the Post Office were unestablished.[28]

Yet another device which enabled the government to keep down its wages bill was "substitution." This meant that workers were employed "temporarily" on supervisory duties appropriate to a higher grade or class but were not promoted to the higher position and were not allowed sufficient extra pay for performing the higher duties. For example, Post Office workers who were employed temporarily on the duties of a higher grade received the minimum pay of this grade only after six months' time, and the amount of extra pay they could earn in this way was limited to £20 a year.[29]

Finally, the government resorted to a practice known to its workers as "speeding up." That is, their duties were becoming increasingly complex and arduous, but they were not receiving compensatory pay increases. Post Office counter clerks in particular complained of the increasing number of postal regulations which they had to know and enforce, and a special grievance was that they had to make good any losses they incurred in money transactions over the counter, even though such losses often resulted from the pressure of the work rather than from the workers' ignorance or carelessness. One woman postal worker reported having had £1 deducted from her weekly pay to cover losses, while a friend of hers had lost £10 in one day. In addition, the Post Office manipulative workers were liable to fines and to stoppage of their annual increments and also to extra unpaid duty by way of punishment for mistakes they made during their work. Another example of speeding up, so telephone operators claimed, was that too many trunk lines were being assigned to one person, and they resented the official system of dividing up the staff into teams and of computing the average answering times of each, with reprimands for those proving to be the slowest.[30] In short, civil servants generally claimed that they were not being paid enough in view of the amount and quality of work they had to perform.

After low pay, the greatest grievance of civil servants was that of their limited prospects of promotion, and here women were at a special disadvantage for their chances of rising to higher, better-paid positions were considerably more restricted than men's. Men, in theory at least, could rise from one grade of the service to another until they reached the First Division, the highest grade. On the other hand, the women's clerical and typing grades were "watertight compartments," strictly separate and distinct from comparable men's grades. As a result, women could not obtain promotion to higher grades of the service like men but were restricted to the supervisory classes within their own grades. This bore especially heavily upon women clerks and typists employed outside the Post Office who, being scattered in small groups among a variety of departments, had only a very limited number of supervisory positions open to them and therefore almost no prospect of promotion. Yet even in the Post Office, where many women in the clerical grades were employed and where the number of supervisory positions was consequently much larger, the rate of promotion was very slow. In one year only eighteen women out of 281 rose from the second class to the first class, which represented a mere 12 per cent of the total staff. In like manner, the great majority of first-class women clerks, 75 per cent, remained stationary at the maximum for their class, the number of promotions from their class to the supervisory class of principal clerks averaging only three a year. Women sorters had a special grievance with regard to promotion because, although there were a few "senior sorters" in their grade receiving special supervisory allowances, most supervisory positions were held by women clerks. In addition, the salaries of women in supervisory positions were much lower than the salaries of men in comparable positions. For example, by 1914 women superintendents of typists received a flat pay rate, without annual increments, of 35s. weekly or £91 a year, and chief superintendents

INVENTION FOR ATTRACTING THE NOTICE OF POST-OFFICE LADIES.

(Patent applied for.)

of typists received usually 40s. weekly or £104 a year, while men in such supervisory positions might earn £250-350.[31]

Even where women were not segregated from men but worked in grades with them and performed the same duties, as in the case of telegraphists, women were not eligible for promotion to all the supervisory classes within these grades. Instead, men workers were supervised only by men, women by women, and the higher positions were accordingly strictly divided between the sexes. Also, the number of higher positions for women was not so large in proportion to the number of workers employed as was the number of men's supervisory posts; that is, women supervisors were responsible for larger numbers of workers than men supervisors. But at the same time, women supervisors received much lower salaries than men of equivalent status. For example, by 1906 there were for telegraphists in London four supervisory classes for men, with salaries ranging from £170 up to £500, while there were only three supervisory classes for women, with salaries of £100-300; in the provinces, there were five classes of supervisory positions for men below the rank of assistant postmasters, with salaries of £100-500, and for women only two classes of supervisory posts with salaries of £85-170.[32]

In this connection mention must be made of a special disability under which women laboured and which affected not only their prospects of promotion but also their chances of employment generally, namely, the imposition of a marriage bar. As early as 1875 the Post Office laid down a rule that in future only single women and widows would be employed, women who married being compelled to leave the service. In 1894, when the grade of women typists was established, the Treasury regulations governing their conditions of service contained the specific provision that they must retire from the service upon marriage, but allowed the payment to them of marriage gratuities. Women who had served at least six years before their marriage received one month's salary for every year of service, up to a maximum of one year's salary. The following year the Treasury extended the right to receive marriage gratuities to all established women in the service, provided that their resignation upon marriage was required by general departmental regulations, and thereupon the marriage bar was almost universally adopted throughout the service. Interestingly, the imposition of the marriage bar reflected the government's concern to save money, for if women were forced to retire from the service upon marriage, they would neither remain at work long enough to rise very high in the salary scale nor become eligible for pensions.[33]

Women themselves differed in opinion about the marriage bar. Those in the lower ranks employed on routine work, such as typists and telephone operators, generally favoured the marriage bar. Their work was not so absorbing nor their pay so good that they wanted to continue in the service after marriage, and they feared that if the bar were abolished, marriage gratuities would likewise be discontinued. Also, they felt that while they were still in the service their chances of promotion would be materially reduced if married women continued to work and to compete for the higher positions. On the other hand, women in the higher ranks, such as clerks and inspectors, were more likely to want to continue their work after marriage and to resent the marriage bar.[34]

Despite, then, the advantages which they enjoyed as members of a "protected industry," civil servants, and women in particular, had a number of very real grievances. Consequently it was but a matter of time until they, like workers outside the service, began to organize in unions and assert their claims to better conditions of employment.

Trade Unionism in the Civil Service

Civil service trade unionism developed first in the Post Office, where conditions were especially conducive to organization. In the first place, the working conditions of postal employees were generally poorer than those of other service grades, and workers here felt a greater need for active unions than did those in other branches of the service. "Low wages, long hours, inconvenient attendance, stupid supervision, and irritating secrecy . . . all combined in varying degrees to keep the post office in a chronic state of turmoil."[35] Secondly, when it came to organizing, postal employees enjoyed the advantage over other service grades of sheer force of concentrated numbers. The Post Office employed a large army of workers, all with common grievances and all subject to one master, the Postmaster-General.

As early as the 1850's postal employees attempted to combine to protest against their working conditions, but the department dealt severely with agitators, often cancelling their annual salary increments, dismissing some, and prohibiting public meetings. There was a prevailing prejudice against service trade unionism not only among Post Office superiors but also among department heads generally and in Parliament. However, following passage of the government-sponsored Trade Union Act of 1871, the Liberal Postmaster-General declared that he could not forbid unions in his department so long as their rules were "unobjectionable."[36]

The next decade saw a number of attempts and failures of workers to organize effectively. Not until 1881 did the first stable combination of postal employees appear, the Postal Telegraph Clerks' Association, which originally catered chiefly for workers in London. In 1887 the U. K. Postal Clerks' Association was organized to present the case of its members, chiefly provincial workers, before the Royal (Ridley) Commission on Civil Establishments, then hearing evidence. These two postal unions also organized the telephone operators in government service. From their beginning the unions admitted women to membership on an equal footing with men and allowed them special representation on their executives in proportion to their numbers. By 1900 the two unions together claimed about 8,000 members. In 1913 they amalgamated to form the Postal and Telegraph Clerks' Association. Meanwhile, in 1890, letter sorters had organized the Fawcett Association, unique among service unions in bearing the name of an individual, that of the Liberal Postmaster-General who had done so much during his tenure of office to improve the conditions of his workers. In 1891 the Postmen's Federation was organized. By 1900 the Fawcett Association had over 3,000 members and the Postmen's Federation more than 23,000. After the war, in 1919, these three principal postal associations amalgamated to form the giant Union of Post Office Workers, boasting 90,000 members.[37]

In comparison with the postal unions, associations of service clerical workers were slow to develop. Like his fellow outside the service, the government clerk tended to regard trade unionism as "vulgar." He did his duty "in the light of the high though rather dry, ethical tradition of the governing classes, and he did not talk shop."[38] Moreover, except for those employed in the Post Office, service clerical workers faced the practical obstacle to organization of being scattered in relatively small numbers among a wide variety of departments. Still, the perpetual downgrading of their work and the consequent reduction in pay scales and stagnation of promotion aroused such deep discontent that at length the service clerical grades followed the example of postal workers in combining.

Unlike those in the Post Office manipulative grades, women in the clerical grades did not organize in unions together with men. Associations throughout the service were based on different grades of workers, and with the exception of telegraphists and telephone operators, women civil servants were employed in grades separate from men. Moreover, many men in the service were openly hostile to women workers, fearing to be driven out by their cheapness, and consequently were loath to join forces with them.[39]

Among the men's clerical associations which appeared, catering for general, all-service grades, were the Second Division Clerks' Association (1890), the Assistant Clerks' Association (1903), and the Boy Clerks' Association (1911). First Division clerks and the intermediate male clerks remained unorganized. In addition to these general associations, there were a number of associations catering for departmental clerical classes.[40]

The first of the separate women's associations to appear was the Association of Post Office Women Clerks, founded in 1897. The immediate cause of its organization was the sudden reduction in the women's pay, their minimum being lowered from £65 to £55 and their annual increments from £3 to £2 10s. in order to bring them into line with the newly created grade of male assistant clerks. Within a few years the women's Association boasted 1,300 members and was publishing its own journal, *Association Notes*. Gradually, a number of similar associations grew up, representing women clerks in other departments besides the Post Office. In 1903 the Women Sorters' Association was formed, and affiliated with the Fawcett Association of male sorters. The immediate cause of this union's appearance was the women's failure to win a hearing before the Bradford Committee, which was then studying postal workers' conditions of employment and which refused to hear the evidence of unorganized workers. Within only two years this new women's Association had won for its members an increase in their minimum pay. About the same time the female Civil Service Typists' Association was organized to protest the higher pay of men typists, and it soon included about 90 per cent of those eligible for membership. In addition to these service associations, the National Union of Clerks and the Association of Women Clerks and Secretaries also tried to organize women clerical workers in the civil service, but without much success until the great influx into the service of temporary women clerks during World War I. In 1913 all of the women's clerical associations in the service amalgamated to form the Federation of Women Clerks, which in turn, three years later, joined with the Civil Service Typists' Association to form the Federation of Women Civil Servants. By 1914 there were an estimated 13,656 women members of service clerical unions.[41]

Women in the inspectorate apparently formed no associations in this period, probably because they did not share the attitude toward organization of other grades of civil servants. By and large they were women dedicated to a cause, looking upon their work not merely as a means of earning a living but as a career which they had chosen, and for which they had been chosen, because of their special qualifications. Moreover, although their work was very arduous, women inspectors were among the most highly paid working women in the country.

By the last years of the nineteenth century trade unionism in the civil service was fairly well established, especially among postal workers. It remained to be seen how effective the unions would be in winning a sympathetic hearing for their claims, especially their demands for better pay.

The Hearing of Civil Servants' Grievances

The civil servants' traditional method of agitating for better working conditions was the presentation of petitions and memorials to departmental superiors and, if possible, directly to the Treasury. This was all very respectable but not particularly effective. Much depended upon the government in power at the time, the Liberals tending to be more sympathetic to service unions and their demands than the Conservatives, while much also depended upon the personal views of the individual department heads. Consequently Post Office workers, like trade unionists outside the service, hit upon the expedient of taking their complaints to members of Parliament and of canvassing candidates in Parliamentary elections.

The Liberal Postmaster-General Henry Fawcett was the first department head to meet with the representatives of a civil service union, that of the telegraphists in 1881, and to encourage unions he gave permission for them to hold meetings on Post Office premises. Another sympathetic department head was Henry Charles Raikes, Conservative Postmaster-General from 1886 until his death in 1891, who made considerable concessions to his workers with regard to longer holidays and sick leave with full pay, payment for overtime and Sunday work, and salary increases, although these actually satisfied no group of workers. Raikes's successor was Sir James Fergusson, described as a "martinet," who refused to consider the postal unions' demands, prohibited postal employees from canvassing Parliamentary candidates in the upcoming general election, and took disciplinary action against union officials who defied his order, in the interval between the election and the actual takeover of office by the victorious Liberals.[42]

As a result of the unions' campaign for a Parliamentary inquiry into Post Office conditions, the new Liberal government agreed in 1895 to the appointment of a departmental committee which was headed by Lord Tweedmouth, the Lord Privy Seal, and which reported early in 1897, following the Conservatives' return to power. Interestingly, the Tweedmouth Committee's decision to hear only witnesses representing associations of postal workers encouraged recruitment by the unions. The Committee made a number of useful suggestions for improvements which were later adopted, such as those relating to the reduction of "split duties" and long "covering periods," and payment for duty at night and on Sundays and holidays. But to the unions' great disgust, the Committee recommended that annual leave be curtailed, suggested the abolition of the weekly "risk allowance" paid to counter clerks in addition to their regular wages to help cover losses in transactions over the counter, proposed only small pay increases, and acquitted department officials of imposing excessive punishments for breaches of departmental rules. The department itself refused to consider any kind of collective bargaining with the unions.[43]

To consolidate their forces for further action, the four chief postal unions—the Postal Telegraph Clerks' Association, the U. K. Postal Clerks' Association, the Fawcett Association and the Postmen's Federation—set up in 1898 a joint committee, although their alliance was not an easy one. Collectively and individually the unions lobbied for yet another Parliamentary inquiry. "Probably no agitation for Parliamentary action has been so vigourously and ruthlessly pressed," and few M.P.'s escaped badgering. Those sympathetic to the unions were "generously primed with facts and figures for use in the House," while those unsympathetic were appealed to for fair treatment or threatened as to their fate at the next election. Some M.P.'s actually appealed to the Postmaster-General for "protection"![44]

In 1903 the Conservative government agreed to the appointment of a "business committee" headed by Sir Edward Bradford, Chief of the Metropolitan Police, to decide on postal employees' claims. Like the Tweedmouth Committee, the Bradford Committee refused to hear the evidence of any but representatives of organized workers, further encouraging the formation of unions, among them the Women Sorters' Association. Now, so far had opinion swung in the workers' favour and so favourable to them was the Bradford Committee's report, especially its recommendations for substantial wage increases, that the government tried to suppress it. The report was finally published, but the government drastically reduced its recommended wage increases on the ground that postal wages compared favourably with those in similar occupations outside the service. Also, Lord Stanley, then Postmaster-General, denounced as "blackmail" the postal unions' canvassing and harassing of M.P.'s, and his workers were delighted when he was defeated by a Labour candidate at the general election of 1906, which resulted in a landslide victory for the Liberals supported by Labour. Over half the M.P.'s elected were pledged to support the unions' demand for still another committee of inquiry.[45]

With the Liberal government in office, the new Postmaster-General, Sydney Buxton, announced his approval of the postal associations, declaring that "far from the recognition of trade unions leading to friction . . . the stronger and more representative the associations become, the less would be the friction, and the more easy it would be to arrive at a conclusion satisfactory to both sides." He agreed to deal with any duly constituted staff association or federation, both on matters affecting the particular grades which they represented and on those affecting the service as a whole.[46]

Buxton also agreed to the appointment of a select committee of the Commons to study Post Office conditions under the chairmanship of C. E. H. Hobhouse, himself Postmaster-General in later years. Like the Tweedmouth Committee, the Hobhouse Committee made a number of useful suggestions for the benefit of postal employees with regard to night duty, payment for "substitute duty," restriction of postal clerks' liability for counter losses, and the increase of special leave granted workers which enabled them to participate in trade-union activities. Still, the unions were angry at the Committee's rejection of their demand for a seven-hour day or forty-two hour week instead of the existing forty-eight hour standard. They also resented the Committee's refusal to recommend restoration of the annual leave which workers had enjoyed before the report of the Tweedmouth Committee, three weeks' leave after five years' service and a calendar month thereafter, the same as for the service clerical grades (although soon after, this amount of leave was in fact granted). Even more galling to workers were the Committee's recommendations for pay increases which were tiny compared with the unions' demands and which left women's pay still out of all proportion to men's. For example, the Postal Telegraph Clerks' Association had asked a scale for women, after five years' service or beginning at about age twenty-one, of 26-50s., whereas the Committee recommended a scale of 24-40s. for women and 26-65s. for men. Nevertheless, Buxton maintained that he could accept but not go beyond the Hobhouse Committee's recommendations.[47]

Meanwhile, members of the service clerical associations generally "eschewed the violence and occasional vulgarity of postal agitation." They continued to use the time-worn technique of appeals to departmental superiors, usually ineffective since no one department head was competent to take action on grades of workers employed in more than one department, and since department heads generally frowned upon their workers' direct appeals to the Treasury. But following Buxton's endorsement of postal unions in 1906, other Liberal ministers also recognized their workers' unions and agreed to deal with their officials. As a result, seventeen new civil service associations sprang up in 1906, and by 1914 a total of seventy-three were in existence. Still, the Treasury had taken no official stand regarding treatment of these associations and generally rejected their claims on the ground that existing conditions were satisfactory.[48]

In these circumstances the feeling grew among civil servants that those in all grades and departments must unite in order to win a hearing for their continuing grievances. Accordingly, the Civil Service Federation was formed in 1911 by a conference of twenty-two unions and federations which represented the great majority of organized civil servants. Within two years' time the Federation boasted a membership of about 102,000, including between 9,000 and 10,000 women. As a result of the Federation's agitation, the government agreed in 1912 to the appointment of another select committee, under R. D. Holt, to study the special problems of the Post Office, and to the appointment of a royal commission under Lord MacDonnell to survey the rest of the civil service.[49]

During their investigations, both the MacDonnell Commission and the Holt Committee were forced to consider the special problems of women in the civil service. Indeed, their deliberations and reports furnish a good summing-up not of official opinion only but also of public opinion generally on the changed position and problems of middle-class working women. Both bodies heard the evidence of twelve women witnesses. The Holt Committee, like the Hobhouse Committee before it, took evidence from independent spokesmen for women workers as well as from representatives of the women's associations. The MacDonnell Commission heard representatives of the women's associations and also a number of eminent women from outside the service. Among these were Miss R. Oldham, representative of the Head Mistresses' Association; Miss Lilian M. Faithfull, Miss Beale's successor as principal of the Cheltenham Ladies' College; Miss Emily Penrose (later Dame Emily), a distinguished classical scholar, formerly principal of Bedford and of Royal Holloway Colleges and at the time principal of Somerville College; and Mrs. Henry Sidgwick of Newnham. Also, the MacDonnell Commission included among its nineteen members two women, Miss Elizabeth Haldane and Mrs. Lucy Deane Streatfeild, who until her marriage had been a factory inspector and in that capacity had made the special inquiry about shop assistants for the Truck Committee of 1908.

The Association of Post Office Women Clerks, supported by the male Second Division Clerks' Association, put forth the strongest claims for women in the service, demanding before both the MacDonnell Commission and the Holt Committee that all grades of the civil service be opened to women on equal terms with men, including the payment to them of equal salaries and the abolition of the marriage bar. Others of the women's spokesmen did not go nearly so far in their demands. Women clerks outside the Post Office asked only for equal treatment with women clerks in the Post Office. For example, the Board of Education paid its women clerks salaries of £65-110 and there were only two higher positions open to them at salaries of £115-140 and £140-190, while in the Post Office, following the upward revision of their pay scales by the Hobhouse Committee, women second-class and first-class clerks received salaries of £65-140 and could rise to the class of principal clerk with salaries of £150-200 and to the rank of superintendent with maximum salaries of £400. Likewise, the Women Sorters' Association merely claimed for its members equal pay with women telegraphists, and also asked that they be supervised not by women clerks but by a new supervisory class of women sorters. The Postal Telegraph Clerks' Association echoed before the Holt Committee the claim of the women Post Office clerks' association to equality for women in the service generally and, more specifically, demanded a greatly improved pay scale for telegraphists which would be the same for women as for men. Not going quite so far as this, the U. K. Postal Clerks' Association asked a pay scale which was lower than that demanded by the other union and under which women would receive the same minimum pay as men but rise to a lower maximum.[50]

With regard to women in the service, the official investigators had first to deal with the question of whether they should be admitted to the men's grades of the service with the opportunity of rising to the highest positions. In this connection the MacDonnell Commission considered the matter of the inherent capabilities of women. Nearly all of the departmental spokesmen giving evidence declared that although women in the service were doing their present work exceedingly well, they were not capable of performing more responsible duties. This opinion was supported by representatives of the universities who gave their conclusions based upon their observations of men and women students, and who mostly claimed that men possessed greater initiative and originality and were better able to bear strain than women, that it was only the "exceptional" woman who would be able to do administrative work in the government. Only the representatives of London and St. Andrews declared that if higher positions in the service were open to women, there would be capable women a-plenty to fill them.[51]

On the other hand, the women's spokesmen contended that because they were permanently relegated to routine and monotonous work with no chance of promotion to more responsible positions, women had no incentive or opportunity to demonstrate their real abilities, and their mental efficiency and even their health suffered. In addition, they claimed, prospects in the service were too poor to attract women of liberal education and exceptional ability who were best qualified for higher positions. The women's representatives were also quick to point out that the case of the Post Office telegraphists proved that women could measure up to men's standard of efficiency, for men and women took the same examination for admission to the service and women performed exactly the same work as men with the exception of night duty (following the recommendations of the Hobhouse Committee women had been liable to Sunday duty like men).[52]

But government spokesmen generally did not oppose the admission of women to the men's grades in the service because of their unshakeable

conviction of women's basic inferiority to men. Rather, they seemed nerv-
ously afraid of two practical obstacles. The first of these was the question
of open competitive examinations. In this connection Stanley Leathes,
the first Civil Service Commissioner, declared before the MacDonnell
Commission: "I cannot altogether keep out of my mind that all open com-
petitions are bad for women. . . . It is a very revolutionary proposal." To
this Lord MacDonnell replied: "We are living in revolutionary times."
Leathes was then forced to admit that men and women telegraphists and
men and women factory inspectors took the same examinations without ill
effects. Interestingly, some of the women witnesses heard likewise opposed
open competitive examinations, although not because they believed that
these injured women's health nor because it was improper for men and
women to take examinations together, as was often claimed. The real
difficulty, according to Emily Penrose, was that written examinations
could not test such important qualities as tact, practical judgment and the
like, and both she and the representative of the Head Mistresses' Association proposed alternative plans, such as recruitment of women from
among students at recognized secondary schools and at the universities,
followed by a qualifying examination.[53]

Much more serious than the examination problem as an obstacle to
opening men's grades of the service to women was the question of "aggregation" versus segregation, that is, the employment of women together
with men in government offices as opposed to their employment separately
from men. On this subject Leathes declared: "I think it would be rather
awkward to have men and women working together, shoulder to shoulder
in the same Department. I do not wish to see it. If we think of employing
women, we always think, is there a room where we can put them by themselves?" Dating back to the time of the employment of the first women
clerks in the service, this official policy of segregation had a profound
adverse effect on women's prospects in the service. They could be employed only where there was a large amount of work to be done and where
this work, as in the Post Office, could be parcelled out into separate blocks
handled by workers whose duties were not interchangeable. There was
little opportunity for women's employment in the smaller departments,
which required considerable flexibility in apportioning their workers'
duties and which were often hard pressed to find for women workers "a
room where we can put them by themselves." Moreover, the policy of
segregation furnished a convenient justification for women's lower pay,
since the duties on which they were employed separately from men were
always said to be less responsible and less valuable than men's, while the
cost of furnishing separate accommodations for women workers was said
to be met by the economies effected through their lower pay.[54]

Again and again the members of the MacDonnell Commission sympathetic to women's claims demonstrated the illogicality of the official
policy of segregation. Why, they asked, was the employment of men and
women together in government offices more impracticable or improper
than their employment together in business offices outside the service

or together in the Post Office on telegraph work? The Commission also brought to light an interesting example of the devious official mind. The Hobhouse Committee had discovered that in the Savings Bank Department of the Post Office, men and women were performing identical duties but at different rates of pay. As a result, the Department's work was reorganized by transferring to men all the warrant work and to women all the ledger work. Sir Alexander King, Secretary to the Post Office, admitted to the MacDonnell Commission that the reason for this reorganization was to enable officials to say truthfully that men and women were not doing "equal work." Asked by Lord MacDonnell whether this was a "very substantial reason," King had to reply: "No, not very."[55]

In addition to considering the admission of women to the men's grades of the service, the two investigating bodies studied a second major question relating to women, that is, whether they should receive equal pay with men doing the same or similar work. This was somewhat of an academic question for the MacDonnell Commission, since women in the service generally, owing to the official policy of segregation, were not, technically at least, doing equal work with men. But it was a question of immediate and practical concern to the Holt Committee studying the special problems of the Post Office, since women in the manipulative grades, although doing exactly the same work as men, were paid so much less. Women appearing before the MacDonnell Commission vigourously debated the question of equal pay. They contested the basic assumption regarding pay on which the government seemed to operate, that women simply needed less money than men, and maintained that workers should be paid on the basis of the work done and not on the basis of their supposed needs. Married men in the service did not necessarily receive higher pay than the unmarried, while women might have heavy financial responsibilities like men, especially widows with children who returned to work. Before the Holt Committee the Postal Telegraph Clerks' Association stoutly maintained that the pay of some of its women members was not even a living wage. Indeed, the Post Office itself seemed to provide confirmation of this claim. It had instituted a regulation requiring its younger women employees to live with their parents, guardians or relatives or with friends, although department spokesmen admitted that the regulation "was not enforced by dismissal and that enquiries were not made as to whether it was being carried out." Finally, the women argued that the difference in their pay caused mutual distrust and suspicion between men and women, and that this was prejudicial to the general efficiency of government departments.[56]

Spokesmen for the government departments sought to justify women's unequal pay on the ground that women's services generally were less valuable than men's for several reasons, but in each case their arguments were countered by those of the women's supporters. Post Office spokesmen admitted that women manipulative workers did the same work as men but pointed out that since women performed no night duty their employment meant worse hours for men, who must be paid more. On the other hand, the women's spokesmen argued that only social prejudice respected by the government barred women from night duty, which could even be considered desirable. The pressure of work at night was much less than during the day, and men on night duty worked only forty-two hours a week instead of forty-eight and received extra pay as well. Government spokesmen also argued that women took more sick leave than men, and that if they received equal pay with men there would be no economic advantage in employing them. In reply, the women's representatives declared that there was a direct correlation between the greater amount of sickness among women and their having less money than men to spend on food, clothing and recreation, while they often had also some of the routine work of housekeeping to do. In any case, women's average sick leave was only about thirteen days annually, compared with eight days for men, which hardly warranted the wide discrepancies in pay. Finally, officials argued that because women retired from the service upon marriage they never gained the long experience and full efficiency that men did, while the government had the expense of always training new women to replace those who retired. This argument, according to the women's supporters, was patently illogical. Women's retirement from the service upon marriage was compulsory, not voluntary, so that official regulations rather than the employment of women in itself caused the expense involved in the constant training of new workers. In any case, only a tiny proportion of the total number of women employed, 2 to 3 per cent, left the service each year because of marriage.[57]

The women's case had been ably presented, but the report of the Mac-Donnell Commission was very disappointing from the women's point of view. With regard to the women's claim for wider opportunities of employment in the civil service, the Commission stated that it would not be legitimate to open the service freely to women merely to provide them with careers, this in reply to some of the evidence presented to the effect that university women had difficulty finding positions worthy of their qualifications outside of the teaching profession. Instead, the Commission declared, the sole object of recruitment should be to provide the most efficient public service possible, consistent with both economy and satisfactory conditions of service. Further, the Commission maintained that the difference between the sexes could not be ignored in recruiting for the service and that "the evidence shows that in power of sustained work, in the continuity of service, and in adaptability to varying service conditions, the advantage lies with men."[58]

The Commission was generally unsympathetic to women's special complaints. On the question of aggregation versus segregation, the Commission declared: "The indiscriminate employment of men and women in one and the same branch raises a number of questions of discipline and of convenience, no one of which may present any very serious, still less any insuperable difficulty, but of which the cumulative effect leads to some embarrassment and to some expense; and, as a general rule, we see no sufficient reason for incurring either." The Commission likewise approved continuation of the marriage bar, believing that "the responsibilities of married life are normally incompatible with the devotion of a woman's whole-time and unimpaired energy to the Public Service." As for women's complaint about the routine and monotonous nature of their work, the Commission maintained that almost everyone could voice the same complaint, and that at least civil servants had the advantage of relatively short working hours with leisure time to cultivate outside interests. Finally, with regard to women's limited prospects of promotion, the Commission believed that this problem was "less formidable" for them than for men, since they always might marry and leave the service and since, if they did not marry, their financial responsibilities for others tended to decrease as they grew older.[59]

In short, the MacDonnell Commission felt that women generally were less competent than men, that they should not be employed together with men, and that their special grievances were not of great weight. Consequently, the Commission did not recommend that women be admitted to the three new men's grades which it proposed should be established: a Junior Clerical Class, to replace the existing boy clerks and assistant clerks; a Senior Clerical Class, to replace the Second Division and intermediate clerks; and an Administrative Class for the highest positions, analogous to the existing First Division.

Within the existing framework of women's employment in the service, the Commission recommended for women clerks and typists certain changes in their conditions of employment. Women clerks in all departments should, as they had requested, be treated equally with women clerks in the Post Office, receiving minimum salaries of £65 and higher pay for supervisory positions. Women typists should be recruited by open competitive examinations rather than by nomination and qualifying examinations, their pay should be improved, and they should be eligible for promotion to the grade of women clerks. These changes, the Commission believed, would lead to wider employment of women as clerks and typists, a desirable result because, owing to the nature of their work and the remuneration offered, a better class of women than of men could be recruited.[60]

The MacDonnell Commission also believed that there were many competent and experienced women with knowledge of special subjects, such as the care and education of children, the administration of the Poor Law, and industrial conditions and wages, who could be employed with benefit to the service in positions from which they were then excluded and in departments where they were then insufficiently represented. As examples, the Commission pointed out that only forty-three women were employed in higher positions at the Board of Education, only eighteen at the Home Office, and eleven at the Local Government Board. While not presuming "to criticize in detail the requirements of a particular staff," the Commission could not "regard the employment of so small a number [of women] . . . as sufficient for the full discharge of duties of such grave importance." Accordingly, the Commission urged that the Treasury, together with heads of government departments and competent women advisers, determine which administrative posts were suitable for specially qualified women. These women should not, however, take the regular competitive examinations for the proposed new Administrative Class but be nominated for positions on the basis of their university and other achievements. However, a minority of the Commission, including its two women members, dissented from this recommendation, agreeing with the "weighty evidence" heard that the exclusion of women from men's examinations was not "satisfactory or just," and holding that although admission of women to Administrative Class examinations might then be inexpedient, it should not be regarded as permanently so.[61]

Finally, on the question of equal pay the MacDonnell Commission proved surprisingly liberal. The Commission realized that existing differences between men's and women's salaries had not resulted from a general consideration of the problem, citing as an example the fact that highly qualified women inspectors received only about half the pay of men. In rather turgid prose the Commission declared that where the character and conditions of women's work "approximate to identity with the character and conditions of work performed by men, the pay of women should approximate to equality with that of men." The Commission recommended that the Treasury conduct a general inquiry regarding salaries with the object of removing inequalities between men and women not based on proved differences in efficiency. However, a minority of the Commission maintained that women's pay should be lower than men's even if their work were of equal value, on the grounds that women outside the service received lower pay than men, that men were breadwinners and a pay scale adequate for them would be excessive for women, and that equal pay would hinder women's employment because there would be no advantage to the government in employing them instead of men.[62]

Meanwhile, the Holt Committee had gone over much the same ground as the Hobhouse Committee, and now made a number of useful recommendations, subsequently adopted, regarding such perennial grievances as substitute duty, Sunday duty, long covering periods, overtime work, and liability for counter losses. But like its predecessor, the Holt Committee rejected the postal workers' claim to a forty-two hour week including mealtimes and to extended annual leave, recommending instead a forty-five hour week excluding mealtimes and extended leave only for telephone operators to bring them into line with other manipulative workers.[63]

After considering the main problem before it, that of Post Office wages, the Holt Committee concluded that postal workers suffered no disadvantage compared with workers outside the service and pointed out that there was no difficulty in recruiting enough workers. Consequently, the Committee blithely ignored the general demand for equal pay for women and the unions' specific wage demands, and merely suggested a few minor revisions in the pay scales established by the Hobhouse Committee. Including upward revisions for men but not for women, the scale for telegraphists in London was to be 22-65s. weekly or about £57-168 yearly for men, and 18-40s. weekly or about £47-104 yearly for women; in the provinces men's pay was to be 18-58s. a week or £47-150 annually, and women's 15-36s. weekly or £39-94 annually. By way of comparison, the Postal Telegraph Clerks' Association had asked a scale, for men and women alike, with a minimum of £52 annually in both London and the provinces, rising to a maximum of £230 in London and £200 in the provinces, while the U. K. Postal Clerks' Association had asked minimum pay of £46 12s. for both men and women, rising to a maximum of £170 for men and £150 for women. The Committee further recommended improved pay for a few women telegraphists in the supervisory classes and for women clerks. For women sorters the Committee recommended a small rise in their maximum pay, making their scale 14-32s. compared with the 14-40s. they had demanded, but it did approve, as they wished, the creation within their grade of a class of overseers with a pay scale of 32-38s. Still, these concessions were offset by the Committee's suggestion that the women sorters take over more of the routine work of women clerks to eliminate the need for the proposed new grade of "female assistant clerks."[64]

Women in the service were naturally disappointed by the report of the MacDonnell Commission, while postal workers generally were incensed by that of the Holt Committee, the consensus being that women especially had been badly treated. Always more aggressively "trade-unionist" than the clerical workers' organizations, the leading postal associations now rejected the recommendations of the Holt Committee and passed resolutions in favour of a strike policy. But the possibility of a strike was averted when the government accepted a suggestion made in the Commons by Ramsay MacDonald that the Holt Committee's report be revised by a committee of experts. Such a committee was appointed under the chairmanship of Sir George Gibb, but the war intervened before it could report and also before the government could effect the changes in the service recommended by the MacDonnell Commission.[65]

In 1914, then, civil servants generally and women in particular remained a very discontented group of workers. Still, they had brought their problems forcefully to public and official attention, and it proved but a matter of time until many of these problems were solved. The most pressing matters to be decided were those of regrading the civil service so as to bring order out of the welter of different grades and classes that had developed, and of giving civil servants a way of officially stating their claims more effectively than through the cumbersome procedure of appearing before select committees and royal commissions. Both these problems were dealt with immediately after the war when Whitleyism made its appearance in the service and when civil servants themselves, through the Whitley machinery, took part in the reorganization of the service. Whitleyism takes its name from the Rt. Hon. J. H. Whitley, Speaker of the House and chairman of the sub-committee of the Reconstruction Committee which recommended that in industries where organizations fully representing both employers and employees existed, these organizations should establish joint councils for regular and frequent consultation. Wishing to encourage by its example the establishment of Whitley Councils in private industry, the government in 1919 created a National Whitley Council, half of its members appointed by the government and half by the civil servants' associations, whose joint decisions when reported to the cabinet were to become operative.[66] In 1920 the civil service was reorganized along the lines recommended by the National Whitley Council. With the exception of those in special departmental classes, civil servants were to be assimilated into five new general grades, all of them to be recruited in future by open competitive examinations. These grades, in ascending order, were: typists and shorthand-typists; writing assistants (later called clerical assistants); the clerical grade proper; the executive grade; and the administrative grade. As for the place of women in the service, wartime experience of their government work proved their ability to handle duties previously considered suitable only for men, and also showed that segregation of men and women workers was not, after all, a necessity. As a result, women were admitted together with men to all grades of the reorganized service.

Reorganization of the service in turn destroyed the basis of the separate men's and women's associations catering for the old segregated grades of workers, and thereafter new associations representing the new mixed grades made strenuous efforts to recruit women members. Especially active was the Civil Service Clerical Association, organized in 1922, which wooed away many members of the Federation of Women Civil Servants, including the whole Civil Service Typists' Association, and also members of the special civil service section established by the Association of Women Clerks and Secretaries. Today the Civil Service Clerical Association is by far the leading organization catering for workers in the lower grades of the service. To recoup its losses the Federation of Women Civil Servants decided in 1932 to admit unestablished women clerks to membership, and joined with the civil service section of the Association of Women Clerks and Secretaries to form the National Association of Women Civil Servants. This new Association lingered on as a small splinter group, more a feminist organization than a real trade union, but it did good work by forcing the larger mixed associations to pay attention to their women members or risk losing them to special women's associations.[67]

Special attention to women's problems was needed, for the admission of women to all grades of the reorganized civil service and the recruitment of women by the new mixed staff associations by no means put an end to all their long-standing special grievances. In practice women were concentrated in the three lowest grades of the service, the two lowest grades being, in fact, reserved for them, while men continued to fill the higher government posts. Even when they worked in the same grades with men, women continued to be employed on certain kinds of work separately from men and supervised by women superiors, so that they could be promoted only to supervisory posts reserved for them. In addition, far fewer women than men were promoted from their grade of the service to the next highest grade. Only shortly before World War II did the government officially accept the policy of true "aggregation" and of "common seniority lists," that is, work was arranged so as to be interchangeable between men and women and women were considered together with men for promotion to higher positions. As for the marriage bar, it was somewhat modified during the inter-war years for the benefit of specially qualified women in higher positions, was temporarily suspended during World War II, and was completely abolished in 1946. With regard to pay, women, under the service reorganization plan of 1920, received the same minimum salaries as men in the same grade, but men received larger increments so that their maximum salaries were considerably higher than women's. Finally, in 1955, yielding to pressure by the T.U.C. and the National Whitley Council, the government announced its acceptance of a plan presented through the Whitley machinery whereby women's scales of pay would be increased by seven annual increments until, by 1961, they were equal to men's.[68] At last women achieved official recognition of their equality with men in the service of the state.

VIII

AFTER THE WOMEN'S MOVEMENT?

It was once the fashion, in writing of the women's movement in Victorian England, to conclude that it was substantially a success, and that this was aptly illustrated by women's winning of the Parliamentary vote in 1918, the victory which could be said to mark the movement's end. But the passage of time has altered perspectives and brought to light new problems, or revealed the continued existence of old problems, so that in the later twentieth century it is again a question, and by no means an academic one, whether the Victorian women's movement was in fact successful.

This movement represented a revolt against the prevailing patriarchal ideal of society. Feminists denounced the "subjection of women" and all that that phrase implied, and demanded "freedom" for women as equal individuals. To what extent, then, did the women's movement succeed in shattering old ideals and setting up new ones, in inspiring women with a new spirit of independence and self-confidence based upon their proved abilities, especially as tested in the marketplace? Beginning in the 1880's there is considerable evidence that in this respect the movement was enjoying success. For example, one observer wrote:

> The good old days, when our grandmothers worked samplers and studied their recipe books, have passed away long ago; our spinster aunts, who would have died rather than soil their hands with anything that savoured of 'ungentility,' are fast fading out; and the present generation of girlhood, with enlarged ideas as to woman's brain and woman's work, is standing on the threshold of life eager to mingle in life's warfare.[1]

And another declared:

> It is a satisfactory sign of the times, and of the progress of a sensible public opinion, that women are nowadays not ashamed to confess that they support themselves by honest toil. Side by side with this laudable determination on the part of women of limited means to be no longer a burden on their relatives, but to take a share in the actual work, and therefore in the rewards of industry, there has sprung up amongst

the leisured class of women a similar desire to be of some use in the world, to do some good before they pass away, to be something more than mere ornaments of life.[2]

Clearly, the idea that work degraded ladies was passing away.

But it would be too much to say that the feminists' ideal of the New Woman came to be generally and wholeheartedly accepted. Throughout this period complaints continued to be voiced about the lack of foresight of parents in failing to prepare their daughters for a life of work outside the home and about the suffering of middle-class women forced to work for a living but unprepared to do so.[3] It would also be too much to say that the changing ideas of women and about women were solely due to feminist logic and eloquence. As one woman remarked:

> The immense growth of the population, and the excess of the female part, have altered the view for both men and women. . . . For one person who has, by reasoning, convinced himself that it is a per- fectly legitimate thing for women to pursue . . . a profession, to acquire a knowledge of business, to travel about unattended, there are a hundred who have been brought to that conclusion by the plurality of daughters, the establishment of cheap schools and col- leges, the omnibus and tramcar service. Facts convince more speedily than theories.[4]

Also, one authority on the women's movement maintained that the idea that work for middle-class women was "disgraceful" finally disappeared only during the crisis years of World War I.[5]

Still, one cannot fail to be impressed by the effect which feminist ideals did in fact have upon many women. One of them pointed out that few men could understand the importance which middle-class women attached to their economic independence because, for men, earning a living repre- sented "but a tiresome necessity" and not "a hardly won and cherished privilege." Another testified to women's "peculiar joy and lofty idealism in work which are, in part, a reaction from ages of economic and personal dependence." In short, women had attained "a measure of that economic, social, and psychological independence which is the *sine qua non* of free- dom."[6]

As a natural corollary of their demand for the rights of women as free and equal individuals, mid-Victorian feminists had claimed for women the right to receive an education as good as men's in order to develop their capabilities to the fullest extent, and the right to enter upon any career which they chose and for which they proved themselves fitted, unhampered by legal or merely conventional obstacles to their employment. This femi- nist claim was made not merely on theoretical grounds but was advanced also as the obvious solution to a crying practical need in view of the large and ever increasing number of "redundant women," especially those of the middle classes. These were women who could not hope to marry and there- by fit into the conventional niche assigned to them in a patriarchal society, but who would have to support themselves, and perhaps others as well, throughout their lives. In mid-Victorian times such middle-class women could look forward only to loss of status and lives of penury by entering the depressed ranks of governesses. Was, then, that "fair field and no favour" in the labour market which the feminists so ardently desired and preached actually won?

Certainly there was in England in the later nineteenth and early twentieth centuries an impressive increase in the number of middle-class working women, women employed both in such traditionally feminine occupations as teaching and nursing and in such new fields for women as the distributive trades, the clerical occupations and the civil service. And women's achievements in all these fields went far toward blotting out the Victorian picture of the ideal lady as a clinging vine, and toward proving feminist claims that women both could be and should be successful and valuable participants in the work to be done in the world.

Teaching continued to be one of the most popular occupations for middle-class women, but it no longer represented a refuge for "decayed gentlewomen." The state created the elementary-school teachers' profession in that it prescribed the professional training required and registered those teachers duly qualified, and although middle-class women long shunned this branch of teaching, they turned to it in increasing numbers as conditions steadily improved, largely owing to the efforts of the elementary-school teachers' unions, or professional associations, in which women played an active part. In secondary education middle-class women themselves pioneered in transforming the occupation into a real profession, initiating professional training and founding the first professional associations, which, in co-operation with the men's organizations formed in imitation of them, concentrated upon achieving the same improvements in working conditions which elementary-school teachers had won. At the same time, the teaching of special subjects in connection with the country's elementary, secondary and technical schools provided a new field of work for middle-class women, as did the growth of the new women's colleges and the coeducational universities, although to a much more limited extent. And it is noteworthy that the greatest degree of recognized professional training and the most effective professional associations among teachers of special subjects were found in those fields which women monopolized, and that women had formed the only professional association catering for, although not limited to, university teachers.

By 1914 teaching in elementary and secondary schools, in the universities, and in the women's branches of special-subjects teaching definitely ranked as professions, and these professions were tending to coalesce with the growing co-operation among the different associations representing them, especially in connection with the teachers' registration movement. In the field of education women's performance amply justified the early feminist demand for greater freedom for women to perform that work outside the home for which they were pre-eminently suited.

The advance of nursing also demonstrated the great good accruing to society when middle-class women were free to take up work outside their homes for which they were so well qualified. Once considered a repellent form of domestic service, the refuge of the most degraded classes of the community, nursing was completely transformed through the efforts of Florence Nightingale and her many followers into a highly skilled and eminently respectable calling. It was also a very popular calling, providing in its various branches broad opportunities for women to find congenial employment and to rise to the highest positions, such as those of hospital matrons and heads of the nursing services, women who stood second to none in the country's professions in the influence for good which they exerted. By 1914 nurses still had not attained state registration, the final legal hallmark of professionals, but the groundwork of the profession had long since been laid, with the provision of recognized training and the growth of active professional associations, and it was only a matter of time until the already professional nurse became also an "R.N."

In the distributive trades and the clerical occupations, the work became easier of access to all classes of the community, and women workers represented a welcome supply of labour in the face of an ever increasing demand. Indeed, the supply of workers outstripped the demand in these fields, with unfortunate results for the workers. Women were somewhat slow to realize the advantages, the necessity even, of joining trade unions to fight for improvements in their working conditions, but the male shop assistants and clerks realized that the unions they had founded must, if they were to be at all effective, admit women on equal terms. In time women came to play an active part in the unions and won a recognized place in their counsels. If, in the years before the war, the unions' achievements on behalf of their members were meager and disappointing, it was still noteworthy that men and women were working together in relative harmony, and they both could hope for a brighter future.

In the civil service likewise, the work became easier of access and women could help to supply the demand for a large army of workers. And likewise, despite the definite advantages of civil service employment in comparison with work outside the service, trade unions developed to fight for improved working conditions. The organizations of Post Office manipulative workers included women on an equal footing with men from the beginning, for they realized that men and women must advance together, but in the civil service clerical grades, since women were employed separately from men, they formed their own separate unions. At length the Post Office unions and the clerical unions, women's as well as men's, succeeded in winning a hearing for their claims, and although these claims had not been met at the outbreak of war, the civil servants' eventual success seemed assured.

In these five fields of work, then, middle-class working women had made their mark by 1914—in the creation of the professions of teaching and nursing, and in the rise of active trade unions in the distributive trades, the clerical occupations and the civil service. Still, study of these five fields of work shows that the increased employment of middle-class women was not, in fact, due to the force of the women's movement itself.

Rather, the growth in the numbers of middle-class working women was a natural result of the general development of the country's economy, was the answer to the changing needs of an increasingly industrialized and urbanized society. In short, the Victorian women's movement witnessed but did not cause the widening of the avenues of employment for middle-class women.

Moreover, in the later years of this period complaints began to be heard again, reminiscent of those voiced in the 1850's and '60's, about the overcrowding in fields of work open to middle-class women, about their difficulties in finding suitable employment. One woman stated that "most of the avenues to employment recently opened up are practically closed by the crowds which poured into them almost as soon as the fact of their existence was made known." Another declared that "with regard to the well-educated woman, the difficulty of finding congenial work other than teaching, which shall ensure an adequate salary, sufficient recreation, and an old age free from financial worry, is almost as acute as ever."[7] Middle-class working women, once relegated to the field of "governessing," were still restricted to certain occupations only, the traditionally feminine professions of teaching and nursing and a few new fields, such as shop and clerical work and the lower reaches of the civil service, where their cheapness compared with men encouraged their increasing employment. In other words, the Victorian women's movement failed, or society as a whole failed, to open all employment to women equally with men, failed to win for them or to grant to them "fair field and no favour."

Also, even in the relatively small number of occupations now open to middle-class women, they did not receive equal treatment with the men employed. In these circumstances one woman commented: "Our pioneers were full of enthusiasm in their journey to the promised land where sex barriers should be removed and sex prejudices die away. . . . The next generation are coming into the field in new conditions." The woman of this younger generation realized that she had not, in fact, reached the "promised land," and that "there is nothing very glorious in doing work that any average man can do as well, now that we are no longer told we cannot do it." She was coming to realize that she had her "own standpoint . . . which is not that of her husband or her brother, or of the men with whom she works, or even that which these persons imagine must naturally be hers."[8]

The chief grievances of middle-class working women employed in occupations together with men were that their pay was not equal to men's and that their opportunities of rising to more responsible and better-paid positions were more limited than men's. These grievances seemed the result both of history and long tradition and of women's special position in society as, potentially at least, wives and mothers.[9] Women had for so long been considered inferior to men that the general conclusion, or at least the general male conclusion, was that women were worthy only of lower pay or in any case would always be willing to accept it. In addition, and more practically, working women, unlike men, were usually assumed to have only themselves to support, or even to be partly supported by their families and to be working merely for "pin money," so the conclusion was that women simply did not need equal pay with men. Also, since many women gave up their work upon marriage, they would not gain the long experience and full command of their work that men would, and so were considered, at least potentially and in the long run, as being not equal to men in value and therefore not deserving of equal pay. The traditional belief in women's inferiority led also to the conclusion that while women could perform routine work well, they could not fill positions of real responsibility. There was also in this connection the problem of men's unwillingness to work for and under the command of women, and the distaste of women themselves at working for other women. And again, women, as possible labour-market drop-outs because of marriage, were generally regarded as only temporary or part-time workers, to be relegated permanently to subordinate positions where they could be easily replaced if need be. In short, women in the labour market found general sex prejudice working against them and had also to contend with the practical results of the general feeling that men, with families dependent upon them and looking upon their work as a lifetime career, needed and deserved better pay and prospects than did women.

But there were telling arguments that could be marshalled in favour of equal treatment for women at work. Latter-day feminists pointed out the illogicality of the claim that women's abilities were inherently inferior to men's in view of the fact that women were doing exactly the same work that men did, as in teaching and in shop, office and government work. Equally illogical was the claim that although women could perform routine work well they could not perform higher duties for, being always limited to routine work, women had no incentive or opportunity to demonstrate their real abilities. Further, the women's spokesmen pointed out that many working women had dependents to support just as men did, while many men workers did not have dependents to support. With regard to the effect of marriage upon women's position in the labour market, the feminists declared that if women did not continue their work after marriage and look upon it as a lifetime career, it was often not because of their free choice but because of the ban on the employment of married women, whether formal and official as in teaching and the civil service or merely conventional as in shop and clerical work. In any case, they maintained that it was unfair to penalize merely because of their sex those women who did not marry and who, like men, had to regard their work as a life career. In these circumstances, feminists argued the injustice of giving all men better pay and prospects than all women rather than paying "the rate for the job" and opening all higher positions to the best qualified, whether men or women, married or unmarried. Finally, women argued that men themselves suffered from the unequal treatment accorded women workers, for in many fields where they were employed together women represented a standing threat to men because of their lower pay. Indeed, women's lower pay seems to be the basic reason for their increasing employment at the expense of men in such fields as elementary-school teaching, the distributive trades, clerical work and the civil service. To those who claimed that employers would not continue to hire women if they no longer represented a cheaper supply of labour than men, feminists retorted that women had become so indispensable a part of the labour force that equal pay for them would not, in fact, adversely affect their opportunities for employment.

Working women were not only acutely conscious of the special disabilities under which they laboured but they also fought valiantly for equal treatment in their work. Sometimes their male colleagues opposed them, presumably in the belief that support of women's claims for equal treatment on the job would jeopardize men's demands for improved conditions for themselves. Sometimes men supported the women's claims, either because they were genuinely sympathetic to feminist appeals or because they were seeking to guard their own position against unfair competition by lower-paid women. Failing to win over the mixed associations of elementary-school teachers, women in this field formed their own associations to agitate for equal treatment and at last persuaded the mixed associations to adopt this policy, while the men's associations among secondary-school teachers always cordially supported the claims of the women's organizations. The trade unions among clerical workers and among Post Office manipulative workers demanded equal pay and opportunities for their women members, while the men's clerical associations in the civil service often endorsed the claims of the unions representing the women's clerical grades. The shop assistants' unions did work for improved conditions for their women members, but failed to adopt the principle of equal treatment for them. Still, experience proved that men were quite ready to desert the women's cause when it came to the point of insisting upon a whole loaf instead of accepting half, of holding out for equality for women rather than accepting concessions for themselves and continuing inequality for women. So it was that the claims of the earlier feminists for wider opportunities for women to work continued to be heard, while to these were added demands for equal treatment for women in their work.

All this is but another way of saying that the Victorian women's movement was, in fact, a failure, if it is judged in the light of whether it achieved its most basic goal, namely, the complete elimination of sex prejudice and sex barriers, the final destruction of the patriarchal society. Clearly English society and the position of middle-class women in particular were vastly different in 1914 from what they had been in the mid-nineteenth century, yet women were still far from being treated as completely free and equal individuals in all spheres of life. The most basic feminist claim had not been met, the women's movement having tried but failed "to challenge patriarchal ideology at a sufficiently deep and radical level to break the conditioning process of status, temperament and role."[10] In other words, the Victorian patriarchy vanished, but patriarchal ideals lived on and continued to affect profoundly the lives of women of later times.

To be sure, changes in the conditions of women's work for which feminists were clamouring in 1914 have come about. For example, marriage no longer represents the barrier to women's employment that it once did, a fact symbolized by the removal of the formal ban on the employment of married women in teaching in 1944 and in the civil service in 1946. In the early years of the twentieth century married women represented only about 14 per cent of all working women; today they represent nearly three-fifths of all women employed. Yet this development is not so much a "reform" won by feminists as it is a practical accommodation of the labour market to changing demographic patterns. In the earlier twentieth century the average age at marriage was higher than it is now, and upon marriage women retired permanently from the labour force to devote themselves to their families. Today women tend to marry earlier than their grandmothers, continue to work usually till the birth of their first child, have fewer children than their grandmothers did, and return to work once their children are of school age. (See Appendix, Table 6g and comment.)

Another change which was urged by feminists in the early twentieth century and which has come about is the grant to women workers of equal pay with men. In 1955, at the urging of the trade-union movement as a whole and of the workers involved, the Conservative government accepted the principle of equal pay for women teachers and women in the civil service. Still, equality of pay was not granted all at once but only gradually, over a period of seven years. In 1970, likewise under pressure from the trade-union movement and from women workers, the Labour government belatedly honoured a pledge made during the 1964 election campaign by sponsoring the Equal Pay Act. The provisions of this Act give employers till the end of 1975 to eliminate all discrimination in pay based upon the sex of their workers, to grant equal pay to women doing work broadly similar or equivalent to that of men. It remains to be seen whether this reform will be carried out in good faith and whether it is true, as feminists have always claimed, that women are so indispensable a source of labour that equal pay will not hinder them in finding work.

Meanwhile, the picture of the employment of middle-class women in 1914 is, in its broad outlines, little changed today. Middle-class working women are still concentrated in traditionally feminine occupations and in subordinate positions or in the lower grades of these occupations. Women teachers are a large majority of those employed in elementary schools, but less than half of those in secondary schools and only a tiny handful among university teachers. Women nurses, overworked and underpaid, are the lowest among the employees in the country's state-supported medical services. Women's work in shops and offices has become indispensable, but few women indeed rise to responsible executive positions in the firms that employ them. Women continue to be employed largely on routine work in the lowest grades of the civil service. In short, women are still regarded and treated as temporary and part-time workers, with all that that implies with respect to their prospects in the labour market. The problem remains that of winning "fair field and no favour," as the Victorians put it.[11]

"Domesticity and dependence" may no longer be exactly ideals for women today as in Victorian times, but domesticity and dependence are still definitely facts of the economic and social life of women in the later twentieth century. The problems confronting women who wish to combine full-time careers with marriage and motherhood are difficult and discouraging. Still, they are hardly impossible of solution if once approached in a general and meaningful way, even if, as some present-day feminists declare, the solution involves a drastic transformation of the structure of marriage and of family life, perhaps even the abolition of marriage and the family as we have known them.

All this is to say, in sum, that the Victorian women's movement did not really end, either in success or failure, in the early twentieth century, but that it continues in being, although perhaps under another name, such as "the sexual revolution" or "women's liberation." Seeking as it did, and does, a "radical alteration in the quality of life,"[12] it is an uncompleted and ongoing revolution, or evolution, like others which seek to realize in practice such high ideals as liberty, equality and brotherhood—or sisterhood.

APPENDIX

Statistics on the Employment of Teachers, Nurses, Shop Assistants, Clerks and Civil Servants in England and Wales, 1861-1911[1]

1. *Teachers*

The census statistics on teachers employed are complete and comparable throughout the period 1861-1911, but unfortunately the census tables on occupations do not distinguish the different groups of teachers, elementary-school, secondary-school, etc.

Table 1a
Number of Teachers Employed
in England and Wales, 1861-1911 [a]

Year	All Teachers Employed	Men			Women	
		No.	% of All Teachers Employed		No.	% of All Teachers Employed
1861[b]	110,260	30,280	27.5		79,980	72.5
1871	126,930	32,901	25.9		94,029	74.1
1881	168,920	46,074	27.2		122,846	72.8
1891	195,021	50,628	25.9		144,393	74.1
1901	230,345	58,675	25.5		171,670	74.5
1911	251,968	68,670	27.2		183,298	72.8

(a) Figures in this table do not include those in the occupational category of teaching labelled as "others in school service," etc.—i.e., those not clearly described as teachers.

(b) The figures given here for 1861 do not include music masters and mistresses, who were included among teachers in this year but were grouped together with musicians in later census reports.

It is interesting that the proportion of women teachers employed remained remarkably stable throughout the period 1861-1911, men holding their ground in the profession as a whole although losing ground to women in certain branches of the profession, such as elementary-school teaching (see text).

Table 1b
Percentage of Increase in the Number of Teachers
Employed in England and Wales, 1861-1911

Years	Total	Men	Women
1861-1871	15.1	8.7	17.6
1871-1881	33.1	40.4	30.6
1881-1891	15.5	9.9	17.5
1891-1901	18.1	15.9	18.9
1901-1911	9.4	17.0	6.8
1861-1911	128.5	126.8	129.2

By far the greatest decennial increase in the number of teachers employed, both men and women, came in the decade 1871-1881, following the creation of a national system of public elementary schools by the Education Act of 1870.

Today in Britain women still represent about three-fourths of the teachers employed in publicly maintained or assisted elementary schools, but only about two-fifths of those employed in publicly supported secondary schools. Women still form only a very small proportion of those in teaching and research positions in the universities—1.5 per cent of all professors, 7 per cent of readers and senior lecturers, 11 per cent of lecturers, and 28 per cent of other members of the academic staffs.

2. Nurses

The census statistics on nurses employed also are complete and comparable throughout the period 1861-1911. Male nurses, employed chiefly as attendants in mental asylums, were consistently only a very small number, and therefore they have not been included here. The figures for women nurses given in the tables below unfortunately do not reflect accurately the number of truly professional nurses. One hospital authority estimated that of the total number of 74,844 women returned as "nurses" in England, Wales, Scotland and Ireland in 1901, about 9,000 were members of religious sisterhoods engaged in nursing, or casual and occasional untrained nurses caring for elderly and infirm persons and for children. Of the remaining 66,000 women returned as nurses, he estimated that two-thirds could not be considered really trained nurses.[2]

Table 2a
Number of Nurses Employed
in England and Wales, 1861-1911

Year	No.
1861	24,821
1871	28,417
1881	35,175 [a]
1891	53,057 [b]
1901	64,214
1911	77,060

(a) Described in this census report as "subordinate medical service."
(b) This figure includes those returned as midwives. However, they were not a relatively large number—in 1881, 2,646, and in 1901, 3,055.

Table 2b
Percentage of Increase in the Number of Nurses
Employed in England and Wales, 1861-1911

Years	% of Increase
1861-1871	14.5
1871-1881	23.8
1881-1891	50.8
1891-1901	21.0
1901-1911	20.0
1861-1911	210.5

3. *Shop Assistants*

The census figures on shop assistants are quite unsatisfactory for most of the period 1861-1911. Until the census of 1901 no attempt was made to distinguish completely "dealers" from "workers" in the various census categories, nor to distinguish shopkeepers from shop assistants among "dealers." Still, an indea of the increase in the number of dealers during this period can be gained from the first two tables below. These tables show the numbers and percentage of increase for dealers returned as being employed in certain occupational classes which remained constant in the census reports from 1861 to 1911 and for which the figures seem to be comparable throughout the period. It is also interesting to see, as in the third table below, the distribution by "trade" of those returned as dealers. The fourth table below presents the figures on dealers in the various census categories in 1911, distinguishing shopkeepers from shop assistants.

Table 3a
Number of Dealers in Certain Census Classes
Employed in England and Wales, 1861-1911[a]

Year	All Dealers	Men		Women	
		No.	% of All Dealers Employed	No.	% of All Dealers Employed
1861	468,448	381,172	81.4	87,276	18.6
1871	613,771	490,580	79.9	123,191	20.1
1881	667,668	522,689	78.3	144,979	21.7
1891	840,632	625,636	74.4	214,996	25.6
1901	954,606	711,571	74.5	243,035	25.5
1911	1,199,249	832,981	69.5	366,268	30.5

(a) Includes dealers in 26 classes identical in the census reports from 1861 to 1911: 1) coal merchants, dealers; 2) ironmongers, hardware dealers; 3) timber, wood,

cork, bark dealers; 4) earthenware, china, glass dealers; 5) oil and colourmen;
6) chemists, druggists; 7) publishers, book sellers; 8) newspaper agents, ven-
dors, newsroom keepers; 9) stationers, law stationers; 10) drapers, linen drapers, mercers; 11) other dealers in textiles; 12) hosiers, haberdashers; 13) cow-
keepers, milksellers; 14) cheesemongers, provision dealers; 15) fishmongers,
poulterers, game dealers; 16) corn, flour, seed merchants, dealers; 17) butchers, meat salesmen; 18) confectioners, pastrycooks; 19) greengrocers, fruiterers; 20) grocers, tea, coffee, chocolate dealers; 21) wine and spirit merchants; 22) rag gatherers, dealers; 23) animal, dog, bird dealers; 24) pawnbrokers; 25) warehousemen; 26) shopkeepers, general dealers.

Table 3b
Percentage of Increase in the Number of Dealers in Certain Census Classes
Employed in England and Wales, 1861-1911

Years	Total	Men	Women
1861-1871	31.0	28.7	41.2
1871-1881	8.8	6.5	17.7
1881-1891	25.9	19.7	48.3
1891-1901	13.6	13.7	13.0
1901-1911	25.6	17.1	50.7
1861-1911	156.0	118.5	319.6

Table 3c
Distribution by Trade of Those Returned as Dealers
in England and Wales, 1911

Census category(a)	Men		Women	
	No.	% of All Men Dealers	No.	% of All Women Dealers
Products of mines and quarries, metals, machines, implements, conveyances	71,057	6.2	7,922	1.7
Precious metals, jewelry, watches	12,077	1.1	2,829	0.6
Musical instruments, toys, tackle for sports and games	5,115	0.5	2,557	0.5
Timber, wood, bark, cork	9,885	0.9	518	0.1
Furniture, fittings, decorations, works of art	27,528	2.4	5,513	1.1

Table 3c
Distribution by Trade of Those Returned as Dealers
in England and Wales, 1911

Census category(a)	Men		Women	
	No.	% of All Men Dealers	No.	% of All Women Dealers
Brick, cement, pottery, glass	6,933	0.6	4,158	0.9
Chemicals, drugs, paints, dyes, oil, grease, soap, resin	38,974	3.4	6,959	1.5
Skins, leather, hair, feathers	7,274	0.6	1,296	0.3
Books, prints, paper, stationery, newspapers	57,545	5.1	23,558	5.0
Textiles	101,321	8.9	89,818	19.0
Dress	63,780	5.8	35,238	7.4
Food	509,236	45.0	178,978	37.7
Tobacco	11,702	1.0	9,596	2.0
Drink and lodging	76,627	6.8	29,969	6.3
Cattle, sheep, pigs, animals, dogs, birds	6,689	0.6	409	0.1
Pawnbrokers	12,611	1.1	2,517	0.5
Warehousemen	9,794	0.9	941	0.1
Costers, hawkers, street sellers	53,971	4.8	15,376	3.2
Miscellaneous and general (b)	49,222	4.3	57,021	12.0
Total	1,131,341	100.0	475,173	100.0

(a) Categories as given in the census tables are abbreviated here.
(b) Includes: rag gatherers, dealers; knackers, catsmeat dealers; general or un-
classified shopkeepers, dealers; other dealers in sundry industries; multiple
shop, store proprietors, workers; receiving shop, office keepers, assistants
(e.g., laundries, dyers, cleaners).

From Table 3c it can be seen that of the total of 1,606,514 dealers employed in England and Wales in 1911, men represented 70.4 per cent and women 29.6 per cent.

Table 3d
Proportion of Shopkeepers and Shop Assistants
among Those Returned as Dealers
in England and Wales, 1911[a]

	Shopkeepers		Shop Assistants	
Census category	Men	Women	Men	Women
Products of mines and quarries, metals, machines, implements, conveyances	47.3%	32.5%	52.7%	67.5%
Precious metals, jewelry, watches	45.8	13.3	54.2	86.7
Musical instruments, toys, tackle for sports and games	41.7	22.1	58.3	77.9
Timber, wood, bark, cork	63.8	52.0	36.2	48.0
Furniture, fittings, decorations, works of art	38.2	30.7	61.8	69.3
Brick, cement, pottery, glass	42.9	24.6	57.1	75.4
Chemicals, drugs, paints, dyes, oil, grease, soap, resin	34.3	9.8	65.7	90.2
Skins, leather, hair, feathers	34.3	15.3	65.7	84.7
Books, prints, paper, stationery, newspapers	40.1	25.2	59.9	74.8
Textiles	24.2	12.3	75.8	87.7
Dress	31.6	22.8	68.4	77.2
Food	37.5	41.4	62.5	58.6
Tobacco	59.0	36.6	41.0	63.4
Drink and lodging	70.1	35.4	29.9	64.6
Cattle, sheep, pigs, animals, dogs, birds	71.1	57.5	28.9	42.5

Census category	Shopkeepers		Shop Assistants	
	Men	Women	Men	Women
Pawnbrokers	19.1	19.8	80.9	80.2
Warehousemen	1.8	0.3	98.2	99.7
Costers, hawkers, street sellers	72.0	73.8	28.0	26.2
Miscellaneous and general	51.9	32.7	48.1	67.3
Total	41.2	30.6	58.8	69.4

(a) This table is an abbreviation of that in the census report, which distinguishes not two classes of dealers but three. Here "shopkeepers" include those designated in the census table as "employers" and "those working on their own account," while "shop assistants" include those designated as "working for employers."

Table 3d illustrates the decline of independent shopkeepers and the rise of the shop assistant class. In only three categories with relatively few numbers did men and women shopkeepers outnumber men and women shop assistants (timber, etc. dealers, cattle, etc. dealers, and costers, hawkers and street sellers). In three additional categories men shopkeepers but not women shopkeepers outnumbered shop assistants (tobacconists, dealers in drink and lodging, and general and miscellaneous dealers). The table also shows, as would be expected, that the proportion of women shopkeepers was almost invariably lower than the proportion of men shopkeepers and the proportion of women shop assistants higher than that of men. In only three categories was there a slightly higher proportion of women shopkeepers than of men and a lower proportion of women shop assistants (dealers in food, pawnbrokers, and costers, hawkers and street sellers).

4. Clerks

The census statistics on clerical workers seem fairly complete for the period 1861-1911, and are summarized in the first two tables below.

Table 4a
Number of Clerks Employed
in England and Wales, 1861-1911[a]

| | | Men | | Women | |
Year	All Clerks Employed	No.	% of All Clerks Employed	No.	% of All Clerks Employed
1861	92,012	91,733	99.7	279	0.3
1871 [b]	130,717	129,271	98.9	1,446	1.1
1881 [c]	236,125	229,705	97.3	6,420	2.7
1891	370,433	351,486	94.9	18,947	5.1
1901	518,900	461,164	88.9	57,736	11.1
1911	685,998	561,155	81.9	124,843	18.1

(a) Includes those returned as commercial or business clerks; law clerks; bankers, bank officials, clerks; insurance officials, clerks; and railway officials, clerks.
(b) Figures for 1871 do not include law clerks, for whom no separate figure was given in the census tables.
(c) Figures for 1881 do not include railway officials and clerks, for whom no separate figure was given in the census tables.

Table 4b
Percentage of Increase in the Number of Clerks
Employed in England and Wales, 1861-1911

Years	Total	Men	Women
1861-1871	42.1	40.9	418.3
1871-1881	80.6	77.7	344.0
1881-1891	56.9	52.8	195.2
1891-1901	40.1	31.2	204.7
1901-1911	32.2	21.7	116.2
1861-1911	645.6	511.7	44,646.6

It is also interesting to note the distribution of clerks among the different categories of clerical work.

Table 4c
Distribution of Clerks among Different Categories of Work
in England and Wales, 1911

	Men		Women	
Category	No.	% of All Men Clerks Employed	No.	% of All Women Clerks Employed
Commercial or business clerks	360,478	64.2	117,057	93.8
Law clerks	34,106	6.1	2,159	1.8
Bank clerks	39,903	7.1	476	0.4
Insurance clerks	41,866	7.5	4,031	3.2
Railway clerks	84,802	15.1	1,120	0.8
Total	561,155	100.0	124,843	100.0

5. *Civil Servants*

The census statistics on civil servants are complete for the period 1861-1911, but somewhat unsatisfactory in that it is impossible always to distinguish those employed in administrative, clerical and manipulative work. The first two tables below present the numbers and the percentage of increase for those returned as employees of the central government and also, for the purpose of completeness and comparison, those returned as employed in telegraph and telephone service. (The government took over the country's telegraph service in 1870, and gradually expanded its provision of telephone service until in 1911 it assumed complete control.)

Table 5a
Number of Persons Employed by the Central Government
in England and Wales, 1861-1911

Year	All Persons Employed	Men		Women	
		No.	% of All Persons Employed	No.	% of All Persons Employed
1861	50,445	48,363	95.9	2,082	4.1
1871	56,179	52,658	93.7	3,521	6.3
1881	59,687	53,106	89.0	6,581	11.0
1891	94,196	79,965	84.9	14,231	15.1
1901	139,232	113,902	81.9	25,330	18.1
1911	189,445	149,672	79.0	39,773	21.0

Table 5b
Percentage of Increase in the Number of Persons Employed
by the Central Government in England and Wales, 1861-1911

Years	Total	Men	Women
1861-1871	11.3	8.2	69.1
1871-1881	6.2	0.9	86.9
1881-1891	57.8	50.6	116.2
1891-1901	47.8	42.2	78.0
1901-1911	36.1	31.4	57.0
1861-1911	275.5	209.5	1,810.3

It is also interesting to see the distribution of central government employees among different departments and different kinds of work when this is possible, as shown in the table below.

Table 5c
Distribution by Work of Persons Employed
by the Central Government in England and Wales, 1911

Classification	Men		Women	
	No.	% of Men Employed by Gov't	No.	% of Women Employed by Gov't
Telegraph and telephone operators [a]	13,103	8.8	14,328	35.9
Other Post Office officers and clerks	29,873	20.0	20,337	51.0
Postmen	46,333	30.9	1,068	2.8
Post Office messengers, etc.	16,861	11.3	888	2.3
Other civil service officers and clerks	31,340	20.9	1,697	4.2
Other civil service messengers, etc.	12,162	8.1	1,455	3.8
Total	149,672	100.0	39,773	100.0

(a) These figures include 4,245 men and 6,093 women employed by the Post Office, and 8,858 men and 8,235 women employed in non-government service not yet absorbed into the civil service at the time of the census.

Table 5c illustrates the great importance of postal workers among civil servants. Post Office employees accounted for 71 per cent of the men employed by the central government in 1911, and no less than 92 per cent of the women so employed.

By 1970 women numbered 195,000 or 40 per cent of the total, among civil servants in the non-industrial sector. Nearly all typists were women, and more than half those in the clerical grades were women, but women represented only 21 per cent of those in the executive grade of the service, and a mere 9 per cent of the administrative grade.

6. *Summary*

The figures in the foregoing tables should be compared with those in the first two tables below, which show the total numbers of the working population in England and Wales during the period 1861-1911 and the percentage of increase in their numbers.

Table 6a
Total Working Population
in England and Wales, 1861-1911

		Men		Women	
Year	Total No.	No.	% of Total Working Population	No.	% of Total Working Population
1861	9,818,994	6,469,674	65.9	3,349,320	34.1
1871	10,730,286	7,329,123	68.3	3,401,163	31.7
1881	11,187,564	7,783,646	69.6	3,403,918	30.4
1891	12,899,484	8,883,254	68.9	4,016,230	31.1
1901	14,328,727	10,156,976	70.9	4,171,751	29.1
1911	16,284,399	11,453,665	70.3	4,830,734	29.7

Table 6b
Percentage of Increase of Total Working Population
in England and Wales, 1861-1911

Years	Total	Men	Women
1861-1871	9.3	13.3	1.5
1871-1881	4.3	6.2	0.1
1881-1891	15.3	14.1	18.0
1891-1901	11.1	14.3	3.9
1901-1911	13.6	12.8	15.8
1861-1911	65.8	77.0	44.2

It is interesting to see that the proportion of women in the country's labour force was actually lower in 1911 than in 1861. The increase for all women workers was tiny, and considerably below the increase for men, from 1861 to 1881 and from 1891 to 1901. By 1970 women represented about 36 per cent of the total labour force in Britain, slightly more than in 1861.

This picture of employment generally in the period 1861-1911 is quite different from that of employment in teaching, nursing, shop and clerical work and the civil service, as summarized from the separate tables in Sections 1-5 above and presented in the two tables below.

Table 6c
Numbers of Teachers, Nurses, Shop Assistants, Clerks
and Civil Servants Employed in England and Wales, 1861-1911[a]

| | | *Men* | | *Women* | |
Year	All Teachers, etc. Employed	No.	% of All Teachers etc. Employed	No.	% of All Teachers etc. Employed
1861	745,986	551,548	73.9	194,438	26.1
1871	956,014	705,410	73.8	250,604	26.2
1881	1,167,575	851,574	72.9	316,001	27.1
1891	1,553,339	1,107,715	71.3	445,624	28.7
1901	1,907,297	1,345,312	70.5	561,985	29.5
1911	2,403,720	1,612,478	67.1	791,242	32.9

(a) Actually total figures given in this table are too low because of the incompleteness of figures on "dealers" in the census reports for most of this period. Included in the figures for 1901 and 1911 in this table are the numbers of dealers given in Table 3a above, but these are lower than the more accurate figures for 1901 and 1911 given in the census tables for those years—298,360 lower for men, and 108,905 lower for women in 1911 (see Table 3c).

Table 6d
Percentage of Increase in the Numbers of Teachers,
Nurses, Shop Assistants, Clerks and Civil Servants Employed
in England and Wales, 1861-1911(a)

Years	All Teachers, etc.	Men	Women
1861-1871	28.2	27.9	28.9
1871-1881	22.1	20.7	26.1
1881-1891	33.0	30.1	41.0
1891-1901	22.8	21.4	26.1
1901-1911	26.0	12.4	40.8
1861-1911	222.2	192.3	307.0

(a) See note to Table 6c above.

In these five fields of work as a whole, the proportion of women grew steadily, the increase of women compared with the increase of men being higher in every decade, markedly so in 1881-1891 and in 1901-1911.

Actually, Tables 6c and 6d blur distinctions which are brought out in the separate tables on workers in these five fields presented in Sections 1-5 above. The generalization about the higher rate of increase in the employment of women in every decade and the consequently steady increase in the proportion of women employed applies only to shop assistants, clerks and civil servants (with the minor exception that for shop assistants the rate of increase for men was very slightly above that for women in the decade 1891-1901). In teaching, the rate of increase in the employment of men and women varied from decade to decade (see Table 1b above), and the proportions of women and men employed remained stable from 1861 to 1911 (see Table 1a above). In nursing, a women's profession, consideration of the proportion of women to men employed is not applicable, but here too there was a steady increase in the numbers employed at a rate significantly higher than the rate of increase for women workers generally.

At the same time, Table 6c and the separate tables in Sections 1-5 above indicate that complaints in the period 1861-1911 to the effect that men were being driven out of work by women's competition were not precisely accurate. While it was true that the proportion of women employed as shop assistants, clerks and civil servants rose throughout this period, in none of these fields nor in teaching did the absolute numbers of men decline; the numbers of men merely increased at a less rapid rate than did the numbers of women.

The rate of increase for both men and women in the five fields of work considered in this study was substantially higher than the increase for men and women in the total working population. This fact illustrates that noteworthy development of the later nineteenth and twentieth centuries, the growing proportion of workers in "middle-class" occupations compared with those in "working-class" employments. This is summarized in the table below.

Table 6e
Proportion of Teachers, Nurses, Shop Assistants,
Clerks and Civil Servants to Total Working Population
in England and Wales, 1861-1911

Year	% of Total Working Population Represented by All Teachers, etc.	% of Total Male Working Population Represented by Men Teachers, etc.	% of Total Female Working Population Represented by Women Teachers, etc.
1861	7.6	8.5	5.0
1871	8.9	9.6	7.4
1881	10.4	10.9	9.3
1891	12.0	12.5	11.1
1901	13.3	13.2	13.5
1911	14.1	14.1	16.4

An excellent analysis of the growth of middle-class employments compared with working-class employments in the last three decades of this period presents statistics summarized in the table below,[3] which may be compared with Tables 6a-6e above.

Table 6f
Employment in Middle-Class Occupations
and in Working-Class Occupations, 1881-1911

	Number of Workers Employed (in 1000's)			
	1881		1911	
	Men	Women	Men	Women
Middle-class occupations	1,669	427	2,869	1,114
Working-class occupations	6,090	2,976	8,587	3,687

	Percentage of Increase, 1881-1911	
	Men	Women
Middle-class occupations	72	161
Working-class occupations	41	24

	Percentage of Workers Employed			
	1881		1911	
	Men	Women	Men	Women
Middle-class occupations	21.5	12.6	25.0	23.7
Working-class occupations	78.5	87.4	75.0	76.3

Finally, it is interesting to know the marital status of the whole female population and particularly of the working women in England and Wales. The census of 1901 first distinguished among women the unmarried and the married or widowed; that of 1911 distinguished the unmarried, the married and the widowed, as shown in the table below.

Table 6g
Marital Status of Women,
Employed and Not Employed, in England and Wales, 1911

	Total No.	Unmarried		Married		Widowed	
		No.	% of Total No.	No.	% of Total No.	No.	% of Total No.
Females over age 10	14,857,113	6,862,025	46.2	6,630,284	44.6	1,364,804	9.2
Females over age 10 employed	4,830,734	3,739,532	77.4	680,191	14.1	411,011	8.5
Females over age 10 not employed	10,026,379	3,122,493	31.1	5,950,093	59.3	953,793	9.6

From Table 6g it is seen that of the total female population over age 10, 32.5 per cent were employed. These working women included 54.8 per cent of the unmarried women, 10.3 per cent of those married, and 30.1 per cent of those widowed.

The marital status pattern of the population has altered dramatically in the twentieth century. The average age at the time of marriage has fallen and now stands at age 25 for men and age 23 for women. Doubtless this has been largely due to changing attitudes toward work for women and the increasing availability of work for women. Whereas in 1911 only 24 per cent of women aged 20-24 were married, by 1968 about 57 per cent of women in this age group were married. In 1911, of the total female population over age 10, 46.2 per cent were unmarried, 44.6 per cent were married, and 9.2 per cent widowed. By 1970, of the total female population over age 15, about 19 per cent were unmarried, 67 per cent married, and 14 per cent widowed or divorced. Concurrently, there has naturally been a change in the pattern of employment of married women. This likewise has been due to changing attitudes and the increased availability of work, and also to the tendency of women to marry earlier and to return to work after the birth of their children. Whereas in 1911 only 14.1 per cent of working women were married, this percentage rose to about 43 in 1951, to 53 in 1961, and about 59 by 1970.

NOTES

I. *The Women's Movement and Working Ladies*

[1]Theodore Stanton (ed.), *The Woman Question in Europe* (New York: G. P. Putnam's Sons, 1884), 2. See Millicent Garrett Fawcett, *What I Remember* (New York: G. P. Putnam's Sons, 1925). Surprisingly little of value has been written on the women's movement. An old work, but still the best general treatment of the subject, is Ray Strachey's *"The Cause": A Short History of the Women's Movement in Great Britain* (London: G. Bell, 1928), published in the U. S. under the title *Struggle: The Stirring Story of Woman's Advance in England* (New York: Duffield, 1930). More recent general works include: Vera Brittain, *Lady into Woman: A History of Women from Victoria to Elizabeth II* (London: Andrew Dakers, 1953); Josephine Kamm, *Rapiers and Battleaxes: The Women's Movement and Its Aftermath* (London: George Allen and Unwin, 1966); William L. O'Neill, *The Woman Movement: Feminism in the United States and England* (New York: Barnes and Noble, 1969); and Marian Ramelson, *The Petticoat Rebellion* (London: Lawrence and Wishart, 1967).

[2]"The Old and New Ideals of Women's Education," *Good Words*, XIX (1878), 855.

[3]It has been reprinted recently in John Stuart Mill and Harriet Taylor Mill, *Essays on Sex Equality* (ed. Alice S. Rossi; Chicago and London: University of Chicago Press, 1970), which also includes their "Early Essays on Marriage and Divorce," 1832, and Harriet Mill's "Enfranchisement of Women," 1851. See also Mill's *Autobiography* (New York: Columbia University Press, 1924).

[4]See B. L. Hutchins, *Conflicting Ideals: Two Sides to the Woman's Question* (London: Thomas Murby, 1913).

[5]*The Economic Foundations of the Women's Movement . . . By M. A.* (London: Fabian Society, 1914), 5-7.

[6][Mrs.] E. Genna, *Irresponsible Philanthropists, Being Some Chapters on the Employment of Gentlewomen* (London: C. Kegan Paul, 1881), 77; Ivy Pinchbeck, *Women Workers and the Industrial Revolution, 1750-1850* (New York: F. S. Crofts, 1930), 315; "Open Council," *English Woman's Journal* [hereafter cited as *EWJ*] VIII (October 1, 1861), 139. For the changing position of middle-class women, see the valuable study by J. A. and Olive Banks, *Feminism and Family Planning in Victorian England* (New York: Schocken Books, 1964), especially Chap. 6, "The Spread of Gentility."

[7]*Letters of John Stuart Mill* (ed. Hugh S. R. Elliot; 2 vols.; London: Longmans, Green, 1910), II, 60-61.

[8]General accounts of this group are to be found in Alicia E. Gallagher, *A Coterie of Victorian Pre-Suffragists, 1850-1875,* Unpublished M. A. Essay, Columbia University, 1943; and Margaret M. Maison, "Insignificant Objects of Desire," *The Listener,* LXXXVI (July 22, 1971), 105-107. The history of the group can also be traced in the pages of the *English Woman's Journal,* in the *Annual Reports* of the S.P.E.W., and in the *Transactions* of the National Association for the Promotion of Social Science, with which the S.P.E.W. was affiliated. An account of this important and interesting Association is given by Lawrence Ritt, *The Victorian Conscience in Action: The National Association for the Promotion of Social Science, 1857-1886,* Unpublished Ph. D. Dissertation, Columbia University, 1959.

[9]See Hester Burton, *Barbara Bodichon, 1827-1891* (London: John Murray, 1949).

[10]Mrs. Belloc Lowndes left uncompleted at her death an account of her mother's earlier life and feminist activities, but her book *"I, Too, Have Lived in Arcadia": A Record of Love and Childhood* (London: Macmillan, 1941) touches upon these while painting a charming picture of Madame Belloc during her marriage and early widowhood.

[11]For Adelaide Procter, see *DNB* and Margaret M. Maison, "Queen Victoria's Favourite Poet," *The Listener,* LXXIII (April 29, 1965), 636-37. The *DNB* also provides sketches of the lives and work of Miss Boucherett and Miss Rye. An excellent biography is Clara Thomas's *Love and Work Enough: The Life of Anna Jameson* (Toronto: University of Toronto Press, 1967).

[12]"Female Education in the Middle Classes," *EWJ,* I (June 1, 1858), 223; Fawcett in *Good Words,* XIX, 856; W. B. Hodgson, "The General Education of Women," *EWJ,* V (April 1,

1860), 76; Rev. H. W. C., "The Position of Woman. A Lecture Delivered in Glasgow . . . , " *EWJ*, VI (January 1, 1861), 292.

[13]Bessie Rayner Parkes, *Essays on Woman's Work* (London: Alexander Strahan, 1866), 221.

[14]The quotation is from Chap. 13, "Love," in Walter E. Houghton's brilliant and classic study, *The Victorian Frame of Mind* (New Haven: Yale University Press, 1957). The phrase "angel in the house" is the title of Coventry Patmore's celebrated poetical work of the 1860's.

[15]For an interesting juxtaposition and analysis of the ideas and arguments of Mill and Ruskin, see Kate Millett, *Sexual Politics* (Garden City: Doubleday, 1970), 88-108.

[16]"Rights and Wrongs of Women," *Household Words*, ser. 1, IX (April 1, 1854), 159.

[17]Eleanor Marx Aveling and Edward Aveling, "The Woman Question," *Westminster Review*, CXXV (January, 1886), 211; Gladys Jones, "The Rights of the Living," *Westminster Review*, CLXXI (June, 1909), 649; E. Lynn Linton, "The Higher Education of Woman," *Fortnightly Review*, XLVI (October 1, 1886), 508; "Open Council," *EWJ*, IX (June 1, 1862), 284.

[18]Mrs. William Grey, *On the Education of Women. A Paper Read at the . . . Society of Arts . . . 1871* (London: William Ridgway, 1871), and "Men and Women," *Fortnightly Review*, XXXII (November 1, 1879), 684; Emily Davies, "Northumberland and Durham Branch of the Society for Promoting the Employment of Women," *EWJ*, VIII (December 1, 1861), 226, and *Thoughts on Some Questions Relating to Women, 1860-1908* (Cambridge: Bowes and Bowes, 1910), 15-16, 107; A. R. L., "Tuition or Trade?," *EWJ*, V (May 1, 1860), 182; "Special Meetings at Glasgow and Edinburgh, with Reference to the Industrial Employment of Women," *EWJ*, VI (November 1, 1860), 158; "Open Council," *EWJ*, X (September 1, 1862), 70; Emily Faithfull, "On Some of the Drawbacks Connected with the Present Employment of Women," National Association for the Promotion of Social Science, *Transactions* [hereafter cited as N.A.P.S.S., *Trans.*] VI (1862), 809-10; Whately Cooke Taylor, "On Indirect Sources of Advanced Female Education," N.A.P.S.S., *Trans.*, XII (1868), 407; Dorothea Beale, "University Examinations for Girls," N.A.P.S.S., *Trans.*, XVIII (1874), 489; Parkes, *Essays on Woman's Work*, 156; Josephine Butler (ed.), *Woman's Work and Woman's Culture: A Series of Essays* (London: Macmillan, 1869), xxxii-xxxv, 318; [Harriet Taylor], "Enfranchisement of Women," *Westminster Review*, LV (July, 1851), 298 [this article is reprinted in John Stuart Mill and Harriet Taylor Mill, *Essays on Sex Equality*]; Fawcett in *Good Words*, XIX, 855.

[19]Mrs. [Anna] Jameson, *The Communion of Labour: A Second Lecture on the Social Employments of Women* (London: Longman, Brown, Green, Longmans, and Roberts, 1856), 118-19; Davies, *Thoughts on Some Questions Relating to Women*, 16; Queen Victoria is quoted in Margaret Cole, *Women of To-day* (London: Thomas Nelson, 1946), 150-51.

[20]Taylor in *Westminster Review*, LV, 295; Jameson, *The Communion of Labour*, 120-21; J. B. [Jessie Boucherett], "On the Obstacles to the Employment of Women," *EWJ*, IV (February 1, 1860), 363-64; Faithfull in N.A.P.S.S., *Trans.*, VI, 809; "The Suppressed Sex," *Westminister Review*, XC (October, 1868), 457-58.

[21]"The 'Saturday Review' and the 'English Woman's Journal,'" *EWJ*, I (May 1, 1858), 203; "Open Council," *EWJ*, IV (January 1, 1860), 354-56; Boucherett in *EWJ*, IV, 372-74; Charles Bray, "The Industrial Employment of Women," N.A.P.S.S., *Trans.*, I (1857), 545; Beale in N.A.P.S.S., *Trans.*, XVIII, 488-89; Davies, *Thoughts on Some Questions Relating to Women*, 13-14; Butler, *Woman's Work and Woman's Culture*, 340-41.

[22]Parkes, *Essays on Woman's Work*, 55; cf. *Economic Foundations of the Women's Movement*, 2.

[23]"Female Industry," *Edinburgh Review*, CIX (April, 1859), 293-336—cf. [John Duguid Milne], *Industrial and Social Position of Women, in the Middle and Lower Ranks* (London: Chapman and Hall, 1857); Boucherett in *EWJ*, IV, 361; Ellen Barlee, *Friendless and Helpless* (London: Emily Faithfull, Victoria Press, 1863), 135-36; *Economic Foundations of the Women's Movement*, 9; Grant Allen, "Plain Words on the Woman Question," *Fortnightly Review*, LII (October 1, 1889), 454-55. For Miss Martineau, see R. K. Webb, *Harriet Martineau: A Radical Victorian* (New York: Columbia University Press, 1960).

[24]W. R. Greg, "Why Are Women Redundant?" in his *Literary and Social Judgments* (Boston: James R. Osgood, 1873); *Economic Foundations of the Women's Movement*, 9-11;

Allen in *Fortnightly Review*, LII, 454-55; Clara E. Collet (ed.), *Educated Working Women: Essays on the Economic Position of Women Workers in the Middle Classes* (London: P. S. King, 1902), 28-30; B. L. Hutchins, *The Working Life of Women* (London: Fabian Society, 1911), 3, 7; J. B. Mayor, "The Cry of the Women," *Contemporary Review*, XI (1869), 198. On the whole question of the rising costs of marriage among the middle classes, see again Banks, *Feminism and Family Planning in Victorian England*, Chap. 6.

25 *Economic Foundations of the Women's Movement*, 11; Hutchins, *Working Life of Women*, 6-10.

26 *Edinburgh Review*, CIX, 297-98, 335.

27 H. J. Roby in N.A.P.S.S., *Trans.*, XXIII (1879), 386; cf. A. L. Bowley, *Wages and Income in the United Kingdom since 1860* (Cambridge: University Press, 1937), 127; Parkes, *Essays on Woman's Work*, 74.

28 Parkes, *Essays on Woman's Work*, 88; W. B. Hodgson, *The Education of Girls; and the Employment of Women of the Upper Classes Educationally Considered: Two Lectures* (London: Trubner, and Manchester: A. Ireland, 1869), 96 n.; Schools Inquiry Commission, *Parl. Papers*, 1867-68, XXVIII, Vol. 8, 284-85. For governesses in this period, see: Bea Howe, *A Galaxy of Governesses* (London: Derek Verschoyle, 1954); Wanda Fraiken Neff, *Victorian Working Women: An Historical and Literary Study of Women in British Industries and Professions, 1832-1850* (New York: Columbia University Press, 1929), Chap. V, "The Governess"; [Emily Peart], *A Book for Governesses. By One of Them* (Edinburgh: William Oliphant, and London: Hamilton, Adams, n.d.); Alicia C. Percival, *The English Miss To-day and Yesterday: Ideals, Methods and Personalities in the Education and Upbringing of Girls during the Last Hundred Years* (London: George G. Harrap, 1939), Chap. V, "The Governess"; M. Jeanne Peterson, "The Victorian Governess: Status Incongruence in Family and Society," *Victorian Studies*, XIV (September, 1970), 7-26; Katherine West, *A Chapter of Governesses: A Study of the Governess in English Fiction, 1800-1949* (London: Cohen and West, 1949).

29 Barlee, *Friendless and Helpless*, 142, 205-6; Schools Inquiry Commission, *Parl. Papers*, 1867-68, XXVIII, Vol. 6, 557—cf. Peterson in *Victorian Studies*, XIV, 11-12; [Bessie Rayner Parkes], "The Profession of the Teacher. The Annual Reports of the Governesses' Benevolent Institution, from 1843 to 1856," *EWJ*, I (March 1, 1858), 3; "The Governess Question," *EWJ*, IV (November 1, 1859), 166-67; Hodgson, *The Education of Girls and the Employment of Women*, 84-88; Parkes, *Essays on Woman's Work*, 98-99.

30 Parkes in *EWJ*, I, 1; "National Association for the Promotion of Social Science," *EWJ*, VIII (September 1, 1861), 56.

31 Parkes in *EWJ*, I 3-5, and *Essays on Woman's Work*, 91 ff.; "Governesses," *St. James's Magazine*, IV (July, 1862), 501-7.

32 Jameson, *The Communion of Labour*, 11 n., 82; Barlee, *Friendless and Helpless*, 133; Butler, *Woman's Work and Woman's Culture*, xv. For the exaltation of the home and its virtues as a dike against an apparently rising tide of prostitution, see again Houghton, *The Victorian Frame of Mind*, Chap. 13.

33 Mary Carpenter, "On Female Education," N.A.P.S.S., *Trans.*, XIII (1869), 353; Millicent Garrett Fawcett, "The Medical and General Education of Women," *Fortnightly Review*, X (November 1, 1868), 563-65; Linton in *Fortnightly Review*, XLVI, 510; Parkes, *Essays on Woman's Work*, 78-79, 163-64; "Association for Promoting the Employment of Women," *EWJ*, IV (September 1, 1859), 55-57; Boucherett in *EWJ*, IV, 363; "A Woman's Thoughts about Women. Female Handicrafts," *Chambers's Journal*, XXVIII (July 11, 1857), 24.

34 "Report of the Society for Promoting the Employment of Women," *EWJ*, VIII (October 1, 1861), 73; "Meetings of the Month. Society for Promoting the Employment of Women," *EWJ*, XI (August 1, 1863), 420.

35 Emily Faithfull, "Victoria Press. A Paper Read at the Glasgow Meeting of the National Association for the Promotion of Social Science, 1860," *EWJ*, VI (October 1, 1860), 122-24, and "Women Compositors. A Paper Read at the Meeting of the Association for the Promotion of Social Science," *EWJ*, VIII (September 1, 1861), 38-41; "Society for Promoting the Employment of Women," *EWJ*, V (August 1, 1860), 390-94; Jessie Boucherett, "Local Societies. A Paper Read at the Meeting of the Association for the Promotion of

Social Science," *EWJ,* VIII (December 1, 1861), 218-20; "Report of the Society for Promoting the Employment of Women . . . , " *EWJ,* IX (August 1, 1862), 378; Society for Promoting the Employment of Women, *Forty-Seventh Annual Report,* May, 1906, 9.

[36]"Society for Promoting the Employment of Women . . . , " *EWJ,* V, 390-91; N.A.P.S.S., *Trans.,* IV (1860), xx.

[37]"Open Council," *EWJ,* IV (January 1, 1860), 354-56; O. R. McGregor, "The Social Position of Women in England, 1850-1914: A Bibliography," *British Journal of Sociology,* VI (March, 1955), 54-55.

[38]"Work and Women," *Westminster Review,* CXXXI (1888), 278.

[39]A. M. Carr-Saunders and P. A. Wilson, *The Professions* (Oxford: Clarendon Press, 1933), 286, 307, and *passim;* Roy Lewis and Angus Maude, *Professional People* (London: Phoenix House, 1952), 46. A more recent account of professionalization is W. J. Reader's *Professional Men: The Rise of the Professional Classes in Nineteenth-Century England* (New York: Basic Books, 1966).

[40]See David Lockwood, *The Blackcoated Worker: A Study in Class Consciousness* (London: George Allen and Unwin, 1958).

II. *Women and Education*

[1][Bessie Rayner Parkes], *Remarks on the Education of Girls* (London: John Chapman, 1854); Schools Inquiry Commission, *Parl. Papers,* 1867-68, XXVIII (8 vols. in one). For general accounts of the education of girls, see Josephine Kamm, *Hope Deferred: Girls' Education in English History* (London: Methuen, 1965); and Alicia C. Percival, *The English Miss Today and Yesterday: Ideals, Methods and Personalities in the Education and Upbringing of Girls during the Last Hundred Years* (London: George G. Harrap, 1939).

[2]See the excellent biography by Barbara Stephen, *Emily Davies and Girton College* (London: Constable, 1927).

[3]Schools Inquiry Commission, *Parl. Papers,* 1867-68, XXVIII, Vol. 1, 546.

[4]*Ibid.,* 560; Vol. 7, 46, 479-81; Vol. 8, 281.

[5]*Ibid.,* Vol. 1, 559; Vol. 6, 74, 388-90.

[6]*Ibid.,* Vol. 4, 233; Vol. 7, 44.

[7]*Ibid.,* Vol. 1, 546-47; Vol. 8, 806.

[8]*Ibid.,* Vol. 1, 548; Vol. 6, 212-13.

[9]*Ibid.,* Vol. 6, 73, 391; Vol. 8, 801.

[10]*Ibid.,* Vol. 1, 549; Vol. 4, 419; Vol. 6, 381; Vol. 7, 240; Vol. 8, 827.

[11]Royal Commission on Secondary Education, Vol. I, Report of the Commissioners, *Parl. Papers,* 1895, XLIII, 8-9, 76.

[12]Emily Davies, *Thoughts on Some Questions Relating to Women, 1860-1908* (Cambridge: Bowes and Bowes, 1910), 114.

[13]See R. Glynn Grylls, *Queen's College, 1848-1948* (London: Routledge and Kegan Paul, 1948); Shirley C. Gordon, "Studies at Queen's College, Harley Street, 1848-1868," *British Journal of Educational Studies,* III (May, 1955), 144-154; and Margaret J. Tuke, *A History of Bedford College for Women, 1849-1937* (London: Oxford University Press, 1939).

[14]The quotations are from Elizabeth Raikes, *Dorothea Beale of Cheltenham* (London: Archibald Constable, 1908), p. 25, and Annie E. Ridley, *Frances Mary Buss and Her Work for Education* (London and New York: Longmans, Green, 1895), p. 93. For Miss Buss, see also Josephine Kamm, *How Different from Us: A Biography of Miss Buss and Miss Beale* (London: Bodley Head, 1958).

[15]For the reformed girls' schools modelled after Miss Buss's, see Sara A. Burstall and M. A. Douglas (eds.), *Public Schools for Girls: A Series of Papers on Their History, Aims and Schemes of Study by Members of the Association of Head Mistresses* (London: Longmans, Green, 1911); and Percival, *The English Miss To-day and Yesterday,* Chap. VIII, "The High School."

[16]Percival, *The English Miss To-day and Yesterday,* 200.

[17]*Ibid.,* 199.

[18]*DNB.*

[19]See Laurie Magnus, *The Jubilee Book of the Girls' Public Day School Trust, 1873-1923* (Cambridge: University Press, 1923).

[20]John William Adamson, *English Education, 1789-1902* (Cambridge: University Press, 1930), 335, 452-53.

[21]See Raikes, *Dorothea Beale of Cheltenham;* Kamm, *How Different from Us;* and Elizabeth H. Shillito, *Dorothea Beale, Principal of the Cheltenham Ladies' College, 1858-1906* (London: S.P.C.K., and New York: Macmillan, 1920). The quotation is from Shillito, p. 13.

[22]See Percival, *The English Miss To-day and Yesterday,* Chap. IX, "The Public Schools."

[23]See Michael Argles, *South Kensington to Robbins: An Account of English Technical and Scientific Education since 1851* (London: Longmans, 1964); and Stephen F. Cotgrove, *Technical Education and Social Change* (London: George Allen and Unwin, 1958).

[24]John Leese, *Personalities and Power in English Education* (Leeds: E. J. Arnold, 1950), 221.

[25]See Ethel Sidgwick, *Mrs. Henry Sidgwick: A Memoir by Her Niece* (London: Sidgwick and Jackson, 1938).

[26]Royal Comm. on Secondary Education, Vols. VI and VII, Reports of Assistant Commissioners, *Parl. Papers,* 1895, XLVIII, 260.

[27]*Ibid.,* 94-98, 269.

[28]G. A. N. Lowndes, *The Silent Social Revolution: An Account of the Expansion of Public Education in England and Wales, 1895-1935* (London: Oxford University Press, 1950), 105; S. J. Curtis, *History of Education in Great Britain* (4th ed.; London: University Tutorial Press, 1957), 304 n.

[29]Royal Commission on the Civil Service, First Report of the Commissioners, *Parl. Papers,* 1912-13, XV, 103.

III. *Women in the Classroom: The Teaching Profession*

[1]Lance G. E. Jones, *The Training of Teachers in England and Wales: A Critical Survey* (London: Humphrey Milford, 1924), 266, 477. This work is excellent on the subject, as is R. W. Rich, *The Training of Teachers in England and Wales during the Nineteenth Century* (Cambridge: University Press, 1933), and I have drawn heavily on both.

[2]For an idea of the social background of elementary-school teachers, see the statistics on the fathers' occupations of 1,116 boys and 3,697 girls who intended to enter elementary-school teaching, given in Charles H. Judd, *The Training of Teachers in England, Scotland and Germany* (Washington: Government Printing Office, 1914), 26.

[3]National Union of Women Workers of Great Britain and Ireland, *Women Workers. The Papers Read at the Conference Held at Manchester . . . 1907* (London: P. S. King, 1907), 40, 44; *The London Head Teachers' Association, 1888-1938* (London: University of London Press, 1938), 82-83, 101; Miss [Emily] Sheriff [sic—Shirreff], "What Public Provision Ought to Be Made for the Secondary Education of Girls?," National Association for the Promotion of Social Science, *Transactions* [hereafter cited as N.A.P.S.S., *Trans.*], XVI (1872), 270; Harold Hodge, "The Teacher Problem," *Fortnightly Review,* LXXI (May 1, 1899), 854-55.

[4]Rich, *The Training of Teachers,* 213; Shirreff in N.A.P.S.S., *Trans.,* XVI, 267; Louisa M. Hubbard, "Elementary Teaching, a Profession for Ladies," N.A.P.S.S., *Trans.,* XVII (1873), 376-78; Elizabeth Raikes, *Dorothea Beale of Cheltenham* (London: Archibald Constable, 1908), 247-49.

[5]Jones, *The Training of Teachers,* 447.

[6]Shirreff in N.A.P.S.S., *Trans.,* XVI, 271-72.

[7]Liverpool Ladies' Union of Workers among Women and Girls, *Women Workers. Papers Read at a Conference . . . 1891* (Liverpool: Gilbert G. Walmsley, 1892), 22-23; National Union of Women Workers, *Women Workers. The Official Report of the Conference Held at Nottingham . . . 1895* (London: F. Kirby, and Nottingham: James Bell, 1895), 192.

[8]Jones, *The Training of Teachers,* 449.

[9]*Ibid.,* 447; National Union of Teachers [hereafter N.U.T.], *Annual Report,* 1914, xxxiii. Two excellent accounts of the union are: Asher Tropp, *The School Teachers: The Growth of*

the Teaching Profession in England and Wales from 1800 to the Present Day (London: William Heinemann, 1957), and Donna F. Thompson, *Professional Solidarity among the Teachers of England* (New York, 1927).

[10]N.U.T., *Annual Report*, 1914, *passim;* Thompson, *Professional Solidarity*, 113-14.

[11]Hugh Armstrong Clegg, Alan Fox and A. F. Thompson, *A History of British Trade Unions since 1889*, Vol. I, 1889-1910 (Oxford: Clarendon Press, 1964), 224; Adolf Sturmthal (ed.), *White-Collar Trade Unions: Contemporary Developments in Industrialized Societies* (Urbana: University of Illinois Press, 1966), 178.

[12]Tropp, *The School Teachers*, 123-24; Raymond W. Sies, *Teachers' Pension Systems in Great Britain* (Washington: Government Printing Office, 1913).

[13]Thompson, *Professional Solidarity*, 64.

[14]Tropp, *The School Teachers*, 120-23, 130-33, 213-14; Sies, *Teachers' Pension Systems*, 30-31.

[15]Edith J. Morley (ed.), *Women Workers in Seven Professions: A Survey of Their Economic Conditions and Prospects* (London: George Routledge, 1914), 43; Mrs. Sidney Webb, "English Teachers and Their Professional Organization," *New Statesman*, Special Supplement, Part I (September 25, 1915), 8 n.

[16]Jones, *The Training of Teachers*, 122; Morley, *Women Workers in Seven Professions*, 43; N.U.T., *Annual Report*, 1914, xc.

[17]Jones, *The Training of Teachers*, 76; Webb in *New Statesman*, Part II (October 2, 1915), 8.

[18]Clegg, Fox and Thompson, *History of British Trade Unions*, 224. For women inspectors, see Chapter VII.

[19]Morley, *Women Workers in Seven Professions*, 45; see also Tropp, *The School Teachers*, 273.

[20]Jones, *The Training of Teachers*, 216, 267-68.

[21]See, for example, the figures on salaries given in T. W. Berry, *How to Become a Teacher* (London: T. Fisher Unwin, 1904), 17.

[22]Tropp, *The School Teachers*, 203-4; Clegg, Fox and Thompson, *History of British Trade Unions*, 225.

[23]Tropp, *The School Teachers*, 204-9. For the Whitley Council, see Chapter VII.

[24]N.U.T., *Annual Report*, 1914, lxx, xciii-xciv.

[25]"The Metropolitan Board Mistresses' Association," *The Governess*, I (June, 1882), 122; *Women's Industrial News*, December, 1898, 98.

[26]Webb in *New Statesman*, Part I, 8; Tropp, *The School Teachers*, 157.

[27]Webb in *New Statesman*, Part I, 8-9; Tropp, *The School Teachers*, 158; A. M. Carr-Saunders and P. A. Wilson, *The Professions* (Oxford: Clarendon Press, 1933), 255.

[28]Webb in *New Statesman*, Part I, 8.

[29]S. J. Curtis, *History of Education in Great Britain* (4th ed.; London: University Tutorial Press, 1957), 406; Tropp, *The School Teachers*, 216, 249, 254, 274.

[30]Webb in *New Statesman*, Part I, 7; N.U.T., *Annual Report*, 1914, cli; Tropp, *The School Teachers*, 215.

[31]Morley, *Women Workers in Seven Professions*, 5, 38.

[32]Schools Inquiry Commission, *Parl. Papers*, 1867-68, XXVIII, Vol. 1, 568-70.

[33]See M. C. Bradbrook, *'That Infidel Place': A Short History of Girton College, 1869-1969* (London: Chatto and Windus, 1969); and Barbara Stephen, *Emily Davies and Girton College* (London: Constable, 1927), and *Girton College, 1869-1932* (Cambridge: University Press, 1933). See also Miss Davies's works, *The Higher Education of Women* (London and New York: Alexander Strahan, 1866), and *Women in the Universities of England and Scotland* (Cambridge: Macmillan and Bowes, 1896).

[34]See Bertha Clough, *A Memoir of Anne Jemima Clough* (London and New York: Edward Arnold, 1897).

[35]See Mary Agnes Hamilton, *Newnham: An Informal Biography* (London: Faber and Faber, 1936); and Ethel Sidgwick, *Mrs. Henry Sidgwick: A Memoir by Her Niece* (London: Sidgwick and Jackson, 1938).

[36]See her *Degrees by Degrees: The Story of the Admission of Oxford Women Students to Membership of the University* (London: Oxford University Press, 1938).

[37] Board of Education, *The Training of Women Teachers for Secondary Schools* (London, 1912), 7; Special Report from the Select Committee on Teachers' Registration and Organisation Bill, *Parl. Papers*, 1890-91, XVII, 28; Schools Inquiry Commission, *Parl. Papers*, 1867-68, XXVIII, Vol. 6, 396.

[38] Mrs. [Maria Shirreff] Grey, "What Are the Special Requirements for the Improvement of the Education of Girls?," N.A.P.S.S., *Trans.*, XV (1871), 367; Miss D[orothea]. Beale, "On the Training of Teachers for High Schools," N.A.P.S.S., *Trans.*, XXII (1878), 433-34; Sel. Comm. on Teachers' Registration and Organisation Bill, *Parl. Papers*, 1890-91, XVII, 313 ff.; Royal Commission on Secondary Education, Vols. VI and VII, Reports of Assistant Commissioners, *Parl. Papers*, 1895, XLVIII, 266-67; Clough, *Memoir of Anne Jemima Clough*, 268; John William Adamson, *English Education, 1789-1902* (Cambridge: University Press, 1930), 486.

[39] Annie E. Ridley, *Frances Mary Buss and Her Work for Education* (London and New York: Longmans, Green, 1895), 281-84; Clough, *Memoir of Anne Jemima Clough*, 271; Board of Education, *The Training of Women Teachers*, 6.

[40] Stephen, *Emily Davies and Girton College*, 140, 147; Adamson, *English Education*, 326; Ridley, *Frances Mary Buss*, 243-45.

[41] Ridley, *Frances Mary Buss*, 246; Association of Head Mistresses, *Annual Report*, 1895, 22, and *Annual Report*, 1914, 82-95; Sel. Comm. on Teachers' Registration and Organisation Bill, *Parl. Papers*, 1890-91, XVII, 153.

[42] Clough, *Memoir of Anne Jemima Clough*, 271; Ridley, *Frances Mary Buss*, 245-46; Association of Assistant Mistresses in Public Secondary Schools, *Annual Report*, 1914, 44.

[43] Ridley, *Frances Mary Buss*, 290-93; Teachers' Guild, *Constitution and Objects of the Guild, Together with a Report of the Annual General Meeting . . . 1887* (London, 1887), 3-4; Royal Comm. on Secondary Education, Vol. III, Minutes of Evidence, *Parl. Papers*, 1895, XLV, 121; Webb in *New Statesman*, Part I, 14; Sara A. Burstall, *Retrospect and Prospect: Sixty Years of Women's Education* (London and New York: Longmans, Green, 1933), 108.

[44] Clough, *Memoir of Anne Jemima Clough*, 266; Webb in *New Statesman*, Part I, 16 n.

[45] Sel. Comm. on Teachers' Registration and Organisation Bill, *Parl. Papers*, 1890-91, XVII, 142-43; Rich, *The Training of Teachers*, 259, 268-69.

[46] Webb in *New Statesman*, Part I, 14-17; Sel. Comm. on Teachers' Registration and Organisation Bill, *Parl. Papers*, 1890-91, XVII, 224; Royal Comm. on Secondary Education, Vol. III, Minutes of Evidence, *Parl. Papers*, 1895, XLV, 279-80.

[47] Webb in *New Statesman*, Part I, 18; Association of Head Mistresses, *Annual Report*, 1907, 13, *Annual Report*, 1911, 26, 45, *Annual Report*, 1913, 46-47, and *Annual Report*, 1914, 12.

[48] Rich, *The Training of Teachers*, 268-73; R. D. Roberts (ed.), *Education in the Nineteenth Century: Lectures Delivered in the Education Section of the Cambridge University Extension Summer Meeting in August 1900* (Cambridge: University Press, 1901), 183; Royal Comm. on Secondary Education, Vol. I, Report of Commissioners, *Parl. Papers*, 1895, XLIII, 205 ff.

[49] Jones, *The Training of Teachers*, 32, 121-24, 222-23; Board of Education, *The Training of Women Teachers*, 8; Morley, *Women Workers in Seven Professions*, 7.

[50] See, for example, Alfred W. Pollard, "The Governess and Her Grievances," *Murray's Magazine*, V (April, 1889), 505-515; and Mary Maxse, "On Governesses," *National Review*, XXXVII (May, 1901), 397-402.

[51] Teachers' Guild, *Constitution and Objects*, 16, and *Annual Reports*, 1899-1900, 25, and 1911-12, 54; Association of Head Mistresses, *Annual Report*, 1914, 43.

[52] Departmental Committee on the Superannuation of Teachers, Report of the Committee on the Second Reference, *Parl. Papers*, 1914, XXV, 6-7; Association of Assistant Mistresses, *Annual Report*, 1914, 18-19, 37; Teachers' Guild, *Annual Report*, 1911-12, 12-13; Association of Head Mistresses, *Annual Report*, 1914, 60; Morley, *Women Workers in Seven Professions*, 34.

[53] Association of Assistant Mistresses, *Annual Report*, 1914, 20-25; Dept. Comm. on Superannuation of Teachers, *Parl. Papers*, 1914, XXV, 19-20, 33.

[54] Royal Comm. on Secondary Education, Vol. I, Report of Commissioners, *Parl. Papers*, 1895, XLIII, 212-17, and Vol. IV, Minutes of Evidence, *Parl. Papers*, 1895, XLVI, 55; Sara A. Burstall, *English High Schools for Girls: Their Aims, Organisation and Management*

(London and New York: Longmans, Green, 1907), 227; Morley, *Women Workers in Seven Professions*, 33-34.

[55]H. B. V. Vaughan-Evans, *A Handbook of Law for Private School Masters* (London: Butterworth, 1922), 88.

[56]Royal Comm. on Secondary Education, Vols. VI and VII, Reports of Assistant Commissioners, *Parl. Papers*, 1895, XLVIII, 320; Clara E. Collet (ed.), *Educated Working Women: Essays on the Economic Position of Women Workers in the Middle Classes* (London: P. S. King, 1902), 91; Clara E. Collet, "The Age Limit for Women," *Contemporary Review*, LXXVI (December, 1899), 868-69; Webb in *New Statesman*, Part II, 8; Association of Head Mistresses, *Summary of the Work of the Association* (London, 1911), 5-6, and *Annual Report*, 1914, 111-13; Association of Assistant Mistresses, *Annual Report*, 1914, 11.

[57]Alfred W. Pollard, "The Salaries of Lady Teachers," *Murray's Magazine*, IV (December, 1888), 780-81.

[58]Royal Comm. on Secondary Education, Vol. I, Report of Commissioners, *Parl. Papers*, 1895, XLIII, 209-11, 318, and Vol. II, Minutes of Evidence, *Parl. Papers*, 1895, XLIV, 172.

[59]Dept. Comm. on Superannuation of Teachers, *Parl. Papers*, 1914, XXV, 34.

[60]Association of Assistant Mistresses, *Annual Report*, 1914, 10-15.

[61]Webb in *New Statesman*, Part I, 16 n.; Morley, *Women Workers in Seven Professions*, 32; Board of Education, Statistics relating to Annual Income and Expenditure, especially in relation to Salaries of Teaching Staff, in certain Secondary Schools in England . . . , *Parl. Papers*, 1911, LIX, 17.

[62]Webb in *New Statesman*, Part I, 12; Royal Comm. on Secondary Education, Vols. VI and VII, Reports of Assistant Commissioners, *Parl. Papers*, 1895, XLVIII, 315-18, 324.

[63]*A Dictionary of Employments Open to Women* (London: The Women's Institute, 1898), 142; *Women's Employment*, January 17, 1913, 8, April 18, 1913, 6, and June 20, 1913, 8.

[64]Association of Head Mistresses, *The True Cost of Secondary Education for Girls* (London: Blackheath Press, 1908), 2-4; National Union of Women Workers of Great Britain and Ireland, *Women Workers. Papers Read at the Conference Held at Manchester . . . 1907* (London: P. S. King, 1907), 50-51.

[65]Rich, *The Training of Teachers*, 130; Curtis, *History of Education*, 297-98; Webb in *New Statesman*, Part II, 2; Jones, *The Training of Teachers*, 149, 152.

[66]Webb in *New Statesman*, Part II, 11-12; Morley, *Women Workers in Seven Professions*, 62.

[67]Jones, *The Training of Teachers*, 176 n.; Webb in *New Statesman*, Part II, 12; Morley, *Women Workers in Seven Professions*, 60, 64.

[68]Webb in *New Statesman*, Part II, 12; *The Fingerpost. A Guide to Professions for Educated Women* (London: Central Bureau for the Employment of Women, 1906), 69; Morley, *Women Workers in Seven Professions*, 62.

[69]Peter Sandiford, *The Training of Teachers in England and Wales* (New York: Teachers College, Columbia University, 1910), 93; Morley, *Women Workers in Seven Professions*, 52; *Dictionary of Employments Open to Women*, 132-33 and Appendix A; Jones, *The Training of Teachers*, 452.

[70]Sandiford, *The Training of Teachers*, 138; Morley, *Women Workers in Seven Professions*, 53.

[71]Berry, *How to Become a Teacher*, 36-38; Webb in *New Statesman*, Part II, 13; Jones, *The Training of Teachers*, 178.

[72]Webb in *New Statesman*, Part II, 2.

[73]Jones, *The Training of Teachers*, 179.

[74]Webb in *New Statesman*, Part II, 4.

[75]Jones, *The Training of Teachers*, 159-60; Liverpool Ladies' Union, *Women Workers*, 39; Baroness Burdett-Coutts (ed.), *Woman's Mission. A Series of Congress Papers on the Philanthropic Work of Women by Eminent Writers. Royal British Commission, Chicago Exhibition, 1893* (New York: Charles Scribner's Sons, and London: Sampson Low, Marston, 1893), 321; A. Amy Bulley and Margaret Whitley, *Women's Work* (London: Methuen, 1894), 17; Morley, *Women Workers in Seven Professions*, 65-70; Sandiford, *The Training of Teachers*, 97.

[76]Jones, *The Training of Teachers*, 160-63.

77Webb in *New Statesman*, Part II, 7-8.
78*Ibid.*, 4-5; Jones, *The Training of Teachers*, 169, 172.
79Webb in *New Statesman*, Part II, 4-5.
80*Ibid.*, 9-11. For the growth of "commercial education," see Chapter VI.
81*Ibid.*, 6; Dept. Comm. on Superannuation of Teachers, *Parl. Papers*, 1914, XXV, 35.
82Webb in *New Statesman*, Part II, 6-7.
83Morley, *Women Workers in Seven Professions*, 15-16, 23.
84*Ibid.*, 18-19; Margaret J. Tuke, *A History of Bedford College for Women, 1849-1937* (London: Oxford University Press, 1939), 218.
85Morley, *Women Workers in Seven Professions*, 18-20, 23.
86Webb in *New Statesman*, Part II, 19 n.
87For good accounts of this movement, see *ibid., passim;* and G. Baron, "The Teachers' Registration Movement," *British Journal of Educational Studies*, II (May, 1954), 133-144.

IV. *Women in White: The Nursing Profession*

1Cecil Woodham-Smith, *Florence Nightingale, 1820-1910* (New York and London: McGraw-Hill, 1951), 40-41; Sarah A. Tooley, *The History of Nursing in the British Empire* (London: S. H. Bousfield, 1906), 79.
2M. Adelaide Nutting and Lavinia L. Dock, *A History of Nursing: From the Earliest Times to the Present Day* . . . (4 vols.; New York and London: G. P. Putnam's Sons, 1907-1912), II, 204; [Mary Stanley], *Hospitals and Sisterhoods* (2d ed.; London: John Murray, 1855), 22.
3The Lancet Commission on Nursing, *Final Report* (London: The Lancet, 1932), 19; Elizabeth Garrett, "Hospital Nursing," National Association for the Promotion of Social Science, *Transactions* [hereafter N.A.P.S.S., *Trans.*] X (1866), 473; Margaret Lonsdale, "The Present Crisis at Guy's Hospital," *Nineteenth Century*, VII (April, 1880), 679; Percy Flemming, "Hospital Nursing in the Fifties and Sixties," *University College Hospital Magazine*, XIV (August, 1929), 164; Nutting and Dock, *History of Nursing*, II, 204.
4Lonsdale in *Nineteenth Century*, VII, 679; Lancet Commission, *Final Report*, 18; Select Committee of the House of Lords on Metropolitan Hospitals, Second Report, *Parl. Papers*, 1890-91, XIII, 808; Garrett in N.A.P.S.S., *Trans.*, X, 473; Stanley, *Hospitals and Sisterhoods*, 8.
5Stanley, *Hospitals and Sisterhoods*, 8, 21; *Third International Congress of Nurses* (Buffalo: Pan-American Exposition, 1901), 371; Tooley, *Nursing in the British Empire*, 138.
6Stanley, *Hospitals and Sisterhoods*, 8, 42; Woodham-Smith, *Florence Nightingale*, 41; Lonsdale in *Nineteenth Century*, VII, 678; Agnes E. Pavey, *The Story of the Growth of Nursing as an Art, a Vocation, and a Profession* (4th ed.; London: Faber and Faber, 1953), 264-65.
7Nutting and Dock, *History of Nursing*, II, 180; Woodham-Smith, *Florence Nightingale*, 41; Tooley, *Nursing in the British Empire*, 77; Stanley, *Hospitals and Sisterhoods*, 44; Sir Edward Cook, *The Life of Florence Nightingale* (2 vols.; London: Macmillan, 1913), I, 61 n.
8Tooley, *Nursing in the British Empire*, 77; Nutting and Dock, *History of Nursing*, II, 306.
9Tooley, *Nursing in the British Empire*, 170, 194; Jean McKinlay Calder, *The Story of Nursing* (London: Methuen, 1955), 58-59; Florence Nightingale, *Selected Writings* (comp. Lucy Ridgely Seymer; New York: Macmillan, 1954), 105-10.
10Royal Commission on the Poor Laws and Relief of Distress, Report of the Commission, *Parl. Papers*, 1909, XXXVII, 238; Ernest Hart, "The Condition of Our State Hospitals," *Fortnightly Review*, III (December 1, 1865), 218-21.
11Tooley, *Nursing in the British Empire*, 215; M. Trench, "Sick-Nurses," *Macmillan's Magazine*, XXXIV (September, 1876), 427; Louisa Twining, *Recollections of Workhouse Visiting and Management during Twenty-Five Years* (London: C. Kegan Paul, 1880), 159-60; Florence Nightingale, *To the Nurses and Probationers Trained under the "Nightingale Fund"* (London, 1897), 8.
12[Harriet Martineau], "Woman's Battlefield," *Once a Week*, I (December 3, 1859), 475; Woodham-Smith, *Florence Nightingale*, 41.

[13] See: Jane M. Bancroft, *Deaconesses in Europe and Their Lessons for America* (New York: Hunt and Eaton, 1890); Allan T. Cameron, *The Religious Communities of the Church of England* (London: Faith Press, 1918); J. S. Howson, *Deaconesses: or the Official Help of Women in Parochial Work and Charitable Institutions* (London: Longman, Green, Longman, and Roberts, 1862); John Malcolm Ludlow, *Woman's Work in the Church: Historical Notes on Deaconesses and Sisterhoods* (London: Alexander Strahan, 1865); Henry C. Potter, *Sisterhoods and Deaconesses at Home and Abroad* (New York: E. P. Dutton, 1873); and *A Short Account of St. John's House and Sisterhood* (London, n.d.).

[14] The official biography and still the best is Cook, *Life of Florence Nightingale*. An excellent biography of later date is Woodham-Smith, *Florence Nightingale*.

[15] Cook, *Life of Florence Nightingale*, I, 106, 307; II, 366.

[16] *Ibid.*, I, 305-6; Woodham-Smith, *Florence Nightingale*, 179.

[17] *Memorials of Agnes Elizabeth Jones. By Her Sister* (14th ed.; London: James Nisbet, n.d.), xii-xiii.

[18] Nutting and Dock, *History of Nursing*, II, 188 ff.; Cook, *Life of Florence Nightingale*, I, 458-59; Woodham-Smith, *Florence Nightingale*, 232.

[19] Cook, *Life of Florence Nightingale*, I, 461.

[20] Lucy Ridgely Seymer, *A General History of Nursing* (3d ed.; London: Faber and Faber, 1954), 176; Minnie Goodnow, *Nursing History* (9th ed.; Philadelphia and London: W. B. Saunders, 1953), 117.

[21] *Facts Relating to Hospital Nurses; In Reply to the Letter of "One Who Has Walked a Good Many Hospitals," Printed in the Times of 13th April last: Also, Observations on Training Establishments for Hospital and Private Nurses* (London: Richardson Brothers, 1857).

[22] This affair was widely discussed in the press. See, for example, the several articles in the *Nineteenth Century*, VII (1880).

[23] Nightingale, *Selected Writings*, 8-9.

[24] Isla Stewart, "The Case for Hospital Nurses. II," *Nineteenth Century*, LI (May, 1902), 781; Sel. Comm. of Lords on Metropolitan Hospitals, Second Report, *Parl. Papers*, 1890-91, XIII, 748; *The Science and Art of Nursing: A Guide to the Various Branches of Nursing, Theoretical and Practical. By Medical and Nursing Authorities* (4 vols.; London and New York: Cassell, n.d.), I, 46.

[25] A. Amy Bulley and Margaret Whitley, *Women's Work* (London: Methuen, 1894), 28-29.

[26] For hospitals generally, see Brian Abel-Smith, *The Hospitals, 1800-1948: A Study in Social Administration in England and Wales* (Cambridge, Mass.: Harvard University Press, 1964); and A. D. Evans and L. G. Redmond-Howard, *Romance of the British Voluntary Hospital Movement* (London: Hutchinson, 1930).

[27] Sel. Comm. of Lords on Metropolitan Hospitals, Third Report, *Parl. Papers*, 1892, XIII, lxxxvi, ciii.

[28] Edith J. Morley (ed.), *Women Workers in Seven Professions: A Survey of Their Economic Conditions and Prospects* (London: George Routledge, 1914), 180-82; *Hospitals and Charities . . . Being the Year Book of Philanthropy and the Hospital Annual* (ed. Sir Henry Burdett; London: Scientific Press), 1910, 102, and 1911, 105; *The Fingerpost. A Guide to Professions for Educated Women* (London: Central Bureau for the Employment of Women, 1906), 100.

[29] Sel. Comm. of Lords on Metropolitan Hospitals, Report, *Parl. Papers*, 1890, XVI, 477, and Third Report, *Parl. Papers*, 1892, XIII, lxxxi.

[30] Morley, *Women Workers in Seven Professions*, 182-83.

[31] Sel. Comm. of Lords on Metropolitan Hospitals, Second Report, *Parl. Papers*, 1890-91, XIII, 731; *Pensions for Hospital Officers and Staffs. Report of a Sub-Committee of King Edward's Hospital Fund for London* (London: C. and E. Layton, and George Barber, 1919), 21.

[32] See George William Potter, *Ministering Women: The Story of the Royal National Pension Fund for Nurses* (London: "The Hospital," 1891).

[33] Sel. Comm. of Lords on Metropolitan Hospitals, Third Report, *Parl. Papers*, 1892, XIII, ciii; *Pensions for Hospital Officers and Staffs*, 6, 23-27, 30-32.

[34] See Nightingale, *Selected Writings*, 16 ff.; and Ian Hay, *One Hundred Years of Army Nursing: The Story of the British Army Nursing Service from the Time of Florence Nightingale to the Present Day* (London: Cassell, 1953).

[35] G. J. H. Evatt, *Proposal to Form a Corps of Volunteer Female Nurses for Service in the Army Hospitals in the Field . . .* (Woolwich: Royal Military Academy, 1885); Elizabeth S. Haldane, *The British Nurse in Peace and War* (London: John Murray, 1923), 165; *A Dictionary of Employments Open to Women* (London: The Women's Institute, 1898), 102-4; Tooley, *Nursing in the British Empire*, 184, 194-95.

[36] *Third International Congress of Nurses*, 331-33; E. C. Laurence, *A Nurse's Life in War and Peace* (2d ed.; London: Smith, Elder, 1912), 162 ff.; Tooley, *Nursing in the British Empire*, 176.

[37] Report of the Committee Appointed by the Secretary of State to Consider the Reorganisation of the Army and Indian Nursing Service, *Parl. Papers*, 1902, X.

[38] Tooley, *Nursing in the British Empire*, 179-82, 196-98; *Science and Art of Nursing*, I, 153-55, 161-66; Haldane, *British Nurse in Peace and War*, 169; Seymer, *General History of Nursing*, 118.

[39] Royal Comm. on Poor Laws and Relief of Distress, Appendix Volume I, Minutes of Evidence, *Parl. Papers*, 1909, XXXIX, 540-41; *Science and Art of Nursing*, I, 157-59.

[40] Lavinia L. Dock and Isabel M. Stewart, *A Short History of Nursing: From the Earliest Times to the Present Day* (4th ed.; New York and London: G. P. Putnam's Sons, 1938), 345.

[41] See Eleanor F. Rathbone, *William Rathbone: A Memoir* (London: Macmillan, 1905).

[42] See *Memorials of Agnes Elizabeth Jones. By Her Sister.*

[43] *Ibid.*, xiv-xv.

[44] *Ibid.*, ix.

[45] *Ibid.*, xxxix.

[46] For good, first-hand accounts of this campaign, see Louisa Twining, *Workhouses and Pauperism and Women's Work in the Administration of the Poor Law* (London: Methuen, 1898), and her *Recollections of Workhouse Visiting and Management.*

[47] Royal Comm. on Poor Laws and Relief of Distress, Report, *Parl. Papers*, 1909, XXXVII, 239; Cook, *Life of Florence Nightingale*, II, 133, 139; Woodham-Smith, *Florence Nightingale*, 300. See Report of the Committee Appointed to Consider the Cubic Space of Metropolitan Workhouses, with Papers Submitted to the Committee, *Parl. Papers*, 1867, LX, Paper No. XVI by Florence Nightingale on the introduction of trained nurses in Poor Law infirmaries.

[48] Royal Comm. on Poor Laws and Relief of Distress, Report, *Parl. Papers*, 1909, XXXVII, 858-63.

[49] Cook, *Life of Florence Nightingale*, II, 138, 192-94; Woodham-Smith, *Florence Nightingale*, 303; Josephine L. DePledge, "The History and Progress of Nursing in Poor-Law Infirmaries," *Westminster Review*, CXLII (July-December, 1894), 177.

[50] Sir Henry Burdett, *How to Become a Nurse: The Nursing Profession; How and Where to Train* (new and rev. ed.; London: Scientific Press, n.d.), 46; Departmental Committee Appointed by the President of the Local Government Board to Enquire into the Nursing of the Sick Poor in Workhouses, Part II, Minutes of Evidence, *Parl. Papers*, 1902, XXXIX, 156-57; Morley, *Women Workers in Seven Professions*, 188; *Science and Art of Nursing*, I, 135.

[51] Dept. Comm. . . . Nursing of Sick Poor in Workhouses, Part I, Report and Summary of Recommendations, *Parl. Papers*, 1902, XXXIX, 6-7, 12-14.

[52] *Ibid.*, Part I, 31-35, and Part II, 156-57; *Science and Art of Nursing*, I, 101.

[53] Dept. Comm. . . . Nursing of Sick Poor in Workhouses, Part II, *Parl. Papers*, 1902, XXXIX, 56, 96, 117.

[54] *Ibid.*, Part I, 15-17; Royal Comm. on Poor Laws and Relief of Distress, App. Vol. I, Minutes of Evidence, *Parl. Papers*, 1909, XXXIX, 464; Twining, *Workhouses and Pauperism*, 194-95; Louisa Twining, "Poor Law Infirmaries and Their Needs," *National Review*, XIII (July, 1889), 638.

[55] *Science and Art of Nursing*, I, 63-64, 103; Burdett, *How to Become a Nurse*, 23, 437-38; Morley, *Women Workers in Seven Professions*, 192-93; Charles Booth (ed.), *Life and Labour of the People in London* (17 vols.; London: Macmillan, 1889-1903), VIII, 93; Sel.

Comm. of Lords on Metropolitan Hospitals, Third Report, *Parl. Papers*, 1892, XIII, lxxviii-lxxix.

[56]Report from the Select Committee on the Registration of Nurses, *Parl. Papers*, 1905, VII, 148-50, 157, 247-49; Royal Comm. on Poor Laws and Relief of Distress, Report, *Parl. Papers*, 1909, XXXVII, 891-95; Report and Special Report from the Select Committee on the Asylums Officers (Employment, Pensions and Superannuation) Bill, *Parl. Papers*, 1911, VI, iii-iv, 28-29, 36-40, 163; Tooley, *Nursing in the British Empire*, 247-49; *Third International Congress of Nurses*, 182-84; *Science and Art of Nursing*, I, 64; Morley, *Women Workers in Seven Professions*, 201-4; *Pensions for Hospital Officers and Staffs*, 57; Booth, *Life and Labour of the People in London*, VIII, 93-94; *The Fingerpost*, 105.

[57]*Science and Art of Nursing*, I, 135.

[58]See: *Organization of Nursing. An Account of the Liverpool Nurses' Training School, Its Foundation, Progress, and Operation in Hospital, District, and Private Nursing. By a Member of the Committee* (Liverpool: A. Holden, and London: Longman, Green, Reader and Dyer, 1865); William Rathbone, *Sketch of the History and Progress of District Nursing: From Its Commencement in the Year 1859 to the Present Date* (London: Macmillan, 1890); Jubilee Congress of District Nursing, Held at Liverpool . . . 1909, *Report and Proceedings* (Liverpool: D. Marples, 1909).

[59]The Metropolitan and National Nursing Association for Providing Trained Nurses for the Sick Poor, *Report of the Sub-Committee of Reference and Enquiry on District Nursing in London* (2d ed.; London, 1875), 60-61, 75-76, 87.

[60]Annie M. Brainard, *The Evolution of Public Health Nursing* (Philadelphia and London: W. B. Saunders, 1922), 145-46; Nutting and Dock, *History of Nursing*, II, 298-99; Mrs. Dacre Craven, *A Guide to District Nurses* (London: Macmillan, 1889), viii-xii.

[61]Cook, *Life of Florence Nightingale*, II, 253; Nightingale, *Selected Writings*, 314-16; Tooley, *Nursing in the British Empire*, 293; Metropolitan and National Association, *Report of the Sub-Committee*, 9, 35, 78; Rathbone, *History and Progress of District Nursing*, 114; *Science and Art of Nursing*, III, 149-50; Morley, *Women Workers in Seven Professions*, 195.

[62]Tooley, *Nursing in the British Empire*, 303; Cook, *Life of Florence Nightingale*, II, 355; *Science and Art of Nursing*, I, 105-6, III, 148-49, 158; Rathbone, *History and Progress of District Nursing*, 114; Honnor Morten (ed.), *A Complete System of Nursing Written by Medical Men and Nurses* (London: Sampson Low, Marston, 1898), 350.

[63]See Board of Education, *Annual Reports of the Chief Medical Officer of the Board of Education* (London); T. N. Kelynak (ed.), *Medical Examination of Schools and Scholars* (London: P. S. King, 1910); and C. Louis Leipoldt, *The School Nurse: Her Duties and Responsibilities* (London: Scientific Press, 1912).

[64]See: J. H. Aveling, *English Midwives: Their History and Prospects* (London: J. and A. Churchill, 1872); Egbert Morland, *Alice and the Stork, or the Rise in the Status of the Midwife as Exemplified in the Life of Alice Gregory, 1867-1944* (London: Hodder and Stoughton, 1951); Report from the Select Committee on Midwives' Registration Bill, *Parl. Papers*, 1890, XVII; Report from the Select Committee on Midwives' Registration, *Parl. Papers*, 1892. XIV, and 1893-94, XIII; Report of the Departmental Committee Appointed by the Lord President of the Council to Consider the Working of the Midwives Act, 1902, *Parl. Papers*, 1909, XXXIII; and Carolyn Conant Van Blarcom, *The Midwife in England: Being a Study in England of the Working of the English Midwives Act of 1902* (New York, 1913).

[65]Amy Hughes, *Practical Hints on District Nursing* (London: Scientific Press, 1897), 32-33; Agnes Hunt, *Reminiscences* (Shrewsbury: Wilding, 1935), 84; Morten, *Complete System of Nursing*, 353.

[66]Morley, *Women Workers in Seven Professions*, 197; *Science and Art of Nursing*, III, 157.

[67]Hunt, *Reminiscences*, 78.

[68]Tooley, *Nursing in the British Empire*, 277.

[69]Report from Sel. Comm. on Registration of Nurses, *Parl. Papers*, 1905, VII, 70; Hansard, ser. 4, CXCI, 1192-93, and ser. 5, LIX, 271; *Third International Congress of Nurses*, 433; Morley, *Women Workers in Seven Professions*, 186-87.

[70]Report from Sel. Comm. on Registration of Nurses, *Parl. Papers*, 1905, VII, 29; Sel. Comm. of Lords on Metropolitan Hospitals, Third Report, *Parl. Papers*, 1892, XIII,

lxxxviii; *Science and Art of Nursing*, I, 55, 103; Morley, *Women Workers in Seven Professions*, 184-85; Central Bureau for the Employment of Women, *Openings for University Women Other than Teaching* (London, 1912), 6; Nutting and Dock, *History of Nursing*, II, 187.

[71] Report from Sel. Comm. on Registration of Nurses, *Parl. Papers*, 1905, VII, 3, 93, 103; *Third International Congress of Nurses*, 432; Emma L. Watson, "Some Remarks on Modern Nurses," *National Review*, XXVIII (December, 1896), 571; Arthur Turnour Murray, *The Law of Hospitals, Infirmaries, Dispensaries, and Other Kindred Institutions Whether Voluntary or Rate-Supported* (London: John Murray, 1908), 196.

[72] Morley, *Women Workers in Seven Professions*, 185; *Third International Congress of Nurses*, 432-33; Report from Sel. Comm. on Registration of Nurses, *Parl. Papers*, 1905, VII, 174-80; Hansard, ser. 4, CXCI, 1193, and ser. 5, LIX, 271; Eliza Priestley, "Nurses à la Mode," *Nineteenth Century*, XLI (January, 1897), 33.

[73] Tooley, *Nursing in the British Empire*, 271-77; Sel. Comm. of Lords on Metropolitan Hospitals, Report, *Parl. Papers*, 1890, XVI, 452; *Third International Congress of Nurses*, 94-103; Morley, *Women Workers in Seven Professions*, 185-86.

[74] Dock and Stewart, *Short History of Nursing*, 253.

[75] Sel. Comm. of Lords on Metropolitan Hospitals, Report, *Parl. Papers*, 1890, XVI, 545 ff.; Report from Sel. Comm. on Registration of Nurses, *Parl. Papers*, 1905, VII, 109; *Third International Congress of Nurses*, 147-48.

[76] Nutting and Dock, *History of Nursing*, III, 32-39; Tooley, *Nursing in the British Empire*, 372-76.

[77] Nutting and Dock, *History of Nursing*, III, 39; Burdett, *How to Become a Nurse*, 438; *Hospitals and Charities Yearbook*, 1898, 102; Report from Sel. Comm. on Registration of Nurses, *Parl. Papers*, 1904, VI, 27, 105.

[78] For arguments both for and against registration, see the evidence given before the Lords' Committee on the Metropolitan Hospitals, *Parl. Papers*, 1890, XVI, 1890-91, XIII, and 1892, XIII, and before the Select Committee on the Registration of Nurses, *Parl. Papers*, 1904, VI, and 1905, VII. For further arguments against registration, see, for example: Eva C. Lückes, *What Will Trained Nurses Gain by Joining the British Nurses' Association?* (London: J. and A. Churchill, 1889), and *Nineteenth Century*, LV (May, 1904), 827-839; and Sydney Holland, *Talk to the Staff Nurses, Private Nurses, and Probationers of the London Hospital* (London, 1905), and *Nineteenth Century*, LXVIII (July, 1910), 143-147. For further arguments in favour of registration, see the articles by Mrs. Fenwick, Isla Stewart and Lord Ampthill in *Nineteenth Century*, XLI (1897), LV (1904), and LXVII and LXVIII (1910).

[79] Hansard, ser. 4, CXCVI, 13-14.

[80] Pavey, *Growth of Nursing*, 357.

[81] Florence Nightingale, *Florence Nightingale to Her Nurses: A Selection from Miss Nightingale's Addresses to Probationers and Nurses of the Nightingale School at St. Thomas's Hospital* (ed. Rosalind Nash; London: Macmillan, 1914), 140-43; "Nursing as a Calling," *Spectator*, LXXIX (September 4, 1897), 305; Report from Sel. Comm. on Registration of Nurses, *Parl. Papers*, 1904, VI, 37.

[82] Report from Sel. Comm. on Registration of Nurses, *Parl. Papers*, 1904, VI, 76, 87, and 1905, VII, 109; Nutting and Dock, *History of Nursing*, III, 57, 60; Hansard, ser. 4, CLXXXVIII, 179 ff.

[83] Nutting and Dock, *History of Nursing*, III, 45-51.

[84] Sel. Comm. of Lords on Metropolitan Hospitals, Report, *Parl. Papers*, 1890, XVI, 555; *Third International Congress of Nurses*, 374.

[85] *Third International Congress of Nurses*, 436; Nutting and Dock, *History of Nursing*, III, 52-53; Report from Sel. Comm. on Registration of Nurses, *Parl. Papers*, 1904, VI, 15; Burdett, *How to Become a Nurse*, 440.

[86] *Third International Congress of Nurses*, 109, 437-39; *Science and Art of Nursing*, I, 66; Nutting and Dock, *History of Nursing*, III, 54.

[87] Margaret Breay (comp.), *The History of the International Council of Nurses, 1899-1925* (n.p., n.d.); Nutting and Dock, *History of Nursing*, III, 54-55; *Third International Congress of Nurses*, 440.

[88]Helen Munro Ferguson, "The State Registration of Nurses," *Nineteenth Century,* LV (February, 1904), 312.

[89]Mary S. Cochrane, *Nursing* (London: Geoffrey Bles, 1930), 88-89; Tooley, *Nursing in the British Empire,* 386; Nutting and Dock, *History of Nursing,* III, 56-58; Report from Sel. Comm. on Registration of Nurses, *Parl. Papers,* 1905, VII; Helen Munro Ferguson, "The Problem of the Trained Nurse," *National Review,* XLVI (October, 1905), 317.

[90]Cochrane, *Nursing,* 91; Ethel Gordon Fenwick, "State Registration of Trained Nurses," *Nineteenth Century,* LXVII (June, 1910), 1058; Hansard, ser. 4, CXCVI, 11; Nutting and Dock, *History of Nursing,* III, 59.

V. *Women behind the Counter: The Distributive Trades*

[1]"How to Utilize the Powers of Women," *English Woman's Journal* [hereafter *EWJ*] III (March 1, 1859), 35; "Association for Promoting the Employment of Women," *EWJ,* IV (September 1, 1859), 57-60; "Society for Promoting the Employment of Women . . . ," *EWJ,* V (August 1, 1860), 394; Jessie Boucherett, "On the Education of Girls, with Reference to Their Future Position . . . , " *EWJ,* VI (December 1, 1860), 221; "Passing Events," *EWJ,* VII (June 1, 1861), 286; "Report of the Society for Promoting the Employment of Women," *EWJ,* VIII (October 1, 1861), 74; Jessie Boucherett, "Local Societies. A Paper Read at the Meeting of the Association for the Promotion of Social Science . . . , " *EWJ,* VIII (December 1, 1861), 220.

[2]An excellent account of this revolution in the distributive trades and of the earlier conditions is given in James B. Jefferys' *Retail Trading in Britain, 1850-1950: A Study of Trends in Retailing with Special Reference to the Development of Co-operative, Multiple Shop and Department Store Methods of Trading* (Cambridge: University Press, 1954). For other general accounts of the distributive trades, see: Alison Adburgham, *Shops and Shopping, 1800-1914* (London: Allen and Unwin, 1964); Thelma H. Benjamin, *London Shops and Shopping* (London: Herbert Joseph, 1934); and Dorothy Davis, *Fairs, Shops and Supermarkets: A History of English Shopping* (Toronto: University of Toronto Press, 1966).

[3]Joseph Hallsworth and Rhys J. Davies, *The Working Life of Shop Assistants: A Study of Conditions of Labour in the Distributive Trades* (Manchester: The National Labour Press, 1910), 2. For the development of large-scale trading, see Jefferys, *Retail Trading in Britain;* for the persistence of the small trader, see Hermann Levy, *The Shops of Britain: A Study of Retail Distribution* (London: Kegan Paul, Trench, Trubner, 1948).

[4]Report from the Select Committee on the Shops (Early Closing) Bill . . . , *Parl. Papers,* 1895, XII, 8, 123.

[5]*Women's Industrial News,* April, 1915, 324.

[6]*Ibid.;* Factory and Workshops Acts Commission, Report of the Commissioners Appointed to Inquire into the Working of the Factory and Workshops Acts . . . , Minutes of Evidence, *Parl. Papers,* 1876, XXX, 797; Report and Special Report from the Select Committee on the Shop Hours Bill, *Parl. Papers,* 1892, XVII, 84, 87, 205; M. Jeune, "The Ethics of Shopping," *Fortnightly Review,* LXIII (January 1, 1895), 125-27; "Association for Promoting the Employment of Women," *EWJ,* IV (September 1, 1859), 57-58.

[7]*Women's Industrial News,* April, 1915, 322.

[8]Departmental Committee on the Truck Acts, Report of the Truck Committee, *Parl. Papers,* 1908, LIX, Vol. 3, 143; Roy Lewis and Angus Maude, *The English Middle Classes* (New York: Alfred A. Knopf, 1950), 8-9; A. L. Bowley, *Wages and Income in the United Kingdom since 1860* (Cambridge: University Press, 1937), 127 and *passim;* M. Mostyn Bird, *Woman at Work: A Study of the Different Ways of Earning a Living Open to Women* (London: Chapman and Hall, 1911), 65.

[9]Thomas Sutherst, *Death and Disease behind the Counter* (London: Kegan Paul, Trench, 1884), 124-25; National Union of Women Workers, *Women Workers. The Official Report of the Conference Held at Glasgow . . . 1894* (Glasgow: James Maclehose, 1895), 57.

[10]Lord Brabazon, *Social Arrows* (London: Longmans, Green, 1886), 281-82; Richard S. Lambert, *The Universal Provider: A Study of William Whiteley and the Rise of the London*

Department Store (London: George G. Harrap, 1938), 33; J. Hallsworth, *Protective Legislation for Shops and Office Employees* (London: George G. Harrap, 1932), 10-12.

¹¹Margaret Bondfield, *A Life's Work* (London: Hutchinson, 1948), 62.

¹²Brabazon, *Social Arrows*, 256; Report from the Select Committee on the Shop Hours Regulation Bill, *Parl. Papers*, 1886, XII, 37, 89-90, 93, 96, 165, 181, 195, 201, 209, 221, 234.

¹³Sutherst, *Death and Disease behind the Counter*, 3; Factory and Workshops Acts Commission, Report of the Commissioners, *Parl. Papers*, 1876, XXIX, xxi; Report from the Select Committee of the House of Lords on the Early Closing of Shops, *Parl. Papers*, 1901, VI, v.

¹⁴Sel. Comm. on Shops (Early Closing) Bill, *Parl. Papers*, 1895, XII, 209.

¹⁵Sel. Comm. on Shop Hours Regulation Bill, *Parl. Papers*, 1886, XII, 272.

¹⁶J. Hallsworth, *Commercial Employees and Protective Legislation* (London: The Labour Publishing Company, 1924), 64; Brabazon, *Social Arrows*, 269; A. Amy Bulley and Margaret Whitley, *Women's Work* (London: Methuen, 1894), 57; Sel. Comm. on Shop Hours Bill, *Parl. Papers*, 1892, XVII, 245.

¹⁷Factory and Workshops Acts Commission, Minutes of Evidence, *Parl. Papers*, 1876, XXX, 799.

¹⁸Sutherst, *Death and Disease behind the Counter*, 6; Sel. Comm. on Shop Hours Regulation Bill, *Parl. Papers*, 1886, XII, 84; Sel. Comm. on Shop Hours Bill, *Parl. Papers*, 1892, XVII, 96; Factory and Workshops Acts Commission, Minutes of Evidence, *Parl. Papers*, 1876, XXX, 799; Bondfield, *A Life's Work*, 62.

¹⁹*Women's Industrial News*, April, 1915, 325-27, 337 ff.; Report of Truck Committee, *Parl. Papers*, 1908, LIX, Vol. 3, 132; Sel. Comm. on Shop Hours Bill, *Parl. Papers*, 1892, XVII, 82; Margaret G. Bondfield, "Conditions under Which Shop Assistants Work," *Economic Journal*, IX (June, 1899), 277.

²⁰Report of Truck Committee, *Parl. Papers*, 1908, LIX, Vol. 3, 114, 355.

²¹*Women's Industrial News*, April, 1915, 331; Sel. Comm. on Shop Hours Bill, *Parl. Papers*, 1892, XVII, 49; Sel. Comm. on Shops (Early Closing) Bill, *Parl. Papers*, 1895, XII, 209; Report of Truck Committee, *Parl. Papers*, 1908, LIX, Vol. 3, 136, 355; William Paine, *Shop Slavery and Emancipation: A Revolutionary Appeal to the Educated Young Men of the Middle Class* (London: P. S. King, 1912), 11.

²²Paine, *Shop Slavery and Emancipation*, 13-14; *Women's Industrial News*, April, 1915, 332; Mary Rankin Cranston, "London's Living-in System," *The Outlook*, LXXVI (February 27, 1904), 516; O. M. E. Rowe, "London Shop-Girls," *The Outlook*, LIII (February 29, 1896), 397; Report of Truck Committee, *Parl. Papers*, 1908, LIX, Vol. 3, 124; Bondfield, *A Life's Work*, 25.

²³*Women's Trade Union Review*, April, 1898, 28; Sel. Comm. on Shop Hours Bill, *Parl. Papers*, 1892, XVII, 246; Report of Truck Committee, *Parl. Papers*, 1908, LIX, Vol. 3, 124-25; Hansard, ser. 4, CLIII, 633, CLIV, 59-60, and ser. 5, XLIII, 1755-56; P. C. Hoffman, *They Also Serve: The Story of the Shop Worker* (London: Porcupine Press, 1949), 61.

²⁴Report of Truck Committee, *Parl. Papers*, 1908, LIX, Vol. 3, 121-23; *Women's Industrial News*, April, 1915, 333-34; Cranston in *The Outlook*, LXXVI, 517.

²⁵*Women's Industrial News*, October, 1910, 18, and April, 1915, 335-36; *Women's Trade Union Review*, April, 1898, 6.

²⁶*Women's Industrial News*, March, 1898, 19-20; Factory and Workshops Acts Commission, Minutes of Evidence, *Parl. Papers*, 1876, XXX, 959; Report of Truck Committee, *Parl. Papers*, 1908, LIX, Vol 2, 47, and Vol. 3, 115; R. Neish, "A Woman's Shopping," *Pall Mall Magazine*, XXIV (July, 1901), 314.

²⁷*Women's Industrial News*, March, 1898, 20, and April, 1915, 330-33; Paine, *Shop Slavery and Emancipation*, 19-22.

²⁸See Margaret Bondfield, *Shop Workers and the Vote* (London: The People's Suffrage Federation, 1911).

²⁹Hallsworth and Davies, *Working Life of Shop Assistants*, 105-7, 110, 114; Sel. Comm. on Shop Hours Regulation Bill, *Parl. Papers*, 1886, XII, 275; Royal Commission on Labour, The Employment of Women, Reports by Miss Eliza Orme, Miss Clara E. Collet, Miss May E. Abraham, and Miss Margaret H. Irwin . . . on the Conditions of Work in Various Industries in England, Wales, Scotland, and Ireland, *Parl. Papers*, 1893-94, XXXVII, Part I, 87;

Report of Truck Committee, *Parl. Papers,* 1908, LIX, Vol. 3, 133; Hallsworth, *Protective Legislation for Shops and Office Employees,* 172.

[30] Report of Truck Committee, *Parl. Papers,* 1908, LIX, Vol. 3, 127; *Women's Industrial News,* April, 1915, 328; Fabian Society, *Shop Life and Its Reform* (London: Fabian Society, 1897), 3.

[31] Fabian Society, *Shop Life and Its Reform,* 2-3; Paine, *Shop Slavery and Emancipation,* 23.

[32] Fabian Society, *Shop Life and Its Reform,* 3-4; Hallsworth and Davies, *Working Life of Shop Assistants,* 117; *Women's Trade Union Review,* July, 1912, 6.

[33] Sel. Comm. on Shop Hours Regulation Bill, *Parl. Papers,* 1886, XII, 192; Royal Comm. on Labour, Employment of Women, *Parl. Papers,* 1893-94; XXXVII, Part I, 89; Report of Truck Committee, *Parl. Papers,* 1908, LIX, Vol. 3, 153; Rowe in *The Outlook,* LIII, 398.

[34] Fabian Society, *Shop Life and Its Reform,* 10; Report of Truck Committee, *Parl. Papers,* 1908, LIX, Vol. 3, 141, 202; Hoffman, *They Also Serve,* 35; Paine, *Shop Slavery and Emancipation,* 25.

[35] Fabian Society, *Shop Life and Its Reform,* 12; Hoffman, *They Also Serve,* 165; Sel. Comm. on Shop Hours Bill, *Parl. Papers,* 1892, XVII, 169; Hallsworth and Davies, *Working Life of Shop Assistants,* 7; Paine, *Shop Slavery and Emancipation,* 12.

[36] Fabian Society, *Shop Life and Its Reform,* 11; Sel. Comm. on Shop Hours Regulation Bill, *Parl. Papers,* 1886, XII, 28; Sel. Comm. on Shop Hours Bill, *Parl. Papers,* 1892, XVII, 169-70, 247; Adolf Sturmthal (ed.), *White-Collar Trade Unions: Contemporary Developments in Industrialized Societies* (Urbana: University of Illinois Press, 1966), 191.

[37] Barbara Drake, *Women in Trade Unions* (London: Labour Research Department, and George Allen and Unwin, 1920), 5; Hoffman, *They Also Serve,* 2-3; Report of Truck Committee, *Parl. Papers,* 1908, LIX, Vol. 3, 114.

[38] Drake, *Women in Trade Unions,* 39, 165; Sel. Comm. on Shop Hours Bill, *Parl. Papers,* 1892, XVII, 173, 182; *Women's Trade Union Review,* January, 1900, 5; Edward Cadbury, M. Cecile Matheson and George Shann, *Women's Work and Wages: A Phase of Life in an Industrial City* (London: T. Fisher Unwin, 1908), 260.

[39] Drake, *Women in Trade Unions,* 63-65, 211.

[40] *Ibid.,* 64, 165, 214-15; *Women's Trade Union Review,* July, 1910, 7.

[41] *Women's Trade Union Review,* April, 1910, 5, January, 1913, 9-10 and October, 1913, 18; *Women's Industrial News,* April, 1915, 341 n.; Drake, *Women in Trade Unions,* 64, 165.

[42] See her autobiography, *A Life's Work,* and Mary Agnes Hamilton, *Margaret Bondfield* (London: Leonard Parsons, 1924).

[43] Catherine Webb (ed.), *Industrial Co-operation: The Story of a Peaceful Revolution* (8th ed.; Manchester: Co-operative Union, 1919), 181-82; Drake, *Women in Trade Unions,* 167-68 and Appendix Table II.

[44] Hugh Armstrong Clegg, Alan Fox and A. F. Thompson, *A History of British Trade Unions since 1889,* Vol. I, 1889-1910 (Oxford: Clarendon Press, 1964), 360, 452; Hallsworth and Davies, *Working Life of Shop Assistants,* 13-14; Margaret Llewelyn Davies, *The Women's Co-operative Guild* (Kirkby Lonsdale, Westmorland: Women's Co-operative Guild, 1904), 70 n.; Webb, *Industrial Co-operation,* 102.

[45] Clegg, Fox and Thompson, *History of British Trade Unions,* 360; Henry Pelling, *A History of British Trade Unionism* (London: Macmillan, and New York: St. Martin's Press, 1963), 225.

[46] Clegg, Fox and Thompson, *History of British Trade Unions,* 452; Hallsworth and Davies, *Working Life of Shop Assistants,* 2, 4, 6-7; Sidney and Beatrice Webb, *The History of Trade Unionism* (London and New York: Longmans, Green, 1920), 503; Drake, *Women in Trade Unions,* 164; *Women's Trade Union Review,* April, 1912, 5, and April, 1913, 10.

[47] Sturmthal, *White-Collar Trade Unions,* 170, 191; Hallsworth, *Commercial Employees and Protective Legislation,* 93.

[48] Factory and Workshops Acts Commission, Minutes of Evidence, *Parl. Papers,* 1876, XXX, 797; Sel. Comm. on Shops (Early Closing) Bill, *Parl. Papers,* 1895, XII, 9, 96, 208.

[49] Factory and Workshops Acts Commission, Report of Commissioners, *Parl. Papers,* 1876, XXIX, xxi, and Minutes of Evidence, *Parl. Papers,* 1876, XXX, 801; Sel. Comm. on Shop Hours Regulation Bill, *Parl. Papers,* 1886, XII, 87-88; Sel. Comm. on Shop Hours

Bill, *Parl. Papers*, 1892, XVII, 98; Sel. Comm. on Shops (Early Closing) Bill, *Parl. Papers*, 1895, XII, 9; Brabazon, *Social Arrows*, 286.

⁵⁰Factory and Workshops Acts Commission, Minutes of Evidence, *Parl. Papers*, 1876, XXX, 953-54, 958; Mrs. Adrian Grant Duff (ed.), *The Life-Work of Lord Avebury (Sir John Lubbock) 1834-1913* (London: Watts, 1934).

⁵¹Factory and Workshops Acts Commission, Minutes of Evidence, *Parl. Papers*, 1876, XXX, 797-98, 800, 958-59.

⁵²Factory and Workshops Acts Commission, Report of Commissioners, *Parl. Papers*, 1876, XXIX, xxii; Sel. Comm. on Shop Hours Regulation Bill, *Parl. Papers*, 1886, XII, 79.

⁵³Sel. Comm. on Shop Hours Regulation Bill, *Parl. Papers*, 1886, XII, iv, 31; Brabazon, *Social Arrows*, 243; *Shop Hours Regulation. Correspondence between the Earl of Wemyss, Chairman, Liberty and Property Defence League, and T. Sutherst, Esq., President, Shop Hours Labour League* (London: Liberty and Property Defence League, 1885), 5 n., 8-9; Sutherst, *Death and Disease behind the Counter*, 73-80.

⁵⁴Sel. Comm. on Shop Hours Bill, *Parl. Papers*, 1892, XVII, 72, 99-101, 175; Hansard, ser. 3, CCCXXIV, 702.

⁵⁵Sel. Comm. on Shop Hours Regulation Bill, *Parl. Papers*, 1886, XII, 154, 172; Sel. Comm. on Shop Hours Bill, *Parl. Papers*, 1892, XVII, 47, 95, 173-80; Sel. Comm. on Shops (Early Closing) Bill, *Parl. Papers*, 1895, XII, 1-3, 13; Drake, *Women in Trade Unions*, 60.

⁵⁶Hansard, ser. 4, XIV, 121, XXXI, 1209-10, and XXXII, 319; *Women's Trade Union Review*, April, 1898, 8-9, January, 1899, 19, and January, 1900, 28; *Women's Industrial News*, September, 1901, 258.

⁵⁷Hansard, ser. 4, LXVII, 178-79, LXXXIII, 864, and CXVIII, 1470; Sel. Comm. on Shops (Early Closing) Bill, *Parl. Papers*, 1895, XII, 54, 81, 117, 127; Sel. Comm. of Lords on Early Closing of Shops, *Parl. Papers*, 1901, VI, 145, 206, 212-13; Lord Avebury, *Essays and Addresses, 1900-1903* (London: Macmillan, 1903), 137; Hallsworth and Davies, *Working Life of Shop Assistants*, 76-79.

⁵⁸*Women's Trade Union Review*, April, 1899, 9-10; Sel. Comm. on Shops (Early Closing) Bill, *Parl. Papers*, 1895, XII, 15-18, 121-25; Sel. Comm. of Lords on Early Closing of Shops, *Parl. Papers*, 1901, VI, 127-29.

⁵⁹Sel. Comm. of Lords on Early Closing of Shops, *Parl. Papers*, 1901, VI, 127-29; Avebury, *Essays and Addresses*, 137.

⁶⁰Hansard, ser. 4, CLIV, 217-18, and CLXXIII, 960 ff.

⁶¹Margaret Hardinge Irwin, "The Shop Seats Bill Movement," *Fortnightly Review*, LXXII (July 1, 1899), 123-131.

⁶²Pelling, *History of British Trade Unionism*, 114; Clegg, Fox and Thompson, *History of British Trade Unions*, 360-61, 375.

⁶³Hallsworth, *Commercial Employees and Protective Legislation*, 42-43, 68-74; Hallsworth and Davies, *Working Life of Shop Assistants*, 132; Hansard, ser. 4, CLXXXVII, 1534 ff.

⁶⁴Hansard, ser. 5, I, 14, and VIII, 1851 ff.; N.A.U.S.A., *Annual Report*, 1909, 3.

⁶⁵Hansard, ser. 5, XXXII, 596; Hoffman, *They Also Serve*, 12.

⁶⁶Hansard, ser. 5, LI, 1166.

⁶⁷Drake, *Women in Trade Unions*, 164-65; Hallsworth, *Commercial Employees and Protective Legislation*, 33-35.

⁶⁸Hansard, ser. 5, LX, 374; Hallsworth, *Protective Legislation for Shops and Office Employees*, 18-21, 141, and *passim*; Hoffman, *They Also Serve*, 13-15.

⁶⁹*Women's Trade Union Review*, April, 1897, 6-7; Hansard, ser. 4, XLIII, 779, 1990-;91; Report from the Standing Committee on Trade . . . , Shipping and Manufactures, on the Truck Bill, *Parl. Papers*, 1896, XIV, 6, 9; Hallsworth, *Commercial Employees and Protective Legislation*, 60-61; *Women's Industrial News*, March, 1898, 17, 21.

⁷⁰*Women's Trade Union Review*, April, 1897, 8, and January, 1900, 28; Hansard, ser. 4, CLII, 1096; Report of Truck Committee, *Parl. Papers*, 1908, LIX, Vol. 3, 135-36.

⁷¹Report of Truck Committee, *Parl. Papers*, 1908, LIX, Vol. 3, 127, 150; Hansard, ser. 4, CLII, 1090, and CLIV, 1067; Hoffman, *They Also Serve*, 46, 50-51.

⁷²Bondfield, *A Life's Work*, 32, 72; Hoffman, *They Also Serve*, 33, 46, 52-53; Report of Truck Committee, *Parl. Papers*, 1908, LIX, Vol. 3, 133.

[73] Report of Truck Committee, *Parl. Papers,* 1908, LIX, Vol. 3, 127, 150; Hoffman, *They Also Serve,* 51, 54-55.

[74] Hoffman, *They Also Serve,* 42.

[75] Report of Truck Committee, *Parl. Papers,* 1908, LIX, Vol. 1, 69, 73-74; Vol. 3, 132-34, 141, 356.

[76] *Ibid.,* Vol. 3, 119-20, 127-28, 152; Hoffman, *They Also Serve,* 52, 60.

[77] Report of Truck Committee, *Parl. Papers,* 1908, LIX, Vol. 1, 71; Vol. 3, 131, 142, 192-93.

[78] *Ibid.,* Vol. 1, 71-72, 75-76; Hoffman, *They Also Serve,* 43.

[79] Report of Truck Committee, *Parl. Papers,* 1908, LIX, Vol. 1, 26-32; *Women's Trade Union Review,* April, 1914, 4; Hallsworth, *Protective Legislation for Shops and Office Employees,* 115.

[80] Report of Truck Committee, *Parl. Papers,* 1908, LIX, Vol. 1, 86-90; *Women's Industrial News,* April, 1915, 331; Hoffman, *They Also Serve,* 63; *The New Survey of London Life and Labour* (9 vols.; London: P. S. King, 1930-1935), V, 152.

[81] Hoffman, *They Also Serve,* 62-63.

[82] *Ibid.,* 58-59, 71; *Women's Industrial News,* April, 1915, 331 n.

[83] Drake, *Women in Trade Unions,* 56; Hallsworth and Davies, *Working Life of Shop Assistants,* 135-36.

[84] Hallsworth and Davies, *Working Life of Shop Assistants,* 136-37; Drake, *Women in Trade Unions,* 56, 168.

[85] Drake, *Women in Trade Unions,* 53-54.

[86] *Ibid.,* 54, 165-66; Hoffman, *They Also Serve,* 77-79; Hallsworth and Davies, *Working Life of Shop Assistants,* 135.

[87] Hoffman, *They Also Serve,* 82-88.

[88] Drake, *Women in Trade Unions,* 54-55, 165-66.

[89] Hoffman, *They Also Serve,* 99-100, 158-60, 214, 247.

VI. *Women in Offices: The Clerical Occupations*

[1] J. H. Clapham, *An Economic History of Modern Britain* (2d ed.; 3 vols.; Cambridge: University Press, 1930-1951), III, 472; "Society for Promoting the Employment of Women . . . ," *English Woman's Journal* [hereafter *EWJ*] V (August 1, 1860), 390-94; Jessie Boucherett, "Local Societies. A Paper Read at the Meeting of the Association for the Promotion of Social Science . . . , " *EWJ,* VIII (December 1, 1861), 218-20; "Report of the Society for Promoting the Employment of Women . . . , " *EWJ,* IX (August 1, 1862), 378.

[2] [W. J. Read], *The Clerks' Charter* (London, 1910), 4.

[3] Grace L. Coyle, *Present Trends in the Clerical Occupations* (New York: The Woman's Press, 1928), 7-8, 11.

[4] For the history of shorthand, see: Isaac Pitman, *A History of Shorthand* (3d ed.; London: Isaac Pitman, 1891); William P. Upham, *A Brief History of the Art of Stenography with a Proposed New System of Phonetic Shorthand* (Salem, Mass.: Essex Institute, 1877); and John Westby-Gibson, *The Bibliography of Shorthand* (London: Isaac Pitman, and Bath: Phonetic Institute, 1887), and *Memoir of Simon Bordley . . . with an Account of All the Script or Sloping-Hand Systems of Shorthand in England . . .* (London: R. McCaskie, 1890). For Pitman's work, see: David Abercrombie, *Isaac Pitman: Pioneer in the Scientific Study of the Language* (London: Sir Isaac Pitman, 1937); and Alfred Baker, *The Life of Sir Isaac Pitman (Inventor of Phonography)* (New York: Isaac Pitman, 1908).

[5] *Transactions of the First International Shorthand Congress Held in London . . . 1887* (London: Isaac Pitman, 1888), 202, 380.

[6] See: Bruce Bliven, Jr., *The Wonderful Writing Machine* (New York: Random House, 1954); G. Tilghman Richards, *Handbook of the Collection Illustrating Typewriters: A Brief Outline of the History and Development of the Correspondence Typewriter . . .* (London: Board of Education, Science Museum, 1938); *The Story of the Typewriter, 1873-1923* (Herkimer, New York: Herkimer County Historical Society, 1923); and Charles E. Weller, *The Early History of the Typewriter* (La Porte, Indiana, 1921).

[7] Coyle, *Present Trends in the Clerical Occupations,* 9-10, 17.

[8]*Ibid.*, 19-20.

[9]*Ibid.*, 26-27, 32-33.

[10]"The Practical Side of Commercial Education," *Chambers's Journal*, LXXIX (March 22, 1902), 247-50. For other works on commercial education, see: Frederick Hooper and James Graham, *Commercial Education at Home and Abroad: A Comprehensive Handbook Providing Materials for a Scheme of Commercial Education for the United Kingdom* (London: Macmillan, 1901); Charles H. Kirton, *The Day Commercial School* (London: Sir Isaac Pitman, 1934), and *The Principles and Practice of Continuation Teaching: A Manual of Principles and Teaching Methods Specially Adapted to the Requirements of Teachers in Commercial and Continuation Schools* (London: Sir Isaac Pitman, n.d.); A. T. Pollard, "Commercial Education," in *Thirteen Essays on Education by Members of the XIII* (London: Percival, 1891); *Report on Commercial Education Presented to the Associated Chambers of Commerce* (London: Isbister, 1887); *The Teaching of Commercial Subjects* (London: Sir Isaac Pitman, 1921); and E. E. Whitfield, *Commercial Education in Theory and Practice* (London: Methuen, 1901).

[11]Kirton, *The Day Commercial School*, 56; Countess of Aberdeen (ed.), *Women in Professions, Being the Professional Section of the International Congress of Women, London, July, 1899* (2 vols.; London: T. Fisher Unwin, 1900), II, 117; *The Fingerpost. A Guide to Professions for Educated Women* (London: Central Bureau for the Employment of Women, 1906), 181.

[12]*The Fingerpost*, 185.

[13]Fred Hughes, *By Hand and Brain: The Story of the Clerical and Administrative Workers' Union* (London: Lawrence and Wishart, 1953), 11; F. D. Klingender, *The Condition of Clerical Labour in Britain* (London: Martin Lawrence, 1935), 62; Richards, *Handbook of the Collection Illustrating Typewriters*, 5; *Story of the Typewriter*, 134 ff.; *Women in Offices* (London: The Labour Publications Department, 1936), 1.

[14]Aberdeen, *Women in Professions*, II, 103; Royal Commission on the Poor Laws and Relief of Distress, Appendix Volume IV, Minutes of Evidence, *Parl. Papers*, 1909, XLI, 83-84; Coyle, *Present Trends in the Clerical Occupations*, 14.

[15]Countess of Warwick (ed.), *Progress in Women's Education in the British Empire: Being the Report of the Education Section, Victorian Era Exhibition. 1897* (London: Longmans, Green, 1898), 186; Clapham, *Economic History of Modern Britain*, III, 473; London Chamber of Commerce, *Report of Proceedings at a Conference on Commercial Education . . . 1898*, 17.

[16]Royal Comm. on Poor Laws and Relief of Distress, App. Vol. IV, Minutes of Evidence, *Parl. Papers*, 1909, XLI, 86.

[17]See: "Clerks. By One of Them," *Chambers's Journal*, LIV (September 8, 1877), 573; "Without Benefit of Clergy," *Spectator*, LXVIII (April 30, 1892), 601; Janet E. Hogarth, "The Monstrous Regiment of Women," *Fortnightly Review*, LXVIII (December, 1897), 933-34; Florence B. Low, "The Educational Ladder and the Girl," *Nineteenth Century*, LXII (September, 1907), 397.

[18]Klingender, *Condition of Clerical Labour in Britain*, 2.

[19]*Ibid.*, and Read, *The Clerks' Charter*, 4; cf. the earlier work entitled *The City Clerks: The Difficulty of Their Position, and Its Causes, with Some Suggestions How to Remove Them. By One of Them* (London, 1878).

[20]*Chambers's Journal*, LIV, 571; B. L. Hutchins, "An Enquiry into the Salaries and Hours of Work of Typists and Shorthand Writers," *Economic Journal*, XVI (September, 1906), 447-48.

[21]Read, *The Clerks' Charter*, 11; Hutchins in *Economic Journal*, XVI, 448.

[22]*Women's Industrial News*, June, 1898, 45; Edith J. Morley (ed.), *Women Workers in Seven Professions: A Survey of Their Economic Conditions and Prospects* (London: George Routledge, 1914), 285-87.

[23]Henry Lloyd and R. E. Scouller, *Trade Unionism for Clerks* (London: Cecil Palmer and Hayward, n.d.), 11-12; J. J. Findlay, "The Genesis of the German Clerk," *Fortnightly Review*, LXXII (September, 1899), 533-35; Hooper and Graham, *Commercial Education at Home and Abroad*, 10-14; *Report on Commercial Education Presented to the Associated Chambers of Commerce*, 44-46; Read, *The Clerks' Charter*, 2.

[24]Klingender, *Condition of Clerical Labour in Britain*, 76; Barbara Drake, *Women in Trade Unions* (London: Labour Research Department, and George Allen and Unwin, 1920), 175; Annual Report of the Chief Inspector of Factories and Workshops for the Year 1910, Special Report . . . on the Hours and Conditions of Work in Typewriting Offices, *Parl. Papers*, 1911, XXII, 197-98.

[25]Royal Commission on the Civil Service, First Appendix to the Fourth Report of the Commissioners, *Parl. Papers*, 1914, XVI, 21; Klingender, *Condition of Clerical Labour in Britain*, 20; Drake, *Women in Trade Unions*, Appendix Table II.

[26]A Member of the Association of Shorthand Writers and Typists, "Discussion. I. The Outlook for Typists," *Socialist Review*, III (July, 1909), 394; M. Mostyn Bird, *Woman at Work: A Study of the Different Ways of Earning a Living Open to Women* (London: Chapman and Hall, 1911), 128, 134; Aberdeen, *Women in Professions*, II, 115; *The Fingerpost*, 180; Morley, *Women Workers in Seven Professions*, 283; Madeleine Greenwood, "Supply and Demand: A Good Field for Employment for Efficient Workers," *Westminster Review*, CLVII (February, 1902), 209-10.

[27]Hogarth in *Fortnightly Review*, LXVIII, 932; Klingender, *Condition of Clerical Labour in Britain*, 20.

[28]Read, *The Clerks' Charter*, 3; *Socialist Review*, III, 395.

[29]G. B. Shaw in preface to Lloyd and Scouller, *Trade Unionism for Clerks*, 6; G. B. Shaw, *Major Barbara*, Act III, Scene 1; Hughes, *By Hand and Brain*, 11; cf. David Lockwood, *The Blackcoated Worker: A Study in Class Consciousness* (London: George Allen and Unwin, 1958), 34-35.

[30]*Chambers's Journal*, LIV, 572; Lloyd and Scouller, *Trade Unionism for Clerks*, 5; Klingender, *Condition of Clerical Labour in Britain*, 19.

[31]Hughes, *By Hand and Brain*, 13-16, 70.

[32]*Ibid.*, 29, 37, 40, 76-77; Royal Comm. on Civil Service, Appendix to Second Report, *Parl. Papers*, 1912-13, XV, 154; Drake, *Women in Trade Unions*, 171-72; Klingender, *Condition of Clerical Labour in Britain*, 24.

[33]Hughes, *By Hand and Brain*, 18-19, 33, 115-16; Drake, *Women in Trade Unions*, 203.

[34]Sidney and Beatrice Webb, *The History of Trade Unionism* (London and New York: Longmans, Green, 1920), 504; Adolf Sturmthal (ed.), *White-Collar Trade Unions: Contemporary Developments in Industrialized Societies* (Urbana: University of Illinois Press, 1966), 183-84, 190-94.

[35]Sturmthal, *White-Collar Trade Unions*, 169-70, 191; Hughes, *By Hand and Brain*, 95-96; cf. Lloyd and Scouller, *Trade Unionism for Clerks*, 22 ff.

[36]Sturmthal, *White-Collar Trade Unions*, 171.

[37]Read, *The Clerks' Charter*, 14-15.

[38]*Ibid.*, 15; Morley, *Women Workers in Seven Professions*, 290-91; Hughes, *By Hand and Brain*, 33; *Women's Employment*, June 6, 1913, 6.

[39]*Spectator*, LXVIII, 601; Read, *The Clerks' Charter*, 7-9; Morley, *Women Workers in Seven Professions*, 290.

[40]Lawrence R. Dicksee and Herbert E. Blain, *Office Organisation and Management, Including Secretarial Work* (London: Sir Isaac Pitman, 1911), 10-13; Read, *The Clerks' Charter*, 8.

[41]Dicksee and Blain, *Office Organisation and Management*, 13; Hughes, *By Hand and Brain*, 34.

[42]Hughes, *By Hand and Brain*, 30-31.

[43]*Ibid.*, 31-33, 40-41; Klingender, *Condition of Clerical Labour in Britain*, 24; Webb, *History of Trade Unionism*, 748-49; Morley, *Women Workers in Seven Professions*, 290; *Women's Employment*, July 4, 1913, 7.

[44]Read, *The Clerks' Charter*, 1.

[45]Hughes, *By Hand and Brain*, 21, 56, 74-75.

[46]Hansard, ser. 5, V, 1370; VI, 737-38, 759.

[47]Special Report on Hours and Conditions of Work in Typewriting Offices, *Parl. Papers*, 1911, XXII, 197-200; *Women's Industrial News*, June, 1898, 47-48.

[48]*Parl. Papers*, 1911, V.

[49]*Ibid.*

[50]*Parl. Papers*, 1911, IV.

[51] *Parl. Papers*, 1912-13, II; 1913, V; 1914, VI.

[52] Hughes, *By Hand and Brain*, 24, 33.

[53] *Ibid.*, 19-20, 25; Drake, *Women in Trade Unions*, 173-75; Lloyd and Scouller, *Trade Unionism for Clerks*, 18.

[54] Hughes, *By Hand and Brain*, 25, 28, 40, 47-48; Drake, *Women in Trade Unions*, 175.

VII. *Women in the Service of the State: The Civil Service*

[1] Moses Abramovitz and Vera F. Eliasberg, *The Growth of Public ·Employment in Great Britain* (Princeton: Princeton University Press, 1957), 62-65; B. V. Humphreys, *Clerical Unions in the Civil Service* (London: Blackwell and Mott, 1958), 1. Both these books are excellent on the subjects which they treat.

[2] Abramovitz and Eliasberg, *Growth of Public Employment*, 38. For the Post Office, see: E. T. Crutchley, *GPO* (Cambridge: University Press, 1938); J. C. Hemmeon, *The Story of the British Post Office* (Cambridge, Mass.: Harvard University Press, 1912); and Howard Robinson, *The British Post Office: A History* (Princeton: Princeton University Press, 1948).

[3] M. S. R. [Maria Susan Rye], "The Rise and Progress of Telegraphs," *English Woman's Journal*, IV (December 1, 1859), 261.

[4] Report from the Select Committee on Post Office Servants (Wages and Conditions of Employment), *Parl. Papers*, 1913, X, 64, 77.

[5] Quoted in Georgiana Hill, *Women in English Life: From Mediaeval to Modern Times* (2 vols.; London: Richard Bentley, 1896), II, 179.

[6] Crutchley, *GPO*, 106-7; Minutes of Evidence Taken before the Select Committee on Post Office Servants, *Parl. Papers*, 1906, XII, 278-80; *The Development of the Civil Service. Lectures Delivered before the Society of Civil Servants, 1920-21* (London: P. S. King, 1922), 117.

[7] First Report of the Civil Service Inquiry Commission, *Parl. Papers*, 1875, XXIII, 176; "Employment of Women in the Public Service," *Quarterly Review*, CLI (January, 1881), 184-87; Hilda Martindale, *Women Servants of the State, 1870-1938: A History of Women in the Civil Service* (London: George Allen and Unwin, 1938), 176-80; Gertrude Tuckwell, *Constance Smith: A Memoir* (London: Duckworth, 1931); Dorothy Evans, *Women and the Civil Service: A History of the Development of the Employment of Women in the Civil Service, and a Guide to Present-Day Opportunities* (London: Sir Isaac Pitman, 1934), 2-3; Edith J. Morley (ed.), *Women Workers in Seven Professions: A Survey of Their Economic Conditions and Prospects* (London: George Routledge, 1914), 262-63.

[8] Morley, *Women Workers in Seven Professions*, 264-66; *The Fingerpost. A Guide to Professions for Educated Women* (London: Central Bureau for the Employment of Women, 1906), 195; Evans, *Women and the Civil Service*, 3.

[9] Martindale, *Women Servants of the State*, 25; G. H. Stuart-Bunning, "Women in Employment," *Public Administration*, XVIII (1940), 196-97.

[10] Royal Commission on the Civil Service, Appendix to Second Report, *Parl. Papers*, 1912-13, XV, 129, 239 ff., 291 ff.; First Appendix to Fourth Report, *Parl. Papers*, 1914, XVI, 14 ff.; Second Appendix to Fourth Report, *Parl. Papers*, 1914, XVI, 72-73; Evans, *Women and the Civil Service*, 12, 20; Martindale, *Women Servants of the State*, 48-49; Morley, *Women Workers in Seven Professions*, 268-69.

[11] Emmeline W. Cohen, *The Growth of the British Civil Service, 1780-1939* (London: George Allen and Unwin, 1941), 151; Second Report of the Royal Commission Appointed to Inquire into the Civil Establishments of the Different Offices of State, *Parl. Papers*, 1888, XXVIII, 251 ff.; Royal Comm. on Civil Service, App. to 2d Report, *Parl. Papers*, 1912-13, XV, 62-64, and 4th Report, *Parl. Papers*, 1914, XVI, 89; Sir John Craig, *A History of Red Tape: An Account of the Origin and Development of the Civil Service* (London: Macdonald and Evans, ·1955), 190; Evans, *Women and the Civil Service*, 3; Martindale, *Women Servants of the State*, 68; Humphreys, *Clerical Unions in the Civil Service*, 32.

[12] Edward Carleton Tufnell. For his letter commenting on Mrs. Senior's report and her rejoinder, see *Parl. Papers*, 1875, LXIII.

[13]Martindale, *Women Servants of the State*, 32-35, 180-82; Morley, *Women Workers in Seven Professions*, 236.

[14]Martindale, *Women Servants of the State*, 36-38; Morley, *Women Workers in Seven Professions*, 245; H. E. Boothroyd, *A History of the Inspectorate. Being a Short Account of the Origin and Development of the Inspecting Service of the Board of Education* (London: Board of Education Inspectors' Association, 1923), 73-79.

[15]Violet Markham, *May Tennant: A Portrait* (London: Falcon Press, 1949); Gladys Boone, *The Women's Trade Union Leagues in Great Britain and the United States of America* (New York: Columbia University Press, 1942); Royal Commission on Labour, The Employment of Women, Reports by Miss Eliza Orme, Miss Clara E. Collet, Miss May E. Abraham, and Miss Margaret H. Irwin (Lady Assistant Commissioners), on the Conditions of Work in Various Industries in England, Wales, Scotland, and Ireland, *Parl. Papers*, 1893-94, XXXVII, Part I; Adelaide Mary Anderson, *Women in the Factory: An Administrative Adventure, 1893 to 1921* (London: John Murray, 1922); Rose E. Squire, *Thirty Years in the Public Service: An Industrial Retrospect* (London: Nisbet, 1927); Hilda Martindale, "Adelaide Anderson," in *Some Victorian Portraits and Others* (London: George Allen and Unwin, 1948); *Women's Trade Union Review*, April, 1914, 27; Countess of Warwick (ed.), *Progress in Women's Education in the British Empire, Being the Report of the Education Section, Victorian Era Exhibition, 1897* (London: Longmans, Green, 1898), 206 ff.

[16]Morley, *Women Workers in Seven Professions*, 249-51; Martindale, *Women Servants of the State*, 50, 60-63.

[17]Morley, *Women Workers in Seven Professions*, 239-40.

[18]*Ibid.*, 240; Martindale, *Women Servants of the State*, 33-35, 41-42; Boothroyd, *History of the Inspectorate*, 76-78; Warwick, *Progress in Women's Education*, 215; Royal Comm. on Civil Service, 4th Report, *Parl. Papers*, 1914, XVI, 88.

[19]Guy Routh, "Civil Service Pay, 1875 to 1950," *Economica*, XXI (August, 1954), 202-3; Abramovitz and Eliasberg, *Growth of Public Employment*, 99; Sel. Comm. on P. O. Servants, *Parl. Papers*, 1913, X, 134, 138, 148; E. Colston Shepherd, *The Fixing of Wages in Government Employment* (London: Methuen, 1923), 111.

[20]Return Showing the Changes in the Wages and Conditions of Service of Post Office Servants . . . in connexion with the Reports of the Select Committees on Post Office Servants, 1907 and 1913, *Parl. Papers*, 1914, LXXI, 42-43; Sel. Comm. on P. O. Servants, *Parl. Papers*, 1913, X, 203.

[21]Morley, *Women Workers in Seven Professions*, 272; Cohen, *Growth of the British Civil Service*, 197-98.

[22]Humphreys, *Clerical Unions in the Civil Service*, 194, 202; Shepherd, *Fixing of Wages in Government Employment*, 164.

[23]Humphreys, *Clerical Unions in the Civil Service*, 48; Craig, *History of Red Tape*, 190; E. N. Gladden, *The Civil Service: Its Problems and Future* (2d ed.; London and New York: Staples Press, 1948), 49; 1st Report of Civil Service Inquiry Commission, *Parl. Papers*, 1875, XXIII, 176; Evans, *Women and the Civil Service*, 2; Cohen, *Growth of the British Civil Service*, 135; Royal Comm. on Civil Service, App. to 2d Report, *Parl. Papers*, 1912-13, XV, 62-64, 4th Report, *Parl. Papers*, 1914, XVI, 89, 1st App. to 4th Report, *Parl. Papers*, 1914, XVI, 23.

[24]Sel. Comm. on P. O. Servants, *Parl. Papers*, 1906, XII, 188-89, 966; Morley, *Women Workers in Seven Professions*, 264; Royal Comm. on Civil Service, 1st App. to 4th Report, *Parl. Papers*, 1914, XVI, 18, and 2d App. to 4th Report, *Parl. Papers*, 1914, XVI, 356.

[25]Changes in Wages and Conditions of Service of P. O. Servants, *Parl. Papers*, 1914, LXXI, 11-17, 29-31; Sel. Comm. on P. O. Servants, *Parl. Papers*, 1913, X, 66.

[26]Royal Comm. on Civil Service, App. to 2d Report, *Parl. Papers*, 1912-13, XV, 125.

[27]Morley, *Women Workers in Seven Professions*, 251; Royal Comm. on Civil Service, 1st App. to 4th Report, *Parl. Papers*, 1914, XVI, 157.

[28]Changes in Wages and Conditions of Service of P. O. Servants, *Parl. Papers*, 1914, LXXI, 11-13; Shepherd, *Fixing of Wages in Government Employment*, 105-7.

[29]Changes in Wages and Conditions of Service of P. O. Servants, *Parl. Papers*, 1914, LXXI, 45.

[30]*Ibid.*; Sel. Comm. on P. O. Servants, *Parl. Papers*, 1906, XII, 369; Sel. Comm. on P. O. Servants, *Parl. Papers*, 1913, X, 155-56.

[31] Royal Comm. on Civil Service, App. to 2d Report, *Parl. Papers,* 1912-13, XV, 61-62, 247, 1st App. to 4th Report, *Parl. Papers,* 1914, XVI, 23; Sel. Comm. on P. O. Servants, *Parl. Papers,* 1906, XII, 964-67; Sel. Comm. on P. O. Servants, *Parl. Papers,* 1913, X, 155-56.

[32] Sel. Comm. on P. O. Servants, *Parl. Papers,* 1906, XII, 775; Changes in Wages and Conditions of Service of P. O. Servants, *Parl. Papers,* 1914, LXXI, 23-29.

[33] Martindale, *Women Servants of the State,* 147-49.

[34] Evans, *Women and the Civil Service,* 61-62; Cohen, *Growth of the British Civil Service,* 190-91.

[35] Leonard D. White, *Whitley Councils in the British Civil Service: A Study in Conciliation and Arbitration* (Chicago: University of Chicago Press, 1933), 243.

[36] Humphreys, *Clerical Unions in the Civil Service,* 2, 33-34; Bernard Newman, *Yours for Action* (London: Herbert Jenkins, 1953), 20.

[37] White, *Whitley Councils in the British Civil Service,* 245; Hugh Armstrong Clegg, Alan Fox and A. F. Thompson, *A History of British Trade Unions since 1889,* Vol. I, 1889-1910 (Oxford: Clarendon Press, 1964), 31, 215-20; Humphreys, *Clerical Unions in the Civil Service,* 32; *Women's Trade Union Review,* January, 1904, 42-43; Sidney and Beatrice Webb, *The History of Trade Unionism* (London and New York: Longmans, Green, 1920), 508.

[38] A. M. Carr-Saunders and P. A. Wilson, *The Professions* (Oxford: Clarendon Press, 1933), 243-44.

[39] Humphreys, *Clerical Unions in the Civil Service,* 55, 153.

[40] For a complete list of service clerical associations, see *ibid.,* 234-37.

[41] *Ibid.,* 55, 89, 153; Sel. Comm. on P. O. Servants, *Parl. Papers,* 1906, XII, 189-92; Royal Comm. on Civil Service, App. to 2d Report, *Parl. Papers,* 1912-13, XV, 61; Barbara Drake, *Women in Trade Unions* (London: Labour Research Department, and George Allen and Unwin, 1920), Appendix Table I.

[42] Clegg, Fox and Thompson, *History of British Trade Unions,* 216-19; Adolf Sturmthal (ed.), *White-Collar Trade Unions: Contemporary Developments in Industrialized Societies* (Urbana: University of Illinois Press, 1966), 177.

[43] Report of the Inter-Departmental Committee on Post Office Establishments . . . , *Parl. Papers,* 1897, XLIV, 6-7; Clegg, Fox and Thompson, *History of British Trade Unions,* 217-20.

[44] Clegg, Fox and Thompson, *History of British Trade Unions,* 217, 358-60; Shepherd, *Fixing of Wages in Government Employment,* 120-21.

[45] Report . . . of the Committee Appointed to Enquire into Post Office Wages, *Parl. Papers,* 1904, XXXIII; Memorandum of the Postmaster-General . . . 1905, setting forth changes about to be made in the Wages of certain Classes of Post Office Servants, *Parl. Papers,* 1905, XLIV; Clegg, Fox and Thompson, *History of British Trade Unions,* 358-59.

[46] White, *Whitley Councils in the British Civil Service,* 247; J. W. Bowen, "Trade Unionism in the Civil Service," *Public Administration,* XV (1937), 425; Humphreys, *Clerical Unions in the Civil Service,* 41.

[47] Sel. Comm. on P. O. Servants, *Parl. Papers,* 1906, XII, 276, and 1907, VII, 10-12, 15, 19-21, 33, 36; Clegg, Fox and Thompson, *History of British Trade Unions,* 398.

[48] Clegg, Fox and Thompson, *History of British Trade Unions,* 222-23; White, *Whitley Councils in the British Civil Service,* 247; Webb, *History of Trade Unionism,* 508; Humphreys, *Clerical Unions in the Civil Service,* 57.

[49] Humphreys, *Clerical Unions in the Civil Service,* 68-69, 91-93; Royal Comm. on Civil Service, App. to 3d Report, *Parl. Papers,* 1913, XVIII, 130, 134.

[50] Royal Comm. on Civil Service, App. to 2d Report, *Parl. Papers,* 1912-13, XV, 10-12, 2d App. to 4th Report, *Parl. Papers,* 1914, XVI, 160, 374; Sel. Comm. on P. O. Servants, *Parl. Papers,* 1913, X, 69-75, 103, 200-3.

[51] Royal Comm. on Civil Service, App. to 3d Report, *Parl. Papers,* 1913, XVIII, 214-17, 234, 262, 275, 278; 2d App. to 4th Report, *Parl. Papers,* 1914, XVI, 421.

[52] Royal Comm. on Civil Service, 2d App. to 4th Report, *Parl. Papers,* 1914, XVI, 582; Sel. Comm. on P. O. Servants, *Parl. Papers,* 1913, X, 75.

[53] Royal Comm. on Civil Service, App. to 2d Report, *Parl. Papers,* 1912-13, XV, 10, 28-29; 2d App. to 4th Report, *Parl. Papers,* 1914, XVI, 582, 587.

[54] Royal Comm. on Civil Service, App. to 2d Report, *Parl. Papers,* 1912-13, XV, 10; 1st App. to 4th Report, *Parl. Papers,* 1914, XVI, 18.

[55] Royal Comm. on Civil Service, App. to 2d Report, *Parl. Papers,* 1912-13, XV, 23, 28-29, 247, 268; 2d App. to 4th Report, *Parl. Papers,* 1914, XVI, 353.

[56] Royal Comm. on Civil Service, 1st App. to 4th Report, *Parl. Papers,* 1914, XVI, 16-17; Sel. Comm. on P. O. Servants, *Parl. Papers,* 1913, X, 75-76.

[57] Sel. Comm. on P. O. Servants, *Parl. Papers,* 1913, X, 75-76; Royal Comm. on Civil Service, 1st App. to 4th Report, *Parl. Papers,* 1914, XVI, 17-18, and 2d App. to 4th Report, *Parl. Papers,* 1914, XVI, 350.

[58] Royal Comm. on Civil Service, 4th Report, *Parl. Papers,* 1914, XVI, 90.

[59] *Ibid.,* 90, 136-37.

[60] *Ibid.,* 92-94.

[61] *Ibid.,* 91-92, 115.

[62] *Ibid.,* 90-91.

[63] Sel. Comm. on P. O. Servants, *Parl. Papers,* 1913, X, 17, 26-29, 37-38, 88-89, 141, 153-54; Changes in Wages and Conditions of Service of P. O. Servants, *Parl. Papers,* 1914, LXXI, 43.

[64] Changes in Wages and Conditions of Service of P. O. Servants, *Parl. Papers,* 1914, LXXI, 11-17, 23-29; Sel. Comm. on P. O. Servants, *Parl. Papers,* 1913, X, 69-75, 200-5.

[65] Humphreys, *Clerical Unions in the Civil Service,* 75. For the reports of the Gibb Committee, see *Parl. Papers,* 1914-16, XXXII, and 1916, XIV.

[66] See White, *Whitley Councils in the British Civil Service,* and J. H. Macrae-Gibson, *The Whitley System in the Civil Service* (London: Fabian Society, 1922).

[67] Humphreys, *Clerical Unions in the Civil Service,* 153-54. For the Civil Service Clerical Association, see Newman, *Yours for Action,* and W. J. Brown, *So Far . . .* (London: George Allen and Unwin, 1943).

[68] Evans, *Women and the Civil Service,* 34-35, 41, 48-49, 56-57, 62-68, 147-48; J. Donald Kingsley, *Representative Bureaucracy: An Interpretation of the British Civil Service* (Yellow Springs, Ohio: Antioch Press, 1944), 181; Martindale, *Women Servants of the State,* 96-98, 110, 152-53, 168, 172-73; Gladden, *The Civil Service,* 15-16, 172-73; Newman, *Yours for Action,* 114-15; Humphreys, *Clerical Unions in the Civil Service,* 191-92.

VIII. *After the Women's Movement?*

[1] "Artistic Professions for Women," *All the Year Round,* new ser., XLIII (September 29, 1888), 296.

[2] Lord Brabazon, *Social Arrows* (London: Longmans, Green, 1886), 57-58. For other similar comments, see: "Common Sense about Women," *Westminster Review,* CXIX (January, 1883), 155-56; "Woman's Work," *Household Words,* ser. 2, IV (April 7, 1883), 454; Bristol and Clifton Ladies' Association for the Care of Girls, *Women Workers. Papers Read at a Conference . . . 1892* (Bristol: J. W. Arrowsmith, and London: Simpkin, Marshall, Hamilton, Kent, 1893), 39; Georgiana Hill, *Women in English Life: From Mediaeval to Modern Times* (2 vols.; London: Richard Bentley, 1896), II, 90-91; Stephen Gwynn, "Bachelor Women," *Contemporary Review,* LXXIII (June, 1898), 866-75; Clara E. Collet (ed.), *Educated Working Women: Essays on the Economic Position of Women Workers in the Middle Classes* (London: P. S. King, 1902), 92, 137-38; Martin Chaloner, "The Solvency of Women," *Edinburgh Review,* CCXIX (January, 1914), 27; Constance L. Maynard, "From Early Victorian Schoolroom to University: Some Personal Experiences," *Nineteenth Century,* LXXVI (November, 1914), 1060-61; Edith J. Morley (ed.), *Women Workers in Seven Professions: A Survey of Their Economic Conditions and Prospects* (London: George Routledge, 1914), 66.

[3] See, for example: Bristol and Clifton Ladies' Association, *Women Workers,* 171; National Union of Women Workers, *Women Workers. The Official Report of the Conference Held at Glasgow . . . 1894* (Glasgow: James Maclehose, 1895), 175, and *Women Workers. The Papers Read at the Conference Held at Manchester . . . 1907* (London: P. S. King, 1907),

135; Countess of Aberdeen (ed.), *Women in Professions: Being the Professional Section of the International Congress of Women, London, July, 1899* (2 vols.; London: T. Fisher Unwin, 1900), I, 38.

⁴Hill, *Women in English Life,* II, 88, 92.

⁵Ray Strachey, *Careers and Opportunities for Women: A Survey of Women's Employment and a Guide for Those Seeking Work* (London: Faber and Faber, 1935), 73.

⁶*The Economic Foundations of the Women's Movement . . . by M. A.* (London: Fabian Society, 1914), 14; Morley, *Women Workers in Seven Professions,* xvi; Kate Millett, *Sexual Politics* (Garden City: Doubleday, 1970), 88.

⁷Bristol and Clifton Ladies' Association, *Women Workers,* 21; Central Bureau for the Employment of Women, *Openings for University Women Other than Teaching* (London, 1912), 1.

⁸Collet, *Educated Working Women,* 142-43; Morley, *Women Workers in Seven Professions,* xii.

⁹For contemporary comments on the subject of working women's special problems, particularly their lower pay, see: Chaloner in *Edinburgh Review,* CCXIX, 14-34; William Smart, *Women's Wages* (Glasgow: James Maclehose, 1892), especially pp. 7-25; National Union of Women Workers, *Women Workers . . . 1907,* 63-64; Dr. Raymond V. Phelan, "Her Wages," *Westminster Review,* CLXXX (September, 1913), 269-70.

¹⁰Millett, *Sexual Politics,* 85.

¹¹For a depressing commentary on the lot of working women in Britain today, including a scathing denunciation of women themselves for their "inertness" and failure to fight for equal rights, see Germaine Greer, *The Female Eunuch* (New York: McGraw-Hill, 1971), chapter entitled "Work."

¹²Millett, *Sexual Politics,* 63.

Appendix

¹These statistics are drawn from the tables on occupations in the decennial census reports on England and Wales, 1861-1911, published in the *Parliamentary Papers* as follows: 1863, LIII, Part I, Section II, Tables XVIII, XIX, XX; 1873, LXXI, Part II, Tables 100, 101, 102; 1883, LXXX, Tables 4, 5; 1893-94, CVI, Tables 4, 5; 1903, LXXXIV, Table XXXV; 1913, LXXVIII, Table 1, Statistics on occupations in 1851 are not comparable with those in the later census reports, because the figures given in the 1851 census tables included the working population of Scotland as well as that of England and Wales.

²Report from the Select Committee on Registration of Nurses, *Parl. Papers,* 1905, VII, 102.

³A. L. Bowley, *Wages and Income in the United Kingdom since 1860* (Cambridge: University Press, 1937), 127-36.

INDEX

DATE DUE